G000078157

The Britain Potential

a politics inspired by a new stage of human consciousness

Jim Cowan has focused on political and social change in Britain for over 40 years. This has been reflected in all areas of his life. Community development, encompassing many different roles, has been at the heart of his work from the early 70s until 2012. Between 1968 and 2005 he acquired five social science degrees, including a PhD. He was also an honorary visiting research fellow for 10 years up until 2016. In his personal life, he has practiced a socially engaged form of Buddhism for over 40 years which has enabled him to develop his consciousness more fully and realise more of his potential. Since 2012 he has been meticulously researching what has been, and is, happening across Britain. All these aspects, work, personal and social, academic study and research come together in this book; and it is these four voices of doing, thinking, being, and researching that you will hear as you read **The Britain Potential**.

The Britain Potential

a politics inspired by a new stage of human consciousness

Jim Cowan

Arena Books

Copyright © Jim Cowan, 2019

The right of Jim Cowan to be identified as author of this book
has been asserted in accordance with the Copyright, Designs and
Patents Act 1988.

First published in 2019 by Arena Books

Arena Books
6 Southgate Green
Bury St. Edmunds
IP33 2BL

www.arenabooks.co.uk

Distributed in America by Ingram International, One Ingram Blvd., P.O. Box
3006, La Vergne, TN 37086-1985, USA.

All rights reserved. Except for the quotation of short passages for the
purposes of criticism and review, no part of this publication may be
reproduced, stored in a retrieval system, or transmitted, in any form or
by any means, electronic, mechanical, photocopying, recording or
otherwise, without the prior permission of the publisher.

Jim Cowan

The Britain Potential *a politics inspired by a new stage of human consciousness*

British Library cataloguing in Publication Data. A Catalogue record
for this book is available from the British Library.

ISBN-13   978-1-911593-40-9

BIC classifications:- JFCA, JFF, JFFJ, JFFP, JFH, JFM, JFSR, JHBA, HRLK, HRE.

Cover design
By Jason Anscomb

Typeset in
Times New Roman

"Our times are moving unmistakably, at the deepest level, toward a focus on human beings and humanism"

Daisaku Ikeda, Soka Gakkai newsletter no 9143

"The universe is made of stories, not of atoms"

Muriel Rukeyser, The Speed of Darkness

The Britain Potential expresses the views of the author alone and does not represent the views of any of the organisations the author is a member of or any of the organisations referred to in the book

CONTENTS

**

Introduction

Each time humanity has developed a more advanced consciousness we have changed how we do things, the kinds of organisations we have, and how government operates (1). That shift of consciousness has entered peoples' lives changing how much potential has been realised. Compare the stifling of potential in the middle ages with the potential realised in the age of reason.

Frederic Laloux has applied this to organisations today (2). He has found a number of next generation organisations and unpacked the kind of consciousness their leaders have. Their consciousness has moved on compared with, for example that of the CEOs of corporates. The organisations which have resulted are a huge improvement. They are light years ahead.

I'm using this approach with Britain itself. When we look back over our more recent history, the consciousness powering the industrial revolution shifted after the second world war, giving birth to welfare state Britain. In 1989 it shifted again giving rise to Britain today, based on markets and money.

So is there a next generation Britain? Is a shift of consciousness occurring which will enable the country to move on from where it is today and for far more potential to be realised? By the time you finish this book, I think you will say yes there is.

According to George Monbiot there is a universal form of story that we have an innate disposition to listen out for (3). This is the negative to positive template which works across religion and politics. We got to the industrial revolution through such a story. We got to welfare state Britain through one too. And the story told by free marketeers was sufficiently compelling to become mainstream by the 80s. *The Britain Potential* shows just how badly market-based Britain is now failing us *and* that there isn't yet that new compelling story. Hence our politics is stuck.

We are longing to hear from politicians who have that next consciousness and the story that goes with it. I haven't heard it yet. But I have been hearing writers and thinkers produce what seem to be elements contributing to such a story. Given my background (explained below) I have felt compelled to join their ranks and write this contribution to that new political narrative.

In *The Britain Potential* I bring out the three 'stories so far' and set them against something we seem to be moving into which I called civil society Britain. And I also examine the kind of consciousnesses that have powered those 'stories so far' and what seems to be powering civil society Britain. This is the 'Big Picture' or the macro part of the story

At the same time the focus on potential provides the opportunity to sharpen understanding of what we can each do, and what kind of ecology of support for realising potential is needed around each of us, so many more people realise far more of their potential. This part of the story begins and ends with the lives of each person. It is the micro part of the story.

What I have found is that Britain is split in two. The big picture is stuck in a past consciousness completely at odds with what I see individuals and groups of people doing with resources that are under their own control. *These* micro stories are about trusting people, relationships, community, leadership, the next consciousness, and realising far more potential. What I argue is that as these micro transformations, in individual lives and in projects, organisations and initiatives, multiply, all this is changing the macro.

Meet the author

There are two other reasons for writing this book. The first is that I have been working on *my* consciousness through practising the SGI form of Buddhism since 1976. I'll explain what this means in a minute. Suffice to say I have experienced first-hand how much more of my potential I have been able to realise. Developing my consciousness has definitely been central to that. Other ways of developing one's consciousness are available!

Secondly, my work has been about contesting what has been powering our consciousness as a country. I have been at the heart of social change in Britain since 1973 when I first came across community development and realised it was my vocation in life.

So let me unpack these two things briefly.

The SGI Buddhist movement in Britain really does have the diversity of the UK population in it. It is socially engaged. SGI Buddhism has enabled me to cultivate a high state of life which is in us all. The awakened heart of the living universe pulses inside each of us. When activated we experience that connectedness with all life *in daily life*. Life gets better, reflecting *our* inner change. SGI stands for Soka Gakkai International. Basically this translates as value that human beings deeply appreciate.

SGI is in 192 countries (4). In the UK it is taking the form of 630 local groups and a membership of 15,000+, spread across the whole country, collectively known as SGI-UK (5). No-one controls these groups, except the people in them. They are autonomous and foster the autonomy of the people in them. Each is working within the unifying framework of Buddhism. SGI-UK continues to grow year on year. In this movement of ordinary people, I know a complete cross section of the British population. I do talks, one to ones, help run courses and seminars, and speak in public. Day to day I see our members fulfilling potential when previously they were stuck. I live this experience of consciousness deepening and at the same time potential of kinds, that I could not have envisaged at the outset, becoming realised. As such this book is a view of Britain and its potential from a British Buddhist. In that sense it probably is a first. It is about trust in ourselves, in others and in life. It is also about the freedom to create our own lives: to be the scriptwriter of one's own life.

Right at my first encounter with community development I sensed it offered a consciousness far ahead of the mainstream culture: people could grow their power by developing really detailed ways to challenge a status quo and move forward together. It didn't need bosses. The power to make something happen could realistically be shared and what would be done would work better. I got first hand experience of this in 1973 by leading a campaign, as a volunteer, to get a zebra crossing. We won over the status quo of the traffic engineers (no mean feat) and a large body of residents of a 1930s estate were no longer cut off from their shops, schools etc.

I also knew it offered a way of doing things that recognised my inner life and who I was. When you are working with people on an equal footing, and there is no authority inherent in the role, the person you really are is what matters. It redefined 'professionalism' in a way I could relate to.

In 1974 I got my first job as a full-time community worker. Since then I have worked with two types of community. I have worked with communities as we would conventionally know them. In my case it has been people living on housing estates, families seeking support, black and white people working together with shared anti-racist aims, and people with disabilities. At the same time, I have mostly been employed to do this work by local authorities. That has given me access to people in the departments of towns halls, people in education, the NHS, care services etc. I have worked with staff inside 'the system' *as if they were also a community*. The most impressive results for all concerned have arisen when these two kinds of communities, with their very different consciousnesses, have worked together. When this has worked well we have seen some serious realising of potential, even within organisations which generally are hostile to people on the ground taking such control.

Sadly, this is not the general direction that the relationship between public services and communities has taken in Britain. The general direction has been polarisation. The community which emerged after the tragic fire at Grenfell Tower experienced how remote and uncaring many public services have become. By finding ways, over 40 years, to buck this trend and actually bring people from these two different cultures together I feel I have something, based on experience, to offer through this book. For an overview of community development in the UK today, the recent work by Local Trust is helpful (6).

These two kinds of experiences in life, as a Buddhist and in social change, have worked extremely well together. The Buddhism has enabled me to maintain a strong sense of freedom in my work. When I have felt confronted by a brick wall at work, Buddhist practice has enabled me to open my eyes to where the cracks were that would eventually open into an unexpected path. If I needed a different perspective one unfailingly began to emerge inside me. I feel extremely grateful to have had creative, meaningful, extremely challenging work, continuously for over 40 years.

Buddhism is not confined to the inner life. Rather it is about the dynamic unfolding of life, moment by moment, between that inner life and everything around that life (7). If I have a high state of life, this will affect all these realities around me. If it is a self-destructive and low state of life so will this. Moreover the 15,000+ members of SGI-UK have a collective, day-to-day experience of how different, refreshing, human, challenging and wonderful an organisation, with *this* kind of consciousness, is.

My work has given me a real-world experience of how Britain is created out across the country. When you work every day, with people inside public services and people in communities, you see how the country works from the ground up, through the eyes of all the people you are working with. You experience the ongoing all-pervasive influence of government. You experience first-hand how things are developing across the country. You further consolidate, year by year, a unifying and more and more comprehensive perspective. Plus, just by living in Britain, through family, friends, the media, and experiences outside work, I have more understanding of what is happening in the country.

I have acquired 5 degrees including a PhD, mostly while doing the day job. This reflects an itch to understand what is going on, not just from multiple perspectives, but to consolidate an overall view. As well as being a community development practitioner, I am a trained social researcher. I have developed the habit of keeping notes which have provided a basis beyond memory recall for some of the material in the book. Having records of many experiences, plus reading widely, has meant I am mixing my own experiences and thinking in with those of many others. It is from thinkers, writers, activists, research and my own life experiences that I have created the book you are about to read.

Because of the very positive stance on the UK's civil society that the book takes, some may think it is arguing for what David Cameron called `the Big Society`. What he was interpreted as saying was that he could further cut spending on local public services and replace them with cheaper services from charities. No doubt this is a distortion of what was intended. However, the whole point of the welfare state has been that the scale of what is needed in the society is never going to be able to be done by civil society organisations alone. *The Britain Potential* is presenting a balanced, comprehensive, and integrating perspective quite unlike the single solution approach of the Big Society.

The book is not anti-capitalist or anarchist. But it is about a new kind of politics which reflects a moving forward of consciousness: one that has a place for both our inner lives and everything around us. This is a book about transforming the undercurrent of society that denies humanity. I hope to have done justice to the solemnity of inner freedom, in a real historical context: one which is receptive to the profound meaning of living. In the process I hope to have made a contribution to a newly emerging type of politics and social action.

1 - Potential and consciousness

".... we are not
problems waiting to
be solved, but
potential waiting to
unfold"

Frederic Laloux (1)

Potential is a wonderful way we look to the future in daily life. We want to encourage children and young people to realise their potential. We want to fulfil our own. But we also talk about potential in a broader way. As I was writing this book, I came across what felt like countless people, in all walks of life, asking me what the book was about. When I said that I thought Britain had the most enormous potential, but that it wasn't being fully realised by a long way, everyone agreed. It was as if I had put into words something they had been feeling but had never expressed clearly to themselves.

What did all these people have in their minds? It could have been a vaguely felt mismatch between how life ought to be and how it actually is. Wendy Brown has found herself expressing this as,

"..a ubiquitous, if unavowed, exhaustion and despair in Western civilisation... ... most of us have ceased to believe in the human capacity to craft and sustain a world that is humane, free, sustainable, and, above all, modestly under human control" (2)

Is this a cry for a shift of consciousness?

Potential is most often talked about in relation to an *individual*. But it is also used to talk about *collectivities* like a country, an organisation, or a community. It can be about *internal* feelings and understandings as well as observable evidence in the *external* world. This gives us four `quadrants` (see Table 1). What these four quadrants give this book is a focus on the *people* potential: moving back and forth between individuals and the country both objectively and `from within`. I think this gives us a really fluid, very human and dynamic way to look at Britain and explore whether indeed it really is fulfilling its potential.

Table 1

The four quadrants

	Internal	External
Individual	Realising potential through how I feel about myself and my perspective on life.	Realising potential through my behaviour and how others see me.
Collective	Realising potential through my relationships with family, friends, communities, and organisations I am part of.	Realising potential through organisations, institutions, and systems that I interact with.

When you factor in shifts of consciousness, the four quadrants become a truly impressive tool helping to synthesise and get an overall view of otherwise baffling and complex realities. This tool comes from the work of Ken Wilber (3). By exploring Britain and its potential though this integrated, or as Wilber calls it, this *integral* lens, I think we get to understand *The Britain Potential* afresh. I hope it feels like waking up

In this book, along with learning to value ourselves, and what kind of consciousness we have, I am focusing on support from others as a practical necessity in realising potential. While it may be that it is us reading, learning, training, being coached, finding something we are good at, overcoming a weakness, and being inspired by someone, we probably come to do this through someone else. I call this the ecology of support that uniquely is within us and surrounds each of us. For us to be realising our own potential, I think that living ecology of support is very important. I would now like to unpack the basic building blocks of that ecology starting with the self, then family and friends, then networks and communities, then organisations and last, but by no means least, the country's politics.

Starting with the self

How do we realise potential? Some of it is internal and some of it is external. Some we do by ourselves. Some we do with others. We may feel trapped or imprisoned by our circumstances. Feeling stuck can be the catalyst for tapping into our inner reservoir and resourcefulness in some new way. Whether we value ourselves plays a big part in feeling able to fill in the application form, go for the interview, and ring someone up we have never met. Realising potential can depend on information, inspiration, or person-to-person support. I am struck by these words,

"We don't live well or fully if we cannot share our thoughts and feelings with others. Inquiry, examination, and collaboration are central to this sharing" (4)

Our relationships with others really matter in living fully. However, that relationship may not be through words. I know one community activist who befriended someone suicidal in a residential home. She visited him frequently. He in turn laid down the ground-rules: nothing simplistic. In fact, he ignored all her words until she *heard* him talking about Vaughan Williams' music. She went away and listened to the pieces and began to realise that he was sharing how he was feeling and also how he wanted to be inspired to feel. Music did it for him. Not words.

I also heard about The Horse Course (5). These are stables with horses that are trained to work with humans. The horse will not come near a human in pain, full of fear or anxiety. But they will respond to directions from that same human when they calm down. These stables have treated large numbers of young offenders for whom talking therapies had not worked. The interaction with the horse tapped into the bodily response and by-passed the thinking mind. It allowed the human to learn to de-escalate or wind down the fear and anxiety so they could do this back home with other humans! Naturally this opens far more possibilities for realising potential.

Here are two stories of people who realised far more of their potential: my own and a young woman I read about.

I stopping drinking alcohol. I gave it up altogether in 1996. The years since then have been like living without the brake permanently on. I have had so much more energy. What I discovered is that the alcohol was not the issue.

The `issue` was me holding back a part of myself because of being emotionally bruised in my childhood and holding up a metaphorical screen inside myself to stop people seeing the mess inside. To say that I had no idea what it really meant to value myself is an understatement. These enormous internal pressures found release in alcohol, which I would sometimes drink to excess.

Not needing to do this anymore has meant I am fulfilling much more of my potential. I really do have a sense of the value of my life. This means my quality of life has shot up. I build better relationships with others. From a holistic viewpoint, I am a much more whole person. I feel much free-er.

The point at which I changed was a point of insight into what was driving me to drink too much. It was an intense engagement with myself. I found myself understanding my younger self from a completely different standpoint: I literally was back at the time, as a young boy, when that emotional bruising took place, realising what I did to protect myself. I remembered that I had decided to hold back a part of myself that I was never going to share with anyone else. If such important people as your father can be taken away from you, what can you rely on? And as I was having this realisation, about what I did, accompanying it was the realisation that I was at that very time able to no longer be controlled by this. The internal `itch` or `cause` of the drinking went resulting in no alcohol since that day! This was a profound shift of consciousness with literally transformational consequences.

Here is an experience from a young woman which seems to me to both speak to the times we live in and illustrate what it could be like to live more of one's potential. By the time she was 14 she was suffering from depression, brought on by being bullied at school from the age of 5. The death of her grandad had added to the depression. She was diagnosed as bipolar and had tried various medications and therapies. Nothing seemed to reach her. By the time she was 16 she wanted to end her life on a daily basis. But encountering a supportive network and starting to practice, *"things began to look like they were improving.....it was a long process and I wasn't sure what happiness felt like"* (6). When I read this, I wondered how many young women in Britain this last line speaks to? It felt like someone was stabbing me in my heart: *"I wasn't sure what happiness felt like"*.

Starting from a very crude state of self-awareness, over several years she evolved into someone with a complex and more dynamic consciousness. So much so that she writes,

"My approach to my depression has now changed. Instead of feeling sorry for myself I see it as a challenge to really transform my life and the life of my family on a deeper level. My episodes now only last a very short time as I refuse to be defeated any more ..I can now say, for the first time, that I truly love and respect my life, and I am able to see the beauty of my life....At the age of 16 I would have never believed that I would still be alive today, let alone feel happy. My heart has changed, and the impossible has become possible" (6)

Beside the text of this experience, was a picture of her getting married. Patently this young woman now has better relationships with others, her quality of life is incomparably better, and she has become whole in some way that was impossible before.

From these examples it is clear that valuing ourselves, our consciousness and the support of others are all important to realising potential. Some of the freedoms in Britain include the press, expression, association, speech, thought, and belief. But I detect a lot of people seeking another freedom: `existential freedom` or being able to become the person I *can* be. By existential freedom I mean feeling free to respond to deeper yearnings, with the time-honoured qualification of not harming others. Living true to ourselves moves us towards realising our potential as individuals. Some people literally build new lives.

We also need material support, especially enough money, to live existential freedoms. Can you really make the kind of changes towards becoming the person you know you could be if you are in poverty, homeless, addicted, in poor health, or have had your benefit cut off or sanctioned? While it may not be impossible in theory, surely it is impossible in reality? These examples made me think of this passage from Parker Palmer,

"If you hold your knowledge of self and world wholeheartedly, your heart will at times get broken by loss, failure, defeat, betrayal, or death. What happens next in you and the world around you depends on how your heart breaks. If it breaks apart into a thousand pieces, the result may be anger, depression, and disengagement. If it breaks open into greater capacity to hold the complexities and contradictions of human experience, the result may be a new life. (7)

The circumstances of too many people in Britain are such that their hearts break apart. Having one of the world's largest economies has not addressed this. *The Britain Potential* is a vision of a Britain where, *if* hearts break, they break *open* because people are coming from a stronger sense of their self-worth, a consciousness which enables them to do this, and that priceless, and very practical, personal ecology of support is there.

The positive upward spiral through self-development is self-fuelling. As we establish our personal integrity through, in part, winning over the challenges to bring potential to fulfilment, we experience a greater wholeness. We find ourselves drawing more and more on positive resources in daily life. And we move towards autonomy.

Autonomy is about learning to govern our own lives so that the autonomy of others is respected. We can't do this without the help of others. Richard Dagger expresses the journey to establish autonomy well,

"This ability grows out of our needs and desires, our talents and limitations, and the opportunities and obstacles in the world around us. No one can develop this ability without the help of others" (8)

We need the assistance of family and friends, neighbours, teachers, workmates and others. But I think Richard Dagger`s key point is that once we have achieved autonomy, *we no longer rely on others to remain autonomous*. In fact, we can support others to become autonomous. This is a self-fuelling, positive, upward spiral of ongoing 'becoming'.

I want to turn now to the collective quadrants

Family and friends

How wonderful if you feel you are moving forward in your life, *and* you have the support of your family as well as your friends. It`s an ideal! How many find themselves at odds with some or all of their family members, precisely because they *are* being the person they can be?

Thankfully gone are the days when it was just assumed that two biological parents are necessary. Single parents have raised children to become mature, independent, happy, and capable adults. Some two parent biological families have proved toxic for their young people. Children can come through surrogates. Same sex marriages can provide great families for children and young people. Today there are complexities of `step` relationships to navigate. Our repertoire of how the family can be is evolving. Any of these diverse arrangements could be toxic or profoundly nurturing.

Today there are enormous possibilities, and complexities in these combinations of family and friend relationships. And for some there is no family, and there may also be no friends. For some it is neighbours, or networks, the community or the internet that prevent them being completely on their own.

Government has invented a new category of family: those that are `just managing`. In 2017 the Centre for Social Justice estimated the cost of family breakdown to be £47 billion (9). The family is, after all, crucial to the wellbeing of the whole society. The levels of loneliness, homelessness, suicide, domestic violence and divorce do suggest that there are circumstances where support for the family is needed. This will be explored further in chapter 3

Networks and community

There is a substantial body of research about the power of supportive and positive networks. In January 2009, The New Scientist reported on research by Nicholas Christakis, a medical sociologist at Harvard Medical School. He found that happiness tends to be spread through social contacts over time, "*..someone`s chances of being happy increase the better connected they are to happy people* " (10).

Peter Totterdell, at the University of Sheffield, found the happiness of nurses, office workers, and players in professional sports teams very much depended on the happiness of the others in the same group. Emotional displays by bank employees had a direct impact on the mood of their customers (11).

Juliet Wakefield, at Nottingham Trent University, in a study of 4,000 people, found that individuals who feel a strong sense of belonging to social groups are much happier people. There is a stronger sense of purpose and security as well as crucial social support during times of stress and crisis, *"it's that subjective sense of belonging that's crucial for happiness"* (12). You may be part of a group growing vegetables sustainably in an urban area. You lose your partner to cancer, and it's the urban farm group who help you through the nightmare.

Youth surely, of all the generations, is most about `potential`. Youth always need role models and networks around them which teach positive values and foster genuine friendships. We need to reflect on this research on networks with the challenges facing our urban youth in mind. Today Britain hardly has a youth service left.

The young woman's experience above, really shows how crucial a network, or community of positive support, can be in breaking through in one's life. The psychological desire to be part of something worthwhile together with others is very fundamental to human beings. We are hardwired for community. Its opposite, loneliness and the pain of involuntary isolation, is strongly associated with depression, paranoia, anxiety, insomnia and fear. Being part of something worthwhile with others can be a powerful route to becoming more of the person you can be. Here is the voice of someone I worked with in my community development work, who began to fulfil much more of her potential through becoming involved with her community,

"I've changed an awful lot personally. You get into the thing of being a housewife and a mum. I'm sure there's an awful lot of people like me. You just don't think about anything. You do things automatically. You stop functioning. When I became involved, I realised there was something else outside the house. Then I just got interested and explored a lot of things. It opened my eyes. I realised, when I was exploring, that councillors and officers do have an effect. They have an involvement in my life, outside of me and the situation I was in. All those influences have a direct effect. I just never thought about it. It's a very gradual process. The realisation or knowing that I could actually do something else. That I was a person in my own right and not only somebody's wife or somebody's mother. And I could write a letter to a councillor or I could get a group of women together." (13)

The research published by Local Trust in 2018 on the future for communities found that some communities need support (14). Poverty, fragmentation, transience, isolation, when they come together, say on an estate, mean that community is unlikely to become self-organising without the right kind of support. I explore more about networks and communities in chapter 4.

Organisations

For Britain to do better at fulfilling its potential, the organisations across the country, of all kinds, need to be working well. Just imagine if the 1.5+ million organisations across the country were working really well [see note (15) for how this was calculated]. Sadly they don't all work well.

Companies get it wrong. Civil society organisations can too. But it is the public services where I think the greatest problems lie in terms of Britain fulfilling far more of its potential. I examine this in chapter 8.

Here is Frederic Laloux's take on organisations today,

"We are increasingly disillusioned by organisational life. For people who toil away at the bottom of the pyramids, surveys consistently report that work more often than not is dread and drudgery, not passion or purpose….….Life at the top of pyramids isn't much more fulfilling. Behind the facade ….……the lives of powerful corporate leaders are ones of quiet suffering too. Their frantic activity is often a poor cover up for a deep sense of emptiness. The power games, the politics and the in-fighting end up taking their toll on everybody. At both the top and the bottom, organisations are more often than not playfields for unfulfilling pursuits of our egos, inhospitable to the deeper yearnings of our souls" (16)

Many organisations are completely stuck, have poor leadership, and actually are extremely ineffective at what they are supposed to be doing. There is enormous alienation here. In some industries we have people cutting corners, making the organisation dangerous. There are just too many poorly run organisations frustrating the people working in them. With organisations in Britain there is a great deal of frustrating of potential. I examine the next generation of organisations in chapter 5.

Politics

What does politics have to do with each of us realising potential? As the woman in the quote earlier said, *"I realised, when I was exploring, that councillors and officers do have an effect"*. Politics sets a framework within which the country functions. The government of the day brings a specific consciousness which binds the people enacting that politics together. Their values spread around the society. The political story of the day impacts on us. George Monbiot, presenting the ideas in his book *Out of the Wreckage*, said, *"The poor blame themselves, it's your fault if you are obese, unemployed or run into debt" (17)*. Politics has a bearing on how some people value themselves and how well the ecology of support is working.

Day to day, we see a politics of firefighting on the surface of things. There is, to say the least, widespread distrust of the political system and those who people it. There is a pervasive sense of politicians not working in the interests of the ordinary man and woman. In 2017 the New Economic Foundation found that 8 in 10 people think they have little or no power over decisions made by the government, councils or local services (18). Voters believe they have extremely limited influence over the key institutions of the country. The formation of parties to rival the two main ones, has done nothing to alter this sense of powerlessness.

There are strengths in our politics. The constituency work of MPs has an open-door policy: anyone can approach an MP in their constituency (fatally exploited in the case of Jo Cox). It is a very positive, taken for granted part of today's Britain that there are freedoms of the press, expression, association, speech, thought, and belief. Moreover, there is the rule of law. Of course, informed people will want to qualify each of these. But the fact is we are nowhere near being merely majoritarian, in which there is no free speech and the rule of law is shaky. We definitely are a democracy (but one that could do with some serious further development).

The current political culture is not very attractive. It is one of aggression, self-absorption, and refusal to reach out beyond its own arguments. It is one of increasing polarisation. It does not help that politicians seem to be able to get away with outright lies and not be in the least accountable (for example *we will ensure nobody is homeless*"). The MPs' expenses scandal reinforced a sense that this representative system is no longer adequate. Around half had no link to their constituency before they became an MP. You do sense there may be one or two conflicts of interest.

Britain today is a complex place. How can politicians, without having their feet properly on the ground, actually know what it is like in Britain? And if there are politicians who do know what it is like, how good will they be at actually getting the right things done? What are the right things? No one seems to know anymore. And this is possibly one of the factors, pulling people back from any real belief in the ability of politicians to make the really substantial changes that are needed.

The dominant political consciousness *does not recognise the inner lives of people*. There is nothing particularly supportive of the spiritual dimensions of life coming through our politics. We do not yet have a politics in Britain *designed* to support individuals, families, networks, communities, and organisations to realise potential. People are looking for a new dimension in politics, which I discuss in chapter 6.

Moving on to consciousness

How am I defining consciousness? I am not talking about the actual mechanics whereby brain matter generates consciousness. This is the stuff of cognitive and neuro science. I am not trying to connect potential with what consciousness in itself is. Rather I am talking about what colours and creates very specific states of awareness of oneself in relation to the world. There's no question that stone age man and woman had very different consciousnesses compared with ourselves. In the stone age, magic and kinship coloured the prevailing consciousness. If by 'today' we take the kind of rational outlook created by 'the enlightenment', then science, technology, and the complexities of inter-personal relatedness (way beyond just kinship) colour the consciousness.

In this use of the word consciousness all four quadrants are engaged in an outlook particular to that stage in human development. Here consciousness is about the social, cultural, and political, as well as personal and collective identity. For example, there are contexts in which large numbers of people share a specific type of consciousness. This can involve the followers of a religion, a political party or people working in a corporation. Your consciousness shapes your stance within the world around you. It gives meaning to living. In this book consciousness is what connects individuals realising potential and the country (or any collectivities within it) realising potential. I am arguing that changing our consciousness is *the* most powerful way to realise more of our own potential. As more of us do this the country better realises potential.

Has anyone developed a way of looking at this very experiential approach to consciousness? Quite a few people have. Here I am going to focus on the colour coded way of talking about consciousness, that I have already touched on, by Ken Wilber and others (19),

"...there are indeed higher and lower (or more or less evolved and aware) structures of consciousness, and that we, as individuals and societies, can grow to higher levels in progressive stages or waves of development" (20)

The merit of drawing on Wilber's definition is that it provides a short hand way to talk about consciousnesses that is fairly well known. It also connects with history and gives insight into why things in the world have developed as they have. I will be using these colours, so readers will need to become familiar with what each colour stands for. To help with this there is a chart below and subsequent chapters explain these consciousnesses through stories, making the differences between them much clearer. Much of the book is focusing on just two: orange and teal.

Table 2

Wilber's consciousnesses

	Description	Examples	Strengths	Weaknesses
Teal	**Integral** Humanistic leadership.	Self-organising autonomous teams.	Holistic problem solving.	Takes effort to develop. In the minority.
Green	**Pluralistic** Non-directive leadership.	Civil rights. Environmental activism. Feminism.	Holistic problem finding.	Endless search for consensus.
Orange	**World centric** Leadership from reason.	Science. Technology. Business.	Universal approaches. Questioning dogma. Responsive to change.	Materialistic. Disconnected from inner life.
Amber	**Ethnocentric** Leadership from rules.	Organised religion. Agriculture. Institutions. Bureaucracies.	Stable. Enduring. Covers a large area.	Strict norms. Inequality. Controlling.
Red	**Egocentric** Leadership of the strong.	Mafia. Prisons. Combat zones.	Can spot opportunities & respond to threats ruthlessly.	Planning/developing strategy.

Before we explore these colours, we need to appreciate that they show the progress humanity has made: from egocentric, to ethnocentric, to world centric, to pluralistic to humanistic. There is a subtlety about that progression: each movement forward rings truer. What has gone before has become problematic. We need to bear in mind that once a consciousness becomes embedded in a particular culture, country, population and time, its centre of gravity or fundamental point may not be so evident. It has become the prevailing way of thinking or the norm. Norms are not easy to see when you are in them and living them. What Wilber's colour coding enables us to do is break out of being submerged within a norm we were not aware of being in!

I am going to start with red: power. These are wolf packs. Red is about the leadership of the strong. It is a very ego centred consciousness. With red we have someone at the centre and foot soldiers and slaves doing the dirty work. Rewards and punishments are understood. You submit to a warlord in return for protection. With red, think mafia, inner city gangs, combat zones, civil wars, and prisons. These ways of being organised are not great at planning or developing strategy. But they can spot opportunities and respond to threats ruthlessly.

The movement on from red is amber. It is stable because of its rules. We are entering the world of organised religion, agriculture, states, institutions, bureaucracies, and the military. Everyone has their proper place. There is more awareness (than with red) of others' feelings and perceptions. But it is ethnocentric. You are with us or against us. For amber religion, there is just one true way. Amber society is about simple morals based on a right way of doing things. Amber is about order, stability, and predictability. There is inequality and strict norms holding that inequality in place. Control is exercised through hierarchies. Amber organisations, such as came into being with the formation of the welfare state, can operate across huge geographical areas. They can scale. They are not only stable, they endure.

Amber may be fine for stable contexts, but once there is turbulence the ability to continually re-appraise and, if necessary, change course, is needed. Breaking out of the straitjacket of amber, humanity has moved on to orange. This can create goals and plans that can shift as circumstances change. This is the great use of reason. It is modernity as progress, success, achievement, and unlimited wealth creation. Set alongside this are ideals for justice, equality and freedom. Whereas amber was ethnocentric, orange is world centric. It wants what is best for everyone. It wants universal approaches.

Orange investigates and harnesses nature's laws for human benefit. The scientific method and continual development of technology is orange. So too is entrepreneurship. Standards of living continually improve. So too does the reckless exploitation of resources. And very crucially for Britain and its culture, *"the subjective realm is fundamentally set apart from the objective realm"* (21). Orange can't connect with peoples' inner lives and instead focuses on observable behaviour. With orange authority, norms, rules and traditions can all be questioned. Religious and political dogma can be questioned without the questioners being imprisoned. But this questioning has its limits. New little ambers also get created like private schools, privileged neighbourhoods, and exclusive clubs. This worldview is materialistic and suspicious of spirituality. With orange think machines. Think the mainstream consciousness in Britain today.

Amber and orange think they are the right way to view and do things. A Britain dominated by amber and orange, in the sixties, gave birth to the next consciousness: green. This consciousness is currently the leading edge.

In the sixties the freedom to question authority reached new heights. This consciousness rejected so much emphasis on reason. Green does not like the materialistic nature of orange. Green seeks fairness, equality, harmony, community, cooperation and consensus. Everything is inter-connected. Think holistic. Greens are seeking close, harmonious bonds. The positive side of green is that it has powered civil rights in America, the worldwide environmental movement, and feminism.

While a strength of green is to see what needs to change, how to achieve this and what path needs to be taken, is not so clear. Thus, the search for consensus can be endless. Although green rejects amber and orange, at the very same time, *"all perspectives deserve respect"*. There is not enough going on within a green consciousness to bring different perspectives together. In fact an absolutist tendency in green will prevent perspectives being heard! Green actually is not really a departure from the *type* of consciousness that has preceded it. Green still thinks it is the correct way to see the world, just like amber and orange. A world which just had amber and orange has now become a world with amber, orange and green. The tendency to polarisation has increased.

Along with these factors, Wilber argues postmodernism has also contributed to the inability of people with a green consciousness to take up leadership positions effectively across society. Where postmodern thinking arrives at a position of 'there is no truth`, to the extent that this filters into green consciousness, it undermines people taking on leadership. Wilber sees green as a 'badly tilted` consciousness in need of greater clarity about making it work positively.

But there is a next colour. This is the consciousness we are moving into and Wilber calls it teal. There is trust in the abundance of life in the universe with teal. Teal is more than world centric, it is able to act on cosmic truths. The ego is not in the driving seat. There is a quest for wholeness, bringing together the ego and deeper parts of the self. A more expansive, embracing self is there. Teal is not fearful and needing to control. Problems become challenges. How can we grow from engaging with this problem? There is a healthy development of self *and* concern and interest in others. Teals develop themselves inwardly, spiritually. But they are able to connect this with complex realities. Life is always teaching us about ourselves and the world. Teal has thinking and rationality, teal has doing, and it also has *being the person I can be*. Teal will tap into all kinds of knowing from analytics to the wisdom to be found through emotion and intuition. With teal there is great leadership, but because it is based on self-organising with this breadth of life, it becomes the most inclusive leadership of any of the consciousnesses. There is a real sense of everything being deeply connected in a living universe (22). We are working together with others to find a deeper place to come from where we can become these more fulfilled people. Think life itself.

Earlier I said that changing consciousness is the *most* important part of realising potential. Wilber characterises teal as a significant quantum leap for humanity. It is of a different order of consciousness compared with those preceding it. What distinguishes teal is an overwhelming sense of the underlying unity of humanity. The workings of life bear equally on everyone and everything in teal. Thus, diversity, though teal, gains a unifying framework, within which the strengths of green, orange, and amber can begin to work together within a shared, larger whole.

Unlike green, for teal, *not all views are equal*. Some views are more true. Depth exists. Teal is able to see the limitations of previous consciousnesses, and their strengths. Teal has the ability to develop a unifying culture in which people with other consciousnesses can work. Laloux`s researches show teal leadership at work in organisations going back 10-20-30 years. So even though teal is being portrayed as the next consciousness, actually teal has been around for some time, as we will see.

Wilber`s profiling is of a society like Britain having a majority in the population with amber or orange, then maybe a quarter with green, and possibly 5% teal. Teal and green are not the majority. In a democracy that might seem to stop the realisation of potential beyond what is being realised now. But we will see in the course of the book that this is just not so. Teal has impact far greater than numbers in the population. Teal is the highest expression of consciousness that we know today that is workable within society on a mass scale.

Mapping potential and consciousness

You can map your own ecology of support for realising potential, together with the consciousnesses, using this self-diagnostic chart. You might be able to see new ways forward.

We can use the example of the young woman earlier in this chapter. Let us call her Susi and that the bullying etc was all around the red consciousness. Her way forward was not, initially, coming from family and friends, but from a very teal community who supported her over a lengthy period to move through stages of internal growth until a teal Susi emerged. In fact, that community offered an organisational framework in which she could play an active part. The community and its organisation enabled her to make a very big change in her consciousness towards teal. There can be enormous power in a committed individual working intensively on themselves while at the same time being part of a community in which very rapid internal development is being supported.

Table 3
Using the self-diagnostic tool

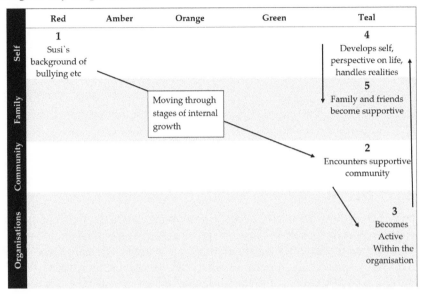

	Red	Amber	Orange	Green	Teal
Self	**1** Susi's background of bullying etc				**4** Develops self, perspective on life, handles realities
Family			Moving through stages of internal growth		**5** Family and friends become supportive
Community					**2** Encounters supportive community
Organisations					**3** Becomes Active Within the organisation

With this one example reader`s can hopefully get a sense of how to use this tool. Other examples might be Joe, with a red consciousness, who hates being in an amber organisation. Or it might be Alice who has developed a green consciousness but feels marginalised, misunderstood and just not taken seriously in an orange family. What parts of their ecology of support might offer them a way forward? The use of this tool will really become more beneficial when it is part of a personal development process shared with others where the rich realities of life can be talked through.

With the teal consciousness, I think there are many more than 5% in Britain. Many have been beavering away on their own. I think there are many people who actually have a teal consciousness but just have not yet named it. So, when you map your ecology of support against consciousnesses you will no doubt be asking yourself whether you are teal? Is this the first time you have named it? Do you know of teal in your ecology of support? Do they know they are teal? Teal gives us a start point for this book: is teal the consciousness that will mean Britain realising its potential? But first let us get to grips with orange Britain.

2 - Market based Britain

"It is a remarkable paradox that, at the pinnacle of human material and technical achievement, we find ourselves anxiety-ridden, prone to depression, worried about how others see us, unsure about our friendships, driven to consume and with little or no community life"

Richard Wilkinson and Kate Pickett (1)

In this chapter I want to take a look at market-based Britain. I am not the only person to have done this. There are three books I would draw attention to. In their different ways they are about us not yet living in a Britain where we can all realise our potential. Implicit in what they are saying is a sense that the prevailing consciousness, the market-oriented orange one, is now undermining the country. The three books are Paul Verhaeghe's *What About Me*, David Marquand's *Mammon's Kingdom*, and George Monbiot's *Out of the Wreckage* (2).

The psychotherapist voice of Verhaeghe gives us orange and teal examples which I draw from in this book. But what I think really distinguishes this work lies in the title. He is expressing immense frustration that our inner lives don't count in an orange world. The sub title is, *"The struggle for identity in a market-based society"*. For Verhaeghe, in a market-based society there is no way we are all able to live with the full radiance of our being.

As the title implies, David Marquand's intellectual voice addresses the materialism pervading Britain, restating some of the fundamentals he sees as essential to a better functioning Britain, but which are being eroded by a market-based society.

George Monbiot, as a well-known journalist, has long addressed what he sees as the worst of all possible worlds continually operating in Britain: the market-based society has literally created a wreckage. What will get us out of the mess? Firstly, rich participating cultures; secondly, developing a stronger sense of ourselves; thirdly, getting people involved in financial decisions; and fourthly, tackling economic neglect. In *Out of the Wreckage* he particularly points to Britain's civil society as a source of renewal.

This book is also contributing to this emerging `this is where we need to go` literature. I wish to contribute the notion of the country having an operating system, which in turn allows us to re-define politics as the struggle over its configuration.

Britain's operating system(OS)

Brian Robertson has given organisations a way to transition from amber/orange/green to teal. He calls it holacracy. He uses the concept of changing the operating system of the organisation, in order to make such a fundamental change.

"...we must move beyond bolting on changes and instead focus on upgrading the most foundational aspects of the way the organisation functions. ....When we change things at this level, we are effectively installing a new organisational operating system, infusing new capacities into the core of how the organisation functions" (3)

Rather than this being a book about bolting on yet more changes to Britain I want to apply this concept to Britain itself by identifying four core elements of the OS. These are civil society, markets/businesses, the state, and the values and consciousness driving the particular configuration of these elements.

When we come to look at our history (chapter 7) we will see that the configuration of civil society, markets and state powering the industrial revolution had radically altered by the time the welfare state was introduced in 1945. Yet another change in Britain's OS took place between 1989 and 1991, when an extremely market oriented central government legislated market reforms into councils, the NHS and many other areas. I lived through that change. It was literally like the earth's magnetic field reversing. Thus began a configuration of power between civil society, markets, and the state driven this time by a radically different consciousness from that which had powered the post-war welfare state. This is the current OS.

Civil society, markets and the state

Because these three elements are so fundamental to this book I want to spell out what I mean by them.

Civil society is where we grow up and where we live. It is our neighbours, our friends, and any involvement we have in communities and networks. Civil society embraces community groups, voluntary associations, religious groups (and their places of worship), community halls and not-for-profits of all kinds. You're going to find a grouping of people doing virtually everything conceivable in our civil society. It is quite incredible.

In Britain's civil society a group of people seeking to do something can always find some way to organise themselves, run something and do something together. The key thing is that the organisations of civil society are, in very many cases, under the control of ordinary people. There is much less 'command and control' than in corporate and public services (although sadly the bigger charities are aping corporates, often as a condition of funding). People learn to work together for a shared purpose. It can be an intensely human experience.

Civil society is where the democratic 'freedom to associate' happens on a truly enormous scale. Generally, people are completely unaware of the significance of being able to freely associate. We take it for granted. Our civil society is vast and very deeply present. There are around 160,000 registered charities employing 821,000 people. But this ignores the large number of community groups which are 'unincorporated associations' and are not registered as charities.

Every day new campaigns are launched, new help lines set up, new services come into being, new sources of advice and support are offered. The internet too is playing a part. When people talk about liking the British way of life, our civil society is one of the things they are talking about. Its freedoms, depth, and breadth help define Britain. This continually evolving sophistication and depth of civil society is a major force helping with the political stability of the country.

Turning to markets, when you are out and about in the 80% of the country we call 'urban', you see shops, and buildings housing the 1.3 million employing organisations in Britain. It is where 26 million work: in shops or for companies or as self-employed. Enterprises are generally visible to us, especially if we use them regularly. Advertising tells us they are there. This is the engine of wealth in the economy. Markets encompass all the different kinds of businesses in all the different industries that exist. It is where we buy and sell anything and everything.

There is a third substantial sphere of activity: the state. For most of us this is much more hidden. Walking around where you live, among the local shops and businesses, you may find the local hospital, care home, homeless project, your child's school, the police station or the town hall. Here is 'the state' at a very local level.

If you earn a reasonable salary, your experience of the state may be limited. You still have to make tax returns (HMRC is a central government agency and part of the civil service), your dustbins are emptied (by the local council), you pay council tax (to your local council), and when you want to build an extension you need approval (from your local council's planning department). For some people that can be about the extent of their dealing with 'the state'.

But if you are claiming benefit you have a much more direct, ongoing connection with the state. If you go and see your GP or you have a child at a state school, your involvement with the state is greater. You may need care, you may need housing, and not be able to buy, in which case your involvement with 'the state' is greater still (even if it is with agencies funded by or contracted by the state).

The state fills gaps left by civil society and markets. In its regulatory role it does what is needed for civil society and markets to work. As we know that is not without controversy. For historians of Victorian Britain this probably sounds far too neutral. In British history the state has, on many occasions, sought to repress popular revolt using violence. In this book I have interpreted making civil society and markets 'work', as getting local public services to work, especially across the big social policy areas like benefits, health, care, housing, education, and criminal justice. This is where the government directs the bulk of public spending. I know there are many many other things the state does, but for me getting public services across the country enacting these five social policy areas well, is a litmus test of the state doing a good job for Britain.

To get an idea why 'the state' might be such a strong influence in British society, when you add up the organisations of the civil service, local authorities, the NHS, education, and criminal justice, they come to something in the region of 30,000 organisations. The state uses just under half of GDP, employing over 5 million of us. So it is a very strong presence in the lives of the people of Britain.

Let us now look at each of these three elements in so far as they reflect the dominating orange conscious of Britain.

Civil society today

Civil society in general is a huge positive for Britain. However a load has been put on it by the state and by markets. As the opening quote for this chapter suggests, civil society, in an orange Britain, is also home to some shocking realities. In Britain we measure things. We produce statistics. Digging around, this is the picture my research has found.

Our civil society is home to a lot of people who have very little income. The Office for National Statistics finds that 10% of our population own nearly half the country's wealth (I don't think the aristocrats even achieved that!). The poorest half of the population own 9% of the wealth. The richest 10% have seen their wealth grow by 20% since 2012. The poorer half just 7%. The UK is now one of the most unequal countries in the world when it comes to wealth, income, and assets (4).

Given this, it is hardly surprising to find we have a lot of people with very little savings or who are in debt. In September 2016 the Money Advice Service found more than 16 million Britons who have less than £100 in savings (5). In Britain today the poorest 10% have debt more than 4 times their income. Based on figures from the Office for National Statistics, the average household in the UK now owes a record amount of £12,887 (6).

The idea that there is a benefits system and that therefore there is no poverty, does not hold up. There is funeral poverty, loss of meals on wheels, malnutrition (yes, malnutrition - more in a moment), food banks, benefits under or incorrectly paid, and 1.5 million children in poverty. There is considerable poverty in the UK, however we define it. The levels of poverty we are seeing in Britain today have not been seen for decades (7).

While it may seem unbelievable that there is malnutrition in Britain, the fact is that the number of meals on wheels in 2010/11 was 75,885 but by 2013/14 it stood at just 29,605 (8). A survey of 10,000 nurses in June 2016 found almost 4 in 10 nurses had treated patients whose health had been affected by malnutrition (9). The biggest growth in voluntary organisations is in foodbanks! Food poverty is at its worst level according to the Trussell Trust. They have distributed the highest number of food parcels in 12 years. Between April to Sept 2016, 519,342 three-day emergency food packs were given out. 36% of them went to children. 44% of these food parcels were needed because of problems with the benefits system (10).

It is the north that has the most vulnerable poor. The cities in the north of England, the Midlands and Scotland have the highest numbers of families in crisis (low income and dealing with complex issues).

Meanwhile there are 40,000 new millionaires from rising house prices (11). So, let us look at whether in British civil society you are going to be able to have somewhere to call home. We need to bear in mind that housing is not a commodity. It is the very basis from which to be able to have a life. It is very very fundamental. Homelessness is not a statistic it is about whether you can live *in* the society.

Just Fair housing reckon 200,000 families are living with other families (12). In 2016, 68,560 families were in temporary accommodation: the highest level since the peak of the financial crisis (13). By January 2017 the number of rough sleepers had doubled since 2010 (14). Major cities are seeing a lot more people sleeping rough and ending up in a cycle of drugs, homelessness, and prison.

Civil society is also the home of a substantial drugs problem. On average in 2016, every five hours someone died through using heroin and/or morphine. Wales, the North West and North East of England have the highest rates. Legal highs or `new psychoactive drugs` reduce people to a zombie-like state. There is a connection between this kind of addiction and crime. The police see the same faces again and again.

There is also considerable stress in Britain today. Continuous stress can raise blood pressure, weaken the immune system and trigger anxiety/depression which in turn can trigger over-eating. If a large part of a working day is stressful, when the brain is overpowered by emotions, there can be outbursts. And stress can be there for children and young people facing exams, especially given the increased use of this form of assessment. All this can be made worse if we don't sleep well.

Health is poor for people leading `difficult lives`: meaning lives of inadequate housing, overcrowding, food poverty, overwork, unemployment, struggling to pay the rent, being threatened with eviction and family breakdown. Dealing with just one of these can take its toll on a person's health.

Mental health really stands out, directly affecting about *a quarter* of the population in any one year (15). Anxiety and depression are the most common forms. Prescriptions for antidepressants were at an all-time high in 2016, and 50% more than 10 years before (16) There are a huge number of complex medical conditions which are added to almost on a daily basis. (see list note 28). About 200 die every day from coronary heart disease. Then there is asthma, stroke, obesity and cancer.

There are shocking levels of violence encompassing domestic violence, race hate, knifings, and violent intolerance in the name of religion. In 2013/14, there were 47,571 'racist incidents' recorded by the police in England and Wales. On average, that is about 130 incidents a day (17). In 2013/14, there were 44,480 hate crimes recorded by police in England and Wales. Of these, 37,484 were recorded as race hate crime. After, the Brexit referendum, race hate spiked ominously (18). Racist attack, however measured, accounts for a substantial amount of the day-to-day violence in Britain.

All this *has* to be impacting negatively on our social fabric. Since the 1950s *"Do you think most people can be trusted?"* has been a staple question in surveys across Europe. In Britain, in the 50s, the answer was 60% yes. Now it's 30%. (19). The social fabric of the country feels like it is being torn. Levels of trust between people are at an all-time low.

All in all we can say that there is a significant body of people in our population living in civil society in Britain today, who are not able to develop their potential because their basic needs are not just unmet; for many they are felt to be unmeetable.

Orange markets/businesses

The great British Class Survey conducted by the London School of Economics, and the work of Guy Standing (School of Oriental and African Studies), tell us there are no less than 7 classes in today's Britain. They are:

The elite 6%;
The established middle class 25%;
A technical middle class 6%;
New affluent workers 15%;
The traditional working class 14%;
Emergent service sector 19%;
and the precariat 15% (See note 20)

If we just take the last two groups, 34% of the population is likely to be in insecure work or on low pay. There are also 'hidden workers'.

In the first part of 2016 the number of people in work approached record levels. But much of the growth in employment has been in insecure or temporary work. While the numbers in self-employment are rising, they work longer hours, are generally low paid, and without pension provision. Although the self-employed may well be the most engaged overall, work doesn't pay enough. For many it is difficult to earn enough to live on. Income inequality statistics, numbers in poverty, families `just managing`, or people homeless means employment is not circulating wealth sufficiently to people at `the bottom of the pile`.

More and more people dislike working for big corporations, finding the culture alienating. Gallup polls tell us very few of us are actually engaged with our work (21). `Working one's way up the ladder` no longer holds the attraction it might have in the past. With the internet, for many, it is no longer necessary.

It is wonderful that we have a vibrant body of companies and businesses of all kinds. Nevertheless, Mike Ashley (Sports Direct) and Phillip Green (BHS) show us that not all are led by trustworthy or responsible individuals. Certain practices should be illegal. Many ask what really is the justification for top CEO pay.

The state in market- based Britain

The welfare state was formed because of the levels of suffering by the poor and working class. It took a monumental struggle to get the state to take this on. Given the great long list of areas of suffering and human vulnerability catalogued above, we have to ask: where are the public services? Prisons are full. Exclusion from schools is pervasive. How schools, health services and social care want to work is being severely hampered. We will see that this is not just about money, although that obviously is very key.

Historically around 40% of GDP is used for public spending. It was just 12% in 1900. By 2016 it was 44%. (22). In November 2015 £742 billion was going on public spending of which:

£217 billion went on the benefit system;
£117 billion on the NHS;
£58 billion on education (23)

So, a major weakness in Britain would seem to be that despite huge expenditure on public services, this enormous range of disturbing realities, which in many cases are clearly weakening the social fabric, seem to be either on the increase, or at very high levels.

Today's OS

In the 1980s the state started to take on board the philosophies and practices that hitherto had been the domain of markets and businesses. Up until that point it was the state that had been dominant. Its public administration (meaning a very bureaucratic approach), had even dominated businesses. Businesses had had to find enterprising ways to avoid being hemmed in by bureaucracy. But by the 80s the government wanted enterprise to be applied to all *state* services.

There were various ways government at that time signalled a move towards market thinking: de-regulating markets; elevating the position of the city; and pre-occupying itself with matters economic, money oriented, financial, and private sector.

So, it was that market thinking came into the ascendant, dominating even the state. It is compelling stuff: how does a modern liberal democracy run a mass society? Is it going to be through bureaucracy or through markets? From the evidence of the welfare state between the second world war and the 70s/80s, the government went for markets as *the* way to run this mass liberal democracy.

And markets exercise colossal power, way beyond national frontiers and the control of governments. We have seen how, through globalisation, a locally elected government in Britain has been powerless to control the impact of currency markets on the pound. Global companies, to some extent, have had free rein over where they base themselves and which government they pay taxes to. And in 2007/8, during the financial crisis, it seemed as if the state had a limitless amount of money with which to bail out failing banks. Government seemed willing to put *any* amount of money into markets. The state put £500 *billion* into the banks in 2008. Films like 'Inside Job' show the capture of the political system by the financial sector in the USA. And many feel something similar may be happening in the UK.

What has become all pervasive in Britain today, is that since the 1980s, government itself has consistently put markets in prime position. Successive governments have been requiring central government departments and local public services to function as if they were businesses in markets.

Figure 1

Today's market-centred configuration

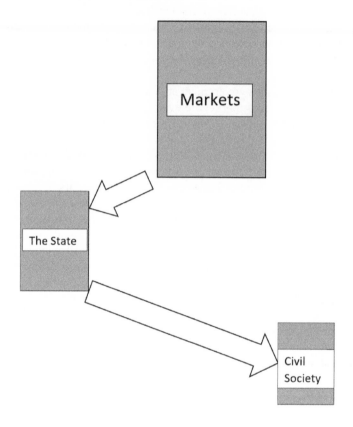

In this diagram of today's operating system, markets/ businesses are centre stage. The state is off to the side, but subjecting *itself* to market-oriented policies. And then the state influences civil society, which is in the most subordinate position within the country.

Having civil society in this subordinate position, shows in the shocking picture we see above. It is like a dumping ground for the failures and worst human indignities of a materialistic and market-oriented culture.

This puts a lot of pressure on ordinary people. There is much more in civil society that requires money. I'm thinking about finding accommodation that enables one's child to go to a school of their/your choice. Or it might mean that finding care for a relative that one can afford is just much harder, given that many families simply can't care for relatives.

The aspiration from the 80s has been that, by becoming like businesses in markets, public services would cost less, money would go further, be better controlled, and that generally, public services would be far more efficient. Interestingly, this thinking came from government!

Because the state championed this thinking, markets and businesses didn't have to. So here is the quid pro quo in this strange, government created and contrived, operating system. Markets will be left in the de facto dominant position by government. Government will be fully supported by markets to create a state/society in which private sector thinking rules. I think we could call this arrangement `cosy`!

The orange consciousness powering this OS

Having worked within state-controlled services, albeit with an unbelievably free rein to do community development work, I have experienced first-hand, from the 90s onwards the vast amount of guidance pouring out of central government onto local public services. It is completely hidden from the public eye. But it controls what is done around the country. When you are on the receiving end of this, year in year out, certain parts of it tell you what kind of thinking or consciousness is at work.

Reviewing many documents, my notebooks, and things I have written over the period, I have been able to distil out what I think has until now remained hidden from view. This is an experience specific to our public services, but once that list of attributes is set out, I have then taken it on to a second stage to suggest the consciousness driving our current OS, more generally.

So here is the quite detailed `specification` of the consciousness driving orange Britain`s public services:

1 Money is primary in regulating human behaviour *and* the performance of organisations (hence benefit sanctions, and payment by results contracts);

2 Human judgment within public services needs to be replaced with standardised measuring (hence questionnaires and scoring). Public services themselves need to be `measured` (hence audits and inspections);

4 Public services require criteria (for eligibility) and standards (that users can expect and staff know they have to provide). What is provided needs to be standardised;

5 Because bureaucracy is inherently inefficient, public provision, wherever possible, should be through contracts, which are transparent and ensure accountability;

6 One of the key ways to do this is by breaking up bureaucracies and market testing what results so that contracted companies take on significant parts of the work;

7 Where this is not possible public services can always be restructured so that they better conform to managerial criteria and become more efficient;

8 All public provision should face challenger alternatives (like academies, rehabilitation trusts etc);

9 `Units` of public service should, as far as is possible, be seen as free standing. Competition between units of public provision is fundamentally good because it helps to shake things up.

Here are the fundamental market values about how public services should operate internally:

1 Human interactions within public services need to conform to centrally laid down criteria and processes. Staff of all kinds need to comply with managements` requirements (the right to manage);

2 Generally, the larger the unit of public service, the better, in terms of reducing unit costs and therefore being more cost-effective (hence the joining together of services across councils, multi academy chains etc etc). The need for support services from outside free-standing units should be reduced as much as possible;

3 An ongoing flow of quantitative/statistical data should be generated by all public provision. The human element should be stripped out so that there is greater reliance on information;

4 Roles need to be adjusted to meet demand within budgets (hence new roles for lower paid staff to take on work that previously required professional qualifications);

5 The model of market oriented public provision requires the feedback mechanism of complaints, as an integral part of the managerial toolbox, in order to measure how well the service is doing and what needs to change.

We can also detect some very specific values relating to finance (bearing in mind the paramount value placed on money as *the* driver of individual and organisational behaviour):

1 All forms of public service should aim to generate a financial surplus and have private sector-like financial management (hence charging wherever possible and cost centres to pay *internal* invoicing etc);

2 Private companies and individual entrepreneurs (for example landlords) who are taking the risk of offering a public service, should not be penalised (hence the difficulty of getting contracts terminated with clearly dysfunctional contractors or of reforming housing benefit in favour of tenants). They are the wealth creators, and should be treated leniently in any funding regime and incentivised wherever possible;

3 Public provision benefits individuals and families and therefore their cost should not just be born by the state. Individuals and families should share in the cost directly by charging (like paying for a child's extra-curricular activity) or indirectly (like being sent home from hospital before having recuperated sufficiently: family and friends have to step in).

Finally there are global elements in this world of market oriented thinking:

1 Comparisons with how completely different industries in any country do things are entirely legitimate because it challenges existing custom and practice and improves efficiency;

2 National and international performance or league tables should be what the managers of public provision base targets on.

We can now take these public sector specifics a stage further and unpack from them a sense of the *overall* values and thinking driving today's operating system. This is what the country has been running on:

- o Money is primary in regulating human behaviour and the performance of organisations;
- o Competition is fundamentally good and should be encouraged at every level;
- o Reward risk takers;
- o Britain needs to compete and therefore comparisons using international league tables need to drive government policy;
- o Services should be through contracts;
- o Staff of all kinds need to comply with managements' requirements (the right to manage).

These values have not created organisations people want to work in. Uncaring, procedurally driven, and unfree working environments have been fostered that alienate staff. These values are directly related to poorly functioning leaders being left in position so long as they appear to operate these values. This in turn results in indignities and human rights abuses being covered up. Because these values are so important to maintaining power, nothing counts as evidence against their validity. It does not seem to matter how bad things get, so long as the model is adhered to.

This brings us to the most serious indictment: this model of human and organisational behaviour lacks any real insight into people. Adherents of market thinking are missing a whole dimension of life: our inner workings as human beings! The human cost of attempting to function in such a model is considerable. The examples below really spell it out. I was told these stories in confidence, recorded them in my notebooks and have left them anonymous. These are people who wanted their lives back.

"I worked part time for Childrens Social Services. Up North a couple wanted to adopt a child. At the panel, I was asked why I hadn't visited them. I work part time. When I worked full time, I had 24 cases. Now I have 20. When do I have time? The chair of the panel said, `I work part time`. That was it. I walked out and never went back. I retired. It took 4 weeks for the dark rings under my eyes and the stress to go. I wear bright clothes for the first time now."

"There is a complex dictionary of definitions I have to conform to and a vast array of instructions. I have to do it in a structured way with people observing me. The freedom to be creative and do it my way has gone. I spend my time complying"

"I was doing a maths lesson. I could do it in my sleep. But I was being observed and knew they would be looking for prescribed outcomes. In fact, I had been given a list of what they were looking for. And it wasn't a very good lesson..trying to make things happen according to these written outcomes. But the fact is I have been able to teach this kind of thing easily and get to all those outcomes. But not this time. This is the kind of thing that will be coming in more and more. I'm close to retirement..so I'm going early. It's not what I want to do."

"As a newly qualified teacher (NQT) they are putting in more and more observations of my teaching in class. Next the head will be coming in. I've looked at their NQT guidelines. This is what they do as preparation for failing an NQT. But this is all additional stress and pressure. None of it actually supports any real improvement in me feeling more confident. I'm leaving before they ruin my future career. In one of my placements I taught exactly the same material in a

genuinely supportive school and was fine. It's really this school's approach which is killing my teaching."

"A woman in her 40s without any prior educational background, but with plenty of life experience got on a community work degree course and got a 2.1. She then got a job as a social worker. After some time the employer 'discovered' she did not have GCSE in maths and required her to take an equivalent while at work. She failed this twice. She had one chance left (you could only take it 3 times). If she failed the third time she would lose the job."

There is one additional insight necessary. This is that such a consciousness supports extreme proposals and practices which have no real connection with the realities they are purporting to influence. These all assume, wrongly, that external financial sanctions will, *in all cases*, affect individual behaviour. This is one of the fatal flaws in trying to run a society on market thinking: the connection between outer and inner is just not understood. It doesn't feature.

In July 2013 fees (aka charging) were imposed in employment tribunals. These tribunals are known to be weighted in favour of employers. By 2013 it was costing up to £1200 for an employee to take an employer to a tribunal. In effect 'the underdog' is having a huge hurdle placed in front of them, in order to access mainstream judicial processes. The union Unison challenged this extreme application of charging in the supreme court and won.

Towards the end of August 2015, the minister for education proposed fining schools whose pupils failed to get at least a C grade in GCSE English or Maths (24). Why I consider this extreme is because it misses what actually creates good education and good exam results.

In March 2014, the leader of Portsmouth Council announced they would charge the parents of the children they took into care. *"It is only £50/ week...it's to show them that they have to take responsibility"* (25). This misses the fact that there are reasons for taking a child into care which are not addressed by financial penalties.

In December 2015, it was decided that the imposition of charges in criminal courts (which has seen magistrates resigning) should cease. The idea being that defendants who plead guilty should face a flat fee penalty of £150 on top of any fines or court costs. Between July and September of 2015, of the potential £22m in such charges, only £1m had been collected (26). Financial penalties self-evidently are not a deterrent. Does a flat fee penalty equate with justice?

In looking to the future, the 'free at the point of use' NHS faces the prospect of charges being used to ration access to GPs. In September 2016, an internet service allowing patients to *buy* a 15-minute session with a GP, was being suggested (27). Extending this would put us back to before there was an NHS, when only those with money could access health care and treatment.

The values identified earlier are not just resulting in the examples of the substantial human cost and extreme incentivising. Market thinking is now in the culture. It is the air we breathe. We will see later that this has been achieved in no small part through the hidden impact of the all-pervasive public services (chapter 8). No one has characterised this `air we breathe` side of market thinking more poingnantly than George Ritzer, with his distinction between `something` and `nothing` (28)!

`Something` is bound up with our real lives, strengthens our sense of self, unites us with others, and treats us as being intelligent, autonomous, and free individuals. `Nothing` is trying to present itself as `something` but everything about it is contrived, mass produced, and essentially the same wherever and whenever. It does nothing for our sense of self, treats us as a consumer and a unit in a market.

`Nothing` is impersonal, even though done between people. The interactions have been created centrally. What is on offer is standardized. Even though you might be able to have choices, they are all within prescribed limits. The `agents` of `nothing` talk to a script. Trying to depart from the script or menu, for example, to consider other options, is generally not acceptable. It all feels homogenous and devoid of any substance.

Celebrating a 40th wedding anniversary with friends and family is definitely `something`. It has real meaning, you feel engaged, and it is something that matters. Or spending a week on the Gower peninsula is definitely `something`. If you stay in a self-catering cottage with its owner next door who feels like a close relative or friend, it is really `something`. It would just not be the same being in a Premier Inn or its equivalent. This would be a bit clinical.

In Soho, London, developers took advantage of Crossrail. Rents went up by 90% and the small shops have now gone. What made it special has gone. It is just like any part of London now. `Something` and `nothing` is there in every aspect of our lives in Britain: from dentistry to B&Bs; from doing a degree to being in a band; from shopping in a supermarket to buying from a couple running a local smallholding; from gardening to buying furniture.

Grenfell Tower is almost an exact metaphor showing the massive load put onto families, friends, networks and communities by an almost non existent state: a series of contracted arrangements that left a community unsafe and with no means of redress. Instead of something they found nothing. There was literally no one for them to engage with in the public sector wasteland in which they found themselves. Grenfell is not an isolated case. It signals the realities that have been building up across the country since the 90s.

Nothing is everywhere!

In sociology, the `iron cage` is a term coined by Max Weber for the increased rationalization inherent in social life, particularly in Western societies (29). Managerial thinking traps individuals in systems based purely on (theoretical) efficiency, rational calculation and control: a modern-day iron cage.

We have only glimpsed the alienation engendered. This is happening in a context where individuals want *more* freedom to become who they can be. This is a powerful contradiction and, ironically a *source of immense energy* to challenge and change the status quo. I believe that the channelling of this energy, creatively and constructively, is one of the challenges of our time. This book is about channelling that considerable energy. This is the teal impulse: not just to be satisfied with critique (which this chapter has largely been), but to go on and show how things can be better by building what has gone before into something new and better. This extreme application, in Britain, of market thinking arose so as to completely do away with bureaucracy and all the values which came with it. Teal is not doing that. Teal is working from within orange, or green or amber towards micro and macro realities which create the connections between inner and outer, where individuals make their collectivities work. Teal is channelling the immense energy for change into unifying efforts. Jean Boulton and others have written a handy synthesis of complexity thinking, in which they say,

"..a complexity worldview sees the world as essentially interconnected and rich with forms and patterns that have been shaped by history and context. A complexity worldview reminds us of the limits to certainty, it emphasizes that things are in a continual process of 'becoming' and that there is potential for startlingly new futures where what emerges can be unexpected and astonishing" (30)

The rest of this book is given over to contrasting orange status quo realities with teal 'becomings'.

3 - Family support

"The same social life pulsated through the house, the street, and the community. The family, and within it, the marital relationship, were part and parcel of a considerably larger conversation. In our contemporary society, each family constitutes its own segregated subworld, with its own controls and closed conversation"
Peter Berger (1)

Family is like bedrock. It is people coming together through life and death, forming lifelong bonds in the face of the daily struggle for survival. These are relationships which cross the generations. At its best it provides a nurturing oasis of humanity and support within a wider world of indifference, danger and risk.

The family is at the root of so much in society. As Peter Berger`s quote (above) suggests, if the family is shut away from a larger conversation, there is reason, as a society, to find acceptable ways to offer support. Those forms of support may not directly be to `the family`. Supporting children, young people, and the elderly indirectly supports `the family`. There is plenty of evidence that such indirect forms of support are needed.

For example, in May 2016 a report gave out a figure of 500 children *a week* being taken into care. The extent of child abuse in all its forms has dominated the news year in and year out (2). For young people, housing is a major issue. The cost of accommodation is pushing young people to stay living with parents. The `bank of mum and dad` is increasingly important. May 2017 figures suggested a total of £6.5 billion coming from family and friends for things like deposits. (3).

On the older end of the spectrum, at the end of 2015, there were just under 12 million aged 65 + in the UK (approaching 20% of the population). The interface between sons and daughters of older people and the institutional arrangements for care really tests many families. It is only recently that such family carers have even been seen as carers in their own right in law, and as needing support in order not just to continue caring, but to have a life.

Acceptable support for families, direct or indirect, brings disproportionate benefit, not just to immediate family members but to society. When the family is working, many other forms of intervention are no longer needed. But adult social services, the NHS, and children's services can't do it. They are overwhelmed. Besides, are they really the best institutions to offer *family* support? Aren't there more acceptable and more effective ways to do this?

If we want the ecology of support for realising potential to flourish in Britain, the family part of it is very crucial. But, as we will see, market-based Britain has proved incapable of grasping this particular nettle. However teal type approaches could readily be brought into being, for very little money.

Here is an orange approach. This is followed by some teal examples.

Market-based support for families

Central government's 'troubled families programme' (TFP for short) was launched in April 2011, as the government's response to the riots across England in the summer of 2011. For a family to be on the programme there had to be:

1. Involvement in crime and antisocial behaviour;
2. Children not attending school;
3. An adult out-of-work on benefits.

Just in this alone we can see how fundamental to the well-being of society the family is.

The aim of this central government initiated and led programme was to 'turn around' the lives of 120,000 families. The treasury estimated these families 'cost' £35 billion annually. That is a quarter of a million per family per year purely as the cost of the services and support coming through local authorities and the welfare state. None of this money actually got to these families.

Local authorities were 'incentivised' to work with troubled families through payment by results: paid first for attaching a family to the scheme, paid later for results achieved. These are local authorities whose adult social services and children services are unbelievably stretched. They also work in very specific ways. The working lives of practitioners in such agencies are now very circumscribed.

Success in TFP speak was judged firstly on some kind of progress in relation to crime, anti-social behaviour and education (call this A). Secondly, continuous employment (call this B). The numbers 'turned around' were initially calculated as A+B! Nothing comes into these equations direct from the families themselves. There is nothing direct from them about any impact on their lives and how they feel they are doing.

Figures, calculated on this basis (A+B) and released at the end of May 2014, showed 44% or 52,833 families of the 120,000 'turned around'. However, and tellingly, only 3.8% or 4,555 families had achieved the work criterion or B

(4). For the vast majority, the definition of `turned around` had been loosened to just A!

As the assessment of `turned around` continued to shift, having one family member come off benefits constituted being `turned around`, as did having any family member with a positive outcome in the two domains.

A Freedom of Information request discovered that three quarters of those families already 'turned around' were still 'committing crime, without jobs and with children still excluded from school` (5). Data from 133 of 152 councils participating in the TFP also found that 1 in 7 families that had been 'turned around' were either 'still on drugs, had children missing from school or involved in criminal acts'. In Birmingham, of the 1,154 'turned around' as of March 2014, 92% were still receiving unemployment benefit (6).

These are families with a complexity of `issues`. If the children have begun attending school, but no one in the family is working, they are still struggling to afford food and clothing, and the mother is suffering from ill-health, has the family been 'turned around'? Until we hear direct from family members, will we ever know?

This whole approach directly reflects many elements of the values unpacked in the previous chapter. In the TFP we can see at work the central assumption that money can regulate the behaviour of organisations like councils. Payments by results contracts were used. Secondly a standardised method of measuring outcomes has removed any possibility of people in these families telling us stories about their inner lives. Finally, we see a desire to convert everything coming out of the programme into `information` reflecting greater value being placed on quantitative data than on human judgment. This is certainly an orange consciousness at work.

The teal approach: an example

Participle`s approach reflected the principles laid out by its founder Hilary Cottam in a ground breaking article on `Relational Welfare`(7). This is no theoretical paper. It is based on 10 solid years of innovating at the local level by creating support networks which major on the relationships developing between ordinary people in the network. It puts the emphasis on peer-to-peer support. Their work was rooted in developing people's capabilities and relationships. Relational welfare demonstrates teal thinking in its ability to bring people in need together as a resourceful community, sharing the running of the network, with very limited but incredibly effective supports in the shape of a few staff and good tech. Participle was about developing structures, practices and processes which functioned well with the people they worked with. They evolved how they did things by listening closely as the community came together.

Participle ran for 10 years and in 2015 closed, posting its learning on the web (see note 7).

Their work in developing the first ever circle of support in Southwark was ground breaking. Southwark Circle supported members aged 50+ to build and sustain strong social bonds and took care of their practical needs. Improving the lives of older people in this way was an indirect form of family support. Here is their account of Circle,

"Circle is a mission driven organisation: its purpose is to support older people to live flourishing independent lives. Circle achieves this through building a broad community and its ability to attract the younger older (members in their 50s and 60s) proved critical to its success since it ensured a community with the strength to support older and frailer members. At the heart of Circle is the shift from a 1950s needs-based service to one which aims to foster a core set of capabilities amongst its members. Circle does not assess its members, it meets them where they are and through its social and practical offer fosters relationships, working and learning and active contribution to the community. Participle's Capability Measurement Index used by Circle measures the success of this capability approach. Key to the success of the Circle model is the relationships members have with each other. New and diverse friendship groups sustained over time offer practical and emotional support in a light touch, everyday way and are there for when the inevitable difficult times emerge". (7)

Participle were always interested in `scaling up`. Starting from 250 people in Southwark they went on to create 3 regional circles (the two others were in Rochdale and Nottingham) and from 2009 these three comprised a national circle network with 5,000 members.

Each Circle in the network was run as a local, independent social enterprise, incorporated as a Community Interest Company employing around 5 people, and led by a full-time director. Members were asked to pay an annual subscription of £30 (intentionally set low given the aim to provide a universal service). This gave access to a local free phone 0800 number for support. The core services offered by each Circle remained those of the initial design: a rich, ever changing social calendar and on demand practical support, provided both by members themselves and paid helpers who were all checked and approved.

With circles, visits to GPs dropped off, people were no longer lonely, and their health was better. Being part of a supportive community transformed lives. How did Participle know? Because all its projects used simple tailored software to keep records and provide a supportive basis: *"the technology makes all the tools available, reduces the burden of reporting and other back office functions"* (7)

Participle also developed a way of working effectively with `troubled families` (without labelling them as such). But these *were* families who met the criteria of the government's troubled families' scheme. Participle's Life programme was born and operated in Swindon, Colchester, Lewisham and Wigan. This work directly supported `the family`. The work started in Swindon,

"In 2008 Participle was approached by Swindon (the Borough Council, Strategic Health Authority and Partners – who we will call Swindon Partners). They asked us if we would work with them to develop a new approach that might stop the cycle of crisis for a number of families they perceived to be falling through the gaps of their existing service provision. Whilst they believed the numbers of these families 'in crisis' were small – about 100 – they knew the cost implications to be large, and moreover, they believed they had a duty of care towards these families" (7).

Participle developed three broad phases of work:

- immersion in the lives of Swindon's families and frontline workers;
- rapid prototyping of new ways of working *developed with families*;
- synthesis of the approach and co-creation of the Life programme.

Just to give you an idea, here is their description of the first phase,

"Eight weeks were spent experiencing the lived reality of the families' lives: doing the school run, shopping on the high street, spending social evenings in the local pub, searching for their children after dark and witnessing negotiations with loan sharks. We also gave families cameras to film 'things we wouldn't know about them' and discovered family members who were keen horse riders, actors, maths whizzes, novel writers and artists. Finally, we sat on their sofas as a succession of policemen, social workers, learning support officers, housing officers and others made their calls". (7)

Angela (anonymised name) lived on a run-down estate in Swindon. The central government TFP was set up to `turn around` 120,000+ families like Angela`s. Participle discovered that Angela`s local authority has 73 services on offer to Angela and families like her. The family is visited regularly by a social worker, a youth worker, a home tutor, a housing officer and the local police officer. *"I just deliver the message and I leave"* is the general approach. None are able to focus on underlying issues. Participle worked out that 86% of the social worker's time is taken up filling in forms and having meetings to discuss them. The remaining face to face time isn't about positive development. It is getting answers to the questions on the forms. It is this system around these families that had been costed at £35 billion. The local public service context, in all its complexities, has now throttled the best of professional intentions.

Here is what Participle did,

"Swindon agreed that a starting point would be to reverse (the usual) ratio. In other words, all those who came into contact with Angela and other families would be able to spend 80 per cent of their time focused on the families rather than the system. Even more radically, the families would decide who was actually in a position to support them.

Angela and another mother were asked to be part of a panel who interviewed and selected a team, from existing front-line workers in Swindon, who could work with one hundred families in similar circumstances. These mothers had no time for those they thought would be 'soft' with them, and even less for those they saw as somehow dehumanised representatives of the system. They chose professionals who confessed that they did not necessarily have the answers, but who convinced them they would stick with it. These were individuals from housing, social work, and the police, who did not rely on jargon or codes. What they offered was driven by their human qualities rather than the rule books.

These new teams have been allotted only a sliver of the former budget. What they can do is spend this money in any way the families decide - on their very first family outings in some cases, in others as a float to start very successful social enterprises. All initiatives are chosen and driven by the families themselves, which is key to transformation. The team is also supported to work in new ways, with space given for supervision, reflection and learning - thereby making the difficult, open and high intensity engagement with families possible to sustain. Investing in relationships and empathy is emotionally costly, and needs its own high-calibre professional support and systems". (7)

Participle proved staff from different employing agencies, *can* work together to the agenda set by members of the community. Local people came inside 'the system' to direct how it worked. This contains a key to future public services that really work.

"We have learnt that it takes an average of two years for a family like Angela's to turn their lives around, and that there will be many steps both forward and backwards. Her children are back in full-time education, and she herself has a job she enjoys, new friendships and, as she describes it, a space within herself to continue growing. (7)

You can see that this sort of approach has not a shred of orange consciousness. It is very teal in the sense of adapting together to create a space for both individual autonomy and the community's autonomy to flourish. It has all four quadrants at work, especially *"a space within herself to continue growing".*

Participle stopped after 10 years. They could not see how the models they had proved to be effective would be taken up and funded around the country. What a tragedy of short sightedness for Britain. What they saw over 10 years was a rejection of their approach by the mainstream and the continued locking up of skills and money in old, outmoded models. The 1945 welfare state model of investing in professionals as the first call on creating scarce people power still prevails.

A second example: family groups

Here is another example of direct support to 'the family' This comes from my own fieldwork. In the late seventies, family groups offered friendship, self-respect and self-reliance, and created community where none had existed. Like Participle's projects, family groups also folded, for exactly the same reasons (8).

Family groups were small, informal groups led by local people, meeting regularly for mutual support and enjoyment. The groups gave their members the care and support like that found in a (positive) extended family. In essence they developed very positive, family-like relationships beyond 'natural' families.

They provided an opportunity to meet people, make friends, gain support and learn to cope with the stresses and strains of life. Through activities members developed new skills and self-confidence. They strengthened the bonds between parents and children. They helped children develop through play, learning new physical and social skills. They helped parents to understand and enjoy their children.

A family group has leaders: someone who works with the adults and someone who works with the children. They work as a team. They are recruited from the neighbourhood the group is in. The group leaders do a preparation course and those selected to become leaders then get going, find their group members, and start weekly meetings. The group leaders are 'paid' on quite modest sessional rates.

When you have a cluster of family groups in a local area, you get new informal networks of friendship and support springing up outside the meetings. People start connecting with education, going back to work, finding things to get involved with, and organising outings.

This was one of the points that I liked about family groups: they were attracting people that professionals were not able to reach. Help came through the interaction of the peer group, through mutual aid, rather than through professional intervention. Help of this kind is more acceptable and probably more durable than that from more formal sources.

I got to know about family groups because between 1979 and 1981 I worked as an action researcher for a 'family groups unit', which at that time was working with clusters of the groups across the country. By 1980 the unit was working with about 40 family groups. I got to understand how these groups worked from the accounts of the people in them. I also witnessed some very tortuous discussions with senior managers in education, health and social care trying to get funding. The groups were easy. Getting them properly funded and supported was not easy. Each agency had its own criteria.

In 1976, family groups became the subject of a European funded project. The research compared the groups working in an inner city with groups in a suburban area. The research highlighted the fact that the leaders were local people, who used the same shops, doctor, school and housing as their members. The leaders were seen as possessing a 'valuable independence of authority' and as providing a service not offered by any other grouping or organisation.

Having a cluster of family groups also helped the leaders support each other and share ideas. Members of the groups could come together for outings and to get courses laid on. They could refer members to other groups.

The purpose of family groups, at this point in their history, was seen as reducing isolation and fostering the growth of new personal networks that could endure beyond the group meetings. They aimed to help people cope with the normal stresses of family life, child rearing, family relationships, budgeting, health and housing problems.

By April 1978 the research project had transformed into the family groups unit. The unit started by visiting all the groups. Half were flourishing and half were moribund. The flourishing ones were all supported by a statutory worker who also provided in-service training. This is another example of the value created when staff in the local state services work together with people in civil society. It is a theme we will encounter again and again. Market based Britain has gone in the opposite direction with staff quite removed, in terms of their procedures and freedom of action, from engaging directly with activists in civil society.

The moribund groups had originally had committees locally to support them but these had disbanded and the group leaders got no support from anyone. In order to activate new resources in civil society, support is needed and committees rarely provide it. Whereas the right staff inside state services, with teal values, know how to support such groups. I saw such staff support clusters of family groups extremely successfully. It did not take much of their time, but made a huge difference. We see here the fundamental importance of the right kind of support.

How do these groups work?

The previous research had not got to grips with how the groups worked. I was seeking to rectify this and felt it could only come from group leaders and members narrating their own experiences. I needed to hear from `inside` the experience. Inspired by Shirley Otto's action research work at the time (9), I hit upon the simple solution of having a contract with the group leaders: I would do

X if they would do Y. They were more than happy with this and great material started pouring out of them.

The group leaders understood that when a new person came to a family group the chain reaction among existing members was critical. The first glances and a group leader who says something like, "Nice to see you", irrespective of appearance, is likely to cue a welcoming chain reaction. What family groups were aiming for was, *"I've never been anywhere where I've been made to feel so welcome. Never experienced such helpfulness"*.

Despite the best efforts of the group leaders and the members, sometimes a group just didn't gel. But these were the exceptions rather than the rule. A group member may do something others feel is just not acceptable, but still welcome the person when they come back after a break. Some people came infrequently but were still welcomed. Group leaders were up against the strong tendency of human beings to form cliques.

I found the groups could even embrace people who had become completely cut off and had very few social skills. For such a person to be recognised by someone else in the street is a huge thing. For them to be invited into someone else's house is massive. Imagine you cannot read or write, or that you don't know how to shop. What an extraordinary thing for that person to reveal there was nothing in the house to eat. Even more extraordinary that the group leader, after the group meeting, went shopping with this person.

This person started a literacy class and eventually joined the local library. Within a short space of time they began functioning independently, really for the first time in their adult life. Sometimes someone just needs a bit of encouragement to overcome a fear of something unknown or something new.

Activities are really crucial to family groups: doing things together. Activities build self-confidence and bring people together. They help people enjoy themselves and create a relaxed atmosphere. They also teach members things they would not otherwise learn and give them something to look forward to each week. They break the ice and get people talking with each other. They draw people into the group and provide fun, entertainment and novelty. Nothing builds self-confidence quite like doing something you have never done before. But at the same time activities have to be freely entered into. Feeling able to keep coming without *having* to join in is key. Some people are not used to making things. Some people are just shy.

With activities, one of the functions of the group leader was to make sure no one felt they were making a fool of themselves. They found out where their group members' individual talents lay and encouraged them to use them. One group member was very shy and never said anything unless spoken to. But this person had tremendous drawing skills and eventually helped the whole group with a drawing activity. They became much less self-conscious.

People who seemed to be on the periphery forever, were suddenly fully involved. Group members were competing with one another to show others how to do something quite challenging and the rest of the group were up for it. Discussions about alcoholism, unemployment, the cost of heating, or making bread might emerge from a keep fit activity or learning how to wire a plug.

Food featured heavily in most groups because cooking and eating are social activities. Group leaders often discovered how little their group members actually knew about cooking great food on a budget. For some group member's a cooking session might be just enjoyable, for others, an opportunity to learn invaluable skills.

Part of the power of the family group was that a play leader worked with the children away from the parents, giving the parents much needed space. Play leaders offered children activities such as painting, pastry, building bricks, garages and cars, puzzles, nursery rhymes, songs and juice time. Some activities were designed to include solitary children and draw them out, to overcome shyness and lack of confidence.

Each group tried, in its own way, to give parents a break from their children and to do it in a way that helped the child's development. Some children were happy to play without their mother on the first day. For others, it might take weeks. It was important for the child to make the decision.

One of the really important things was that children's behaviour often reflected something happening in the family. Children can be very tuned into underlying feelings. A parent in good spirits was likely to be reflected in the behaviour of the child. Likewise, a parent's problems often became reflected in the child's behaviour. A couple of hours in a family group can break that vicious circle.

Parents also learn from play leaders. They pick up new ideas to use at home and bring in ideas for play leaders to use. The way the play leader responds may also influence them. For parents who always shout, it's quite something to see another adult talking calmly and taking an interest.

Perhaps one of the most direct forms of help parents get from family groups is being able to talk with other parents about what they are going through. A parent who thinks their child is abnormal finds that in fact other parents have the same issues going on and they can discuss and exchange ideas.

The family group is a stable thing. Always there, regular as clockwork and always welcoming. Each family group is unique, just as the people in them are. They vary in size and composition, meet in different settings and do different activities. But all of them are aiming to create a warm, supportive environment in which members are able, in some cases for the first time in their lives, to express themselves and make friends. Within the group, once a week, they are able to try things they haven't tried before, without fear of being laughed at or being made to feel inadequate. At any one time, countless problems and setbacks in everyday life prevent members from being fully themselves. Within the group, they can talk about themselves as they are, build on positive experiences and create something new in their lives. Family group members can bring the whole of themselves to the group. And this family-like relating is emulating the kinds of families where you can admit your failings, with people who know you as you are; where there is no need for pretence. Feeling comfortable allows room for growth.

Sometimes group members met outside regular sessions in one another's homes. From there, networks of friendship often started to spread out. Late in 1979 I asked the families of 6 family groups' members what they thought about their family member coming to the group. All responded in the positive.

Family groups were bridge builders in the sense that social workers and health visitors could be 'involved', but at a distance. Families 'at risk' used family groups. The hard-pressed social worker is never going to be able to develop the relationships, through shared activity and informal dialogue, that a group leader could. Health visitors found that by going to family groups, anti-authority parents (who refused to go to a clinic), changed their attitude and made use of services. But group leaders were always wary of taking on direct requests from statutory workers asking them to tell group members something. Rather they might think about creating a situation in the group which might enable members to get the message.

Moving in this teal direction

I think you can sense this kind of thing is not coming from an orange consciousness. It has those teal qualities of heart, very embracing human relationships, people bringing the whole of themselves to the activity, and a simplicity of a community working together without any outside interference. A family group is an autonomous team.

It has been up-hill for other ventures which share an intrinsic similarity to family groups: groups like Home-Start (10). This *has* found a way to be supported by local public services. It is possibly because they represent an incredibly low cost to local state services. Today it has 16,000 volunteers supporting 30,000 families. In addition, their volunteers can be seen, by local services, as professionals offering their services to families on a voluntary basis. Families struggling with post-natal depression, isolation, physical health problems, bereavement and many other issues receive the support of a volunteer who will spend around two hours a week in a family's home supporting them in the ways they need. There are 269 local, independent Home-Starts across the UK.

Googling 'family support' will yield pages of organisations and initiatives. It is all waiting to be built on. These days the internet itself, through social media, websites etc. provides ways to bring support into the lives of individuals and families.

All these initiatives unleash the power of ordinary people to do the very things professionals are unable to do: real care, real one-to-one personal support, and group activities that empower people in their daily lives. What they provide is integration, bonding, overcoming isolation, overcoming fragmentation, learning, developing, realising dreams, and supporting one another. And this adds up to a repairing of the social fabric. They harness the power of positive networks around individuals. They protect people. They provide opportunities. And they spread active participation and meaningful involvement. They do not cost much and can be targeted where needed.

In Britain today, too little has been going into supporting this to happen. And this is an extremely powerful way in which Britain's potential is being stifled. There really are an enormous range of ways families, directly or indirectly, can get acceptable support. Far more than there is space here to present. However, they are likely to share many of the features presented in looking at Participle, family groups and Home Start. In my mind the situation in today's civil society demands we move in this direction.

4 - Networks and communities

"My only fixed truth is a belief in people, a conviction that if people have the opportunity to act freely and the power to control their own destinies, they'll generally reach the right decisions".
Saul Alinsky (1)

Since the stone age, community has been central to human experience. As this passage from Saul Alinsky suggests, a community, *able to act freely*, provides the people in it with a compass in life. It is not the same kind of compass as comes from the family, but involvement within a community brings with it a whole complex of understandings and human connectedness we cannot get in any other way.

Community is extremely hardy, despite being killed off or dying time and time again: sometimes through the actions of the state; sometimes because a market has dried up; sometimes through the internal dynamics within the community; sometimes because the shared consciousness has moved on.

Like families, community, expressing any of the consciousnesses, can be towards the positive or towards the negative. Which it is is very much to do with its leadership as well as the availability of resources necessary for it to function well. Community can be hijacked for ulterior motives by others, politicians for example. From my experience, community, with teal leadership, is sublime. I don't at all wish to suggest complacency. What makes it sublime is its consistency of effort and vigilance to maintain the health of the community throughout its `membership`. These are wanted communities, wanted by the people in them, who actively do their best to support their community. This is community like a fast-flowing stream of clear pure water. But community can also degenerate into the equivalent of stagnant water. And in stagnant water nasty things can grow.

Just what are orange networks and communities? My mind thought of entrepreneurs networking lunches. But then I remembered the enormous community that grew and grew of, *"like-minded people of the free-market persuasion"* (2). Madsen Pirie gives us an insider's account of the community that propelled Margaret Thatcher to power in her account of the setting up of the Adam Smith Institute,

"We used our contacts from the Mont Pelerin Society and the Institute of Economic Affairs, plus free-market academics whose works we had read....." (3).

It is an irony that a community of people, really functioning as a community, shared the ideology of free markets which had no real place for community! I think this gives us some idea of the timeless reality that community brings to human life.

The research Local Trust published in 2018 shows the impact of orange Britain on communities,

"Across the country, we see communities with tremendous unrealised assets – not least the imagination, energy and commitment of local residents. But where those communities have been at the sharp end of social and economic change, who and what can support them in becoming more powerful and changing their lives for the better in the future? How can we ensure that these disadvantaged communities are equipped to meet the challenges of the next decade?" (4)

In other words, they echo the experience of the community that emerged after Grenfell Tower: there is either no support for community or what there is is continually reducing. Some communities experience instability through business closure, austerity public services, and/or the `dumping ground` or `torn social fabric` impacts from market orientation (homelessness, depression, addiction, benefit sanctions, ill health etc etc). It is these communities which tend not to have the resources necessary for them to function.

Local Trust finds that `place`, despite the internet, is still important. And I would add that generally speaking if you live in one of the 10,000+ villages in Britain the fact of community is self-evident. You may not be involved in it, but the chances are it is there, and there with autonomy or the capacity to act freely. Local Trust find `place` is still important in towns and cities. Here there are also networks and communities of `identity`, based on gender, sexuality, race, ethnicity, or even nationality. But community is going to struggle where poverty, transience, fragmentation, and isolation come together. Orange Britain has been particularly harsh for many such communities. Here Local Trust argues for,

"Spaces to come together: to meet, learn, debate, plan, and act – what we have called the 'social infrastructure'. These may be face-to-face or digital, ideally both. Financial support: from seedcorn funding that will cover basic costs to larger-scale investment. Access to support from community development workers or others who can link communities in with developments elsewhere, share information, learning and skills, alert them to new possibilities and challenge them where necessary. Skills and the will on the part of decision

makers to recognise the assets and knowledge within communities and work alongside them to create change." (5)

I would go further with the last sentence and say, *"Enabling community activists to play vibrant meaningful roles inside places like town halls, directly with staff".*

To be in a highly challenging `place`, where community struggles, those few early activists, coming together for the first time, with the right kind of support, can break through, and encourage others to come forward. The two stories, which follow, illustrate this. There is a real role here for community development. Here is Local Trust`s take on key things community development offers,

"Community development approaches support people in communities of place, interest and identity to work together: to identify the changes that they want to see locally; to find ways of addressing them together; and to have more control over the decisions and actions – whether those of the state, business, third sector or media – that affect their lives. They give people in communities the confidence that comes from being listened to and taken seriously. They provide external knowledge and skills to supplement those already in the community and they promote community learning. They help communities to develop structures, organisations and ways of working to achieve their goals. They bring a strategic perspective: 'understanding the strategic context and what's coming down the line, always having that in mind'. Having someone to turn to who is detached from the stresses and strains of day-to-day life is especially important when there are disagreements or when there are difficult conversations to be had." (6)

That, I think is about a teal consciousness. It is a particularly subtle form of leadership which holds the space for community activists to take those early steps, and then more steps with more people and so on.

Below I share two stories which come from my community development work in the 70s and 80s. The first is about place. The second, in the 80s is about identity. Both put flesh on the bones of the above. By the end of these stories you can clearly see far more potential being realised both by an entire network/community as well as by the individuals involved. In both stories having community development input was absolutely critical.

The Estate

Because the Estate had been built on the cheap it was on land nobody else had wanted. It was boxed in by the boundaries between authorities, a cemetery and a railway line. This was home to about 10,000 people. There were a lot of older people and a lot of children and young people (7).

In 1974 I was one of two community workers employed by the local authority responsible for the Estate. As me and my co-worker, Bruce, tuned into the lives and views of tenants on the Estate, it felt to me like they saw their Estate as having a kind of giant but invisible Sylvia Plath bell jar over it (8). Plath's bell jar is a metaphor for a kind of suffocation of existence. It suggests being completely enclosed in an existence in which hope is denied by the all-pervasive oppression bearing down on everybody. And this gets internalised as powerlessness. As the next 4 years showed, this oppression had another side to it. It was a powerful contradiction which could, with the right handling, turn into a source of immense energy among a growing body of activists determined they would bring about changes that were needed.

In 1974 people were trying to get off the estate. The community on this Estate was by no means realising its potential and everybody knew it. By 1978, this was reversing and people were beginning to come back. By 1978 the active people in the community had experienced a series of victories. Whilst some things did not change, there was a far more positive and hopeful spirit among those actively engaged, whose numbers and confidence had grown. Amongst key councillors and officers in the local authority a subtle shift in understanding about the Estate had taken place: less paternalistic and prejudiced.

People sceptical about teal might say, *"But what about conflict, surely you need someone in authority to sort out a deep-seated conflict on a place like this Estate?"* Before I arrived on the Estate, such a conflict flared up. It revolved around a very amber consciousness in the only group on the Estate: the tenant's association. When a child was killed on the road they washed their hands of it. This lit a fuse. It triggered the emergence of a substantial body of people wanting to make something happen for the young people of the Estate. The group who emerged literally hated the tenant's association and would have nothing to do with them. They wanted to take action and decided to run a playscheme over the summer. Before Bruce and I arrived there had been two other community workers Ben and John. Here is a summary of what happened.

At one meeting the playscheme action group decided to go around the Estate holding block meetings. Each block was leafleted and one of the community workers went around with a loud hailer. Kids gathered around and they were asked to deliver leaflets and bang on the door at the same time. Between a quarter and a third of residents came out and stayed on the balcony. Using the loud hailer Ben and John described the activities of the playscheme, ice skating, outings etc. Having got people curious, they would ask them to stay out on the balconies so they could come and talk with them. They then asked if they were prepared to get involved and whether they would pass information about the playscheme to their friends, neighbours etc. Ben and John found about 50 people willing to help this way. They also unearthed about 250 people interested in knowing more about it. Nothing quite like this had happened on the Estate before!

The meetings of the playscheme committee were quite different from those of the tenant's association. The two community workers took on, on an informal basis, chairing and minute taking. The point was to avoid a highly structured committee so that people working together for the first time could operate in their own way unhampered by having to take on externally imposed, unfamiliar roles. Each person got very involved as jobs got taken on in this informal and supportive atmosphere. Everyone who had asked to be sent information had an envelope once a week telling them what was happening. They were asked to read it and pass it on. There was a feeling all over the Estate that something was going to happen.

August was not a dull month out on the Estate. The two infant and junior schools were used for a nursery and junior club. There was a youth club for teenagers. There were regular minibus outings to caves, parks and fun fairs. There were 5 special day outings to different seaside towns. A mini-Olympics was organised as well as roller skating, ice skating, swimming, a beauty contest, a procession, theatre groups, and a film show.

The tenth meeting of the playscheme committee was used to look back on what had happened. 26 adults talked from 8pm to 11pm. The notes of the discussion covered 6 sides of typescript. There could be no doubt they had provided a tremendous programme for the youth and children of the estate. They had turned the bell jar into enormous energy.

After this Ben and John left and Bruce and I got busy. Given the conflict between the playscheme committee and tenant's association, we decided we would support the formation of other independent groups but at the same time work with the tenant's association so that in future it would be able to become an umbrella for all these groups.

I took on working with the parent run youth club (as the playscheme action group had become). Bruce started working with the tenant's association. Bruce was so successful at working with both groups before I arrived, that by the time I started, the two groups had set up joint executive meetings.

Bruce's piece of work, became working with pensioners to set up a new group. The tenant's association gave Bruce a list of 30 or so pensioners they were happy for him to visit.

Bruce and I developed a methodology for forming a new community action group. We would spend a lot of time with the individuals discussing the issue and becoming clear about the extent of real interest that that person had. Not until we had gathered a full picture of how people felt and had taken a long hard look at what it meant as a whole, would we then go back to each person and discuss the idea of a group forming. And in that discussion, we would discuss our role (essentially to support them, to enable or facilitate).

At this point we would call the initial meeting to form the group. We went back to each person and discussed it. We would talk about who else was going to be there, how the meeting should be run, what it needed to cover. We found it was absolutely crucial that that first meeting was productive. Often, we would have an outside speaker to take the edge off things. One or two days before we would put reminders through letter boxes. We definitely did not feature the group's constitution at that first meeting, but worked with the key people to get an appropriate 'ordinary language' constitution in place in the early stages after the first meeting. We very much pitched those first meetings around becoming excited about the concept of the group, and what being involved in it could do.

After these two groups became established, parents with children at the school formed a group. And completely new groups of people formed subsequent annual playschemes. People who had done it in previous years helped find new people each year.

As we came to the end of 1974, Bruce and I got the sense that we were gradually turning a corner and a local civil war was being averted: that the future would not be one of multiple groups continually fighting each other, but one of a network of active involvement which individuals could enter from many different 'points', and once involved, could 'move on' to other parts of the network.

The network of groups that did in fact become inter-connected, included a mother and toddler club, a community centre planning group, a zebra crossing action group, a pensioner club, a youth 'combine', yearly playschemes, a block representatives' group, a parents' association and a welfare rights group and at the centre (so to speak) a revamped tenants association now calling itself a neighbourhood association.

Drilling holes in the bell jar

As the number of active people taking on leadership grew. It became imperative to connect them with key powerful people in the formal world of the local authority and other institutions. We developed a way to communicate with officials, tailor-made for dealing with a maze of bureaucracies. This proved very effective at getting the message across to those in the council and elsewhere.

In the days before computers and email, we encouraged individuals in the groups to send a photocopied letter to the complete range of individuals concerned with an issue. The letter listed who it had been sent to. This meant photocopies of the same letter being sent simultaneously to a range of council officers and councillors. No one could say they hadn't been asked or informed. It also created an expectation among officers that councillors would be contacting them. When a councillor did contact an officer, they would know that the officers already had the letter. When the circulation of such a letter was followed up by personal lobbying, by one of the active people on the Estate, it proved very effective.

A variation on this arose with the block reps' system. Individuals from each block agreed to act as representatives for their block on repairs and maintenance. If a tenant in the block could not get a repair done, the block rep would contact officers further up the hierarchy. They also met as a group and invited representatives of the housing department.

We encouraged tenants, and especially the neighbourhood association, to use a slideshow to structure meetings with housing officers (our 70s version of powerpoint). Skilful officers could be very adept at talking their way through a meeting which obscured what really needed to be done. Tenants could get carried away and deflect attention away from the real issues. Some key things may just not get discussed. Finally, the arguments put may not be that well argued.

So how to tie a meeting together so it is fool-proof? Together with the block reps we developed the use of 35mm colour slides. The first thing was to get all the pictures needed. You also needed a room with a white wall to project to. Thirdly you needed a detailed agenda, itemising slide by slide what the slide is, a summary of why it was a problem, and then the action required. So....

Item 1:   Pram sheds at the corner of block X

The pram sheds have rotted doors, low jutting corroded roofs and dumped household goods. These are dangerous to children and a public health nuisance.

Required: The demolition of the pram sheds since they are no longer serviceable.

This really worked. Tenants loved the technology and the precision with which they got their message across. Nobody wanted to come back to an embarrassing re-run of the slides because the work had not been done!

Thus, it was that officers of the housing department began to put a lot more effort into the management of the Estate.

Shattering the bell jar

Three things shattered the bell jar: getting a zebra crossing, getting control over the modernisation of the flats, and a local history book.

Tenants had tried many times over the years to get a zebra crossing. In some voluntary work, the year before, on a much smaller estate, where I lived, I had successfully led a campaign to get two zebra crossings. This proved to be excellent preparation for the campaign on the Estate.

The previous year I had initially I hit a brick wall. Traffic engineers in the local council were telling me there would not be a high enough volume of traffic on the new road. They kept going on about a formula of PV to the power of 2, where P was the number of pedestrians per hour and V the volume of cars per hour. And if this gave you some huge figure you could have a crossing. If not you couldn`t.

They seemed guided solely by their professional expertise rather than their role as public servants. We were definitely dealing here with highly qualified

professionals who had their own view of the world, cosseted by a seemingly impregnable bureaucracy. Then I stumbled across a new circular (circular 19/74) from the Department of the Environment issued in May 1974 which said,
"there are some situations in which the numerical criteria should be applied flexibly".
Examples given were where:

- a community is divided by a busy road;
- shopping areas mean people have to cross the road;
- older people have to cross;
- children have to go to school.

And this had proved to be the trump card where I lived. It certainly fitted the Estate where I was now working and the active tenants got busy with a campaign armed with this new knowledge.

At the first public meeting, with the chair of the highways committee, a real unity of action could be seen among the activists on the estate. Meetings like this brought people together across the various estate groupings. The highways chairman said he understood how people felt but that previous counts of people and traffic in the past had never established anything like the numbers required for a zebra crossing. A copy of circular 19/74 was then produced and the section on flexibility pointed out. It seemed as if this was news to the chairman. He stopped in his tracks and reading the text for himself concluded by saying his committee would support the application for a crossing and press the case with the regional authority who had the last say. At this point it looked as if the campaign on the Estate would be brief and follow a similar pattern as the one on the estate where I lived.

Like the estate where I lived (small e) it was necessary to meet with the regional authority. This was a small meeting of active people from the groups and the regional councillor. He agreed with the argument about using the flexibilities in the circular. He had just done so with us on the estate where I lived, how could he do otherwise?

And just like the stories we read to children about wicked witches, just when it seemed certain that the Estate would get its zebra crossing, the Borough's traffic engineers mounted a traffic study in the area. They painstakingly measured volumes and proved conclusively that the amount of traffic on the road would not alter with a zebra!

People on the Estate were now very determined. They felt that they were experiencing deliberate delaying tactics, and that the engineers were trying to 'wear people down'. It seemed to the people on the Estate as if the deaths and injury of children were unimportant to the traffic engineers. Bruce and I made sure as many people as possible all over the Estate got the traffic engineer's report. They put together their response to this report and it was copied to every single person on the regional committee, together with a supporting letter from the local school. The regional committee finally agreed to a zebra. The Estate had won. A crossing was laid over a year after the campaign had started. I was working on the Estate until 1978 and at no time over that period did the issue of the safety of children crossing the road come up as an issue. All it took was a single zebra crossing. I used to think about the child or children who would be able to have a life because of what the estate residents did that year.

Controlling modernisation

One of Bruce's major achievements was to get a newly rejuvenated Neighbourhood Association connected up with the General Improvement Area programme. This was run by the council. Its purpose was to slowly move around the estate, modernising it. Bruce focused on linking Chris, the new chair of the neighbourhood association, (yes new leadership made all the difference) to the chair of housing.

Here is an example of the kind of thing this opened up. The most densely populated block had a block of housing in its central courtyard! This had been knocked down and there was just a rough empty space. At an appointed time, the block rep had made sure as many tenants as possible came out to meet the architect who would decide what play equipment would be installed in the empty space. There was a wonderful hour or so in which pictures of equipment were handed out and everybody walked around the space. By the end of it what was needed and where it needed to be had pretty well been sorted out. That was more or less what got done. I went home that night feeling I had done a good day's work!

But there was a far more serious issue raised by modernising the Estate. 'Housing Need' boiled down to four categories of people: the homeless, people on the waiting list, transfer requests, and clearance/improvement people in modernisation areas like the Estate.

The chairman of the housing committee, publicly stated that he wanted to use housing policy to keep the community on the Estate together. But when you bring this intention fully into a real live modernisation programme you get some challenges. Modernisation meant emptying blocks, modernising the block once completely empty, then letting the flats to different tenants. Where did the tenants go when the block was emptied? And who came onto the estate when the modernised flats were let?

The Estate wanted a full blown 'sons and daughters' policy to be operated by the Council (giving priority to sons and daughters of existing residents). But this ran up against the harsh reality that the Estate was just one cog in a massive housing operation. The housing committee did in fact discuss the proposal. Reporting on it, the borough housing officer was clear that they were trying to avoid any future accusations of queue jumping that might skew their system of defining housing need. So just allocating newly modernised flats solely to sons or daughters of existing tenants would not be on.

But, and this did open up the possibility of the estate being seen less and less as a 'dumping ground', they would stop simply allocating flats on the Estate to people in the greatest housing need and open allocations up to *everyone* on the waiting list. In that way they would find sons and daughters who wanted to live there. It was a compromise which attested to the clout the tenants on the estate were developing.

Inspired by the general spirit of activism now permeating the Estate, tenants in a block that was being emptied formed a committee and surveyed themselves. 17 of the 37 tenants wanted to be rehoused on the Estate! They wrote to the director of housing asking what practical arrangements were being made for this to happen? They were offered newly improved flats. By a happy coincidence, flats which had just been modernised became available just at the time their block was being emptied.

At one point the very funding of the modernisation of the Estate got called into question. The Estate went on the offensive contacting the central government housing minister direct. The housing minister wrote back saying, £30 million more was being made available nationally, £2.2 million of which was going to the authority controlling the estate. Since the Estate needed `only` £243,000 they felt they were now in a strong position. A group of selected councillors made the decision about how to use the £2.2million and in competition with 60 items on the agenda, the Estate`s modernisation went ahead.

These victories with the zebra crossing, the maintenance of the estate and the modernisation were being achieved by tenants who had never previously been able to do or say such things: the bell jar was well and truly shattered. Out on the Estate there was, for many, a feeling of liberation.

Endgame

Tenants on the Estate were extremely vocal about what should go in the community centre. There was a very large population of children. There were a lot of pensioners. The council was aiming to build a cheap multi-purpose centre. This would mean pensioners and youth having to share facilities. The tenants visited multi-purpose centres on other large council estates and found they did not work. The tenants were challenging the basic provision that the council had in mind.

The tenants wanted the council to do a further examination of what was needed for their particular Estate. However, the architects' department said it had no staff to do this work. The tenants suggested finding two architecture students to come and live on the Estate over the summer for 3 months. An unused doctor`s surgery was opened up for them to live in. The students would be supervised by the deputy lead architect in the council and a report from them would go to the sub-committee of the main housing committee which dealt with building plans.

The students found the best information was coming from active members of the community action groups.

Once the council agreed to a youth and community centre in two separate parts of the one building, attention then switched to making sure the two major funders talked to each other. And when the architecture students moved out of the doctor's surgery, the community moved in, informing the council it was now being run as a temporary community centre. They felt it should be the trial run for the new centre. It was run for several years with great success. It became an extremely valuable resource centre, consisting of meeting rooms, a room for use by children, and equipment essential for community groups to function on the Estate.

For the future youth and community centre, a sizeable sum was needed. Both organisations needed to make ongoing commitments to the project. Elected members needed to maintain the commitment in the face of competing demands. Like the crossing, the whole community centre issue needed to get to a point where the estate had comprehensively won.

The clincher came left of field.

When you work in a community in a sustained way, you become aware of the `shape` of things. There are threads of discussion, or issues that run through the community in a sustained way. The groups and campaigns were by now all responding to most of these threads. But one still resonated away without finding a response. It was the desire on the part of a few of the original 1930s tenants to tell their story of what the estate was like then and what that meant for today. I started to think about a local history book as a possible piece of work. It was the kind of thing the neighbourhood association would support. Nancy was central to the neighbourhood association and had also moved onto the estate when it first opened. She had her story to tell, *and* she knew all the others who eventually were in the book.

The story was published by the neighbourhood association as a local history book. Their stories wove together into a fantastic insight into real life on the estate. Far from 'problem families' it was a resourceful community full of energy and action as well as human support for one another.

Now it so happened that a rumour went around, just before publication, that the chair of the housing committee was promising the resources earmarked for the community centre on the Estate to another area in the Borough. By now the book was attracting national attention through a freelance writer for the Guardian. This led to the equivalent of the One Show wanting to cover the book launch (so prime time TV coverage).

By now the leading figures on the Estate were quite capable of seeing where this could go. They had soft power political capital. They rang the chair of the housing committee and invited them to launch the book, on one condition, that given the national press interest, a cast iron assurance of the council's commitment to keep the funding in place for the community centre would be given. If they didn't do this the Estate would use the press interest to give them a second story about the failure to honour the commitment to fund a community centre.

This was what happened. The chair of housing made clear to the national press just how much they were committing. The older people present could not have been more moved. Finally, a thirty-years dream was happening through their words. The Estate really had got its youth and community centre. From that point onwards plans turned into bricks and mortar and it was built. The history book was what clinched it.

Launched with local and national media coverage, the book attracted great interest in the local council. The fact that such a publication could come from one of their Estates, meant it also commanded attention inside the housing department. Enough councillors and officers in the local authority had either read the book or were aware of its significance, so that a considerable shift of attitude towards the Estate took place. Through the book, officials in all the agencies started to treat the Estate and its residents with a good deal more humanity and respect. It was viewed more positively and the various initiatives seemed to finally have the wind behind them. Leading councillors moved overall council policy in the direction of mini town halls and the committee paper proposing this acknowledged the Estate book as contributing to this. It was as if the language of the people of the Estate had in the end proved more enduring and insightful than that of the local authority.

I appreciate this story is a little on the long side. But it is a classic. The reason I think it shows a teal-like spirit is the real detail in their efforts and the spirited collaborations between people without any hint of amber or orange consciousness. The groups on the state were like a collection of autonomous teams all working together as well as getting on with their own thing. They developed an inspiring kind of resourcefulness. They wanted the best for their community and working together they did whatever it took to make that happen. Collectively they were evolving a path forward. At the same time, they got tremendous co-operation going with very key individuals who could make a difference to the lives of people on the Estate.

Britain has 248 Estates of 10,000 or more, which post 'right to buy' have in many cases become run down. Unless those living there have got active and become powerful, these estates perform the 21st century version of being the dumping grounds in dealing with overwhelming housing need across the UK. It is a proliferation of 'the bell jar'. Given Grenfell Tower this 70s-experience could hardly be more relevant. There is an alternative.

The anti-racist network

Just as in the 70s, class erupted from within the bedrock of British society, in the 80s it was the turn of race and racism. Locally the old approach to the welfare state carried on, despite the *national* change over to market policies. In fact, bureaucracy, became even more dysfunctional locally. It proved utterly unable to respond to the uprisings by black youth. Local public services in the 80s were sleepwalking into sustained inaction and inertia.

At the heart of anti-racism was an agenda of trying to create responsive public services: ones that worked well for both black and white people. The agenda was to transform institutional racism (9). This became the focus of my community development work throughout the 80s. This was very different from the class politics of the 70s. Institutional racism created totally different power dynamics in which 'accommodating', as happened with class politics, simply could not work (this is explained more below). In the network, which emerged where I was working, we found ways to overcome the central dynamic of racism: denial by white people that it exists. Because we found ways to do this, alliances between black and white people, inside council services, started up to create changes in local services that benefited both black and white people. This could hardly be more relevant today with, for example Reni Eddo-Lodge writing,

"I'm no longer engaging with white people on the topic of race. Not all white people, just the vast majority who refuse to accept the legitimacy of structural racism and its symptoms... You can see their eyes shut down and harden. It's like treacle is poured into their ears, blocking up their ear canals. It's like they can no longer hear us." (10)

The antiracist network in the 1980s was introducing a very real tackling of issues of race and racism. It was introducing a kind of 'the political' that the existing system did not find at all easy to handle. What was so very different was that the anti-racist network saw power as constitutive of all social relations. Therefore, white denial could no longer run through those relationships inside the system because it simply perpetuated institutional racism. What was triggered in powerful people in the system was their retrenching to the use of authority. If power is constituted in everyday actions and relations, merely using authority was taken by the network as a refusal to be part of changing the relationships. Until the network came along, powerful people in the, extremely bureaucratic, structure had been used to accommodation and compromise. But the issue of race took on a whole different complexion: it demanded a change in the power dynamic being experienced within the social relations of daily life. In that sense all members of staff had enormous power! What the old-style welfare state bureaucrats were wanting was to stay above the battle, to neutralise conflict, to have a conflict free working world with a few 'accommodations'. What they were presiding over was a dysfunctional bureaucracy which excluded black people and provided racism as a public service. It was not great for white staff.

It is Chantal Mouffe I think who has best captured this kind of politics,

"A well-functioning democracy calls for a vibrant clash of democratic political positions. If this is missing there is the danger that this democratic confrontation will be replaced by a confrontation among other forms of collective identification, ... Too much emphasis on consensus and the refusal of confrontation lead to apathy and disaffection with political participation. Worse still, the result can be the crystallization of collective   passions   around issues, which cannot be managed by the democratic process and an explosion of antagonisms that can tear up the very basis of civility". (11)

This gives us insight into the relevance of the antiracist network of the 80s to today. In the uprisings of 1981 and again in 1985 the very basis of civility was being torn up precisely because responding constructively on issues of race and racism had not been integral within the system. But the network, by staying true to the nature of racism, itself provoked and drew out of the system it engaged with, its inability to respond. We can either accept a permanent state of conflict, with temporary arrangements that again become challenged, and have to move on (what Mouffe calls an agonistic state of `the political`) or we can try to close things down in order to protect the status quo and find the very basis of civility is exploded. Today with terrorism we again have issues arising up and down the country that can either strengthen and further develop our functioning democracy or force further exclusion and the intensification of violence.

What you are about to read is a story of how a network of people emerged effectively to further strengthen the functioning of our democracy at local level.

As black people took to the streets in the 80s, within councils, black people were getting jobs at officer level for the first time in British history. This gave them a voice in the power structure. In many cases they chose to use it and did so in an extremely coherent manner. These were extraordinary black people. They had the clarity of newcomers *and* the additional force of centuries of racist oppression and colonial tyranny. With remarkable poise, skill and integrity they started to take up the opportunities, now that the 'nastiness' (as Cedric Robinson describes the kernel of racism (12)) could, for the first time on the British mainland, no longer be denied. These were black people who no longer felt that by challenging, nothing would change. They were going to make sure things did change.

Basil was employed in a local authority in response to the uprisings. His work shook me to my core: he was transforming an entire department! Basil explained to me about racism awareness training. He had been running such 3-day courses for some time. He found they created a culture in a local authority department, genuinely supportive of responding on issues of race and racism. Crucially the training located racism in white people without them switching off or deflecting it onto black people. And it acknowledged that racism had a completely different impact on black people. This got my attention. Both black and white were becoming engaged.

What really excited me was that in beginning such a programme Basil had started with the director and the senior management team: that particular programme had been the most challenging he had ever done. But it really had impact right across the organisation.

I enrolled on a 3-day programme so I could get a sense of it for myself. The key trainer was a black man called Tuku Mukherjee. Those three days in 1982 were life changing. I was beginning my journey that Hannah Arendt calls the journey from not being able to discuss to being able to discuss (13). It was inherently liberating and very scary. And there were illuminating publications coming out exactly at this time, which perfectly complemented doing a 3-day programme. During 1982 Routledge published a book with the title "Community Work and Racism" (14). Basil had an article in it and so did Tuku. Also around this time a black activist called Herman Ouseley published a book called `The System` (15). This analysed a council and its services and argued the need for `positive action` in every aspect of any councils' operations.

My experience of Tuku was life changing. I was captivated by the atmosphere of us all engaging with ourselves at a profound level. While, at the same time, hearing and discussing some very challenging accounts of Britain from a black viewpoint. It was intense, often uncomfortable, but also very warm and supportive. It was genuine critical thought shared collaboratively. Those three days enabled me to get a much more coherent perspective on everything I was involved with so far at work: personally, professionally and institutionally. It had that `agonistic` quality so vividly portrayed by Mouffe.

On a personal level, I had a major realisation about an experience, in my family, I had had as a young boy. It was an extremely violent racist incident that I had never unpacked and it still smouldered away inside me. Tuku unearthed it. And I was able, as time went by, to have that experience become one of the reasons I was doing this anti-racist work.

The three days flew by. I loved it. Here we were talking about important things in a good way. And that is rare. It was a well-structured programme in that there was a compelling logic to the sequence of things we did, bolstered by Tuku's extraordinary analytic capabilities. He could unfold the ideology of racism so you were able to touch it and feel it in your own life. Tuku helped us assemble *for ourselves*,

- historical insight (but which shone a bright light on current practices),
- insights on racial identity (I was being asked *"who am I racially?"*)
- an internal language not otherwise available (to use personally, professionally, and institutionally).

It was a mix of head stuff, engaged/embodied understanding, self-exploration, and knowledge, all swirling around inside each of us so that *"what I can do where I am can change. I can see for myself the need for change"* . It moved from self to systems and back again through this powerful lens of the ideology of race which went back in Britain as far as the 12ᵗʰ century. All four quadrants were definitely there. The everyday world suddenly looked and felt very different. Anti-racism training was all about conversations, building relationships and then co-ordinated action. The training was potent, moved our hearts and minds and enabled us to steer different courses of action under our own control that made sense. Overcoming the impacts of racism was *different* for black people and white people. But Britain is home to both and that means a sharing of power. It is no longer a white only country (and in fact never has been (16)).

What had prevented this genuine sharing, was the destructive impact of the ideology of racism operating in the lives of both white and black peoples' lives. Left un-addressed this was a highly divisive and destructive legacy/inheritance. The three days was not just about intellectually `getting` this. It was also about us as individuals freeing ourselves from this conditioning through changing the relationships among us. You left the three days with an imprint of what a racially just Britain was like. It was more than possible. We had all experienced it!

At a turning point in the 3 days, we unpacked something Tuku called `the white norm`. This is the `white world` black people experience, but which white people don't see as white. I immediately `got` the colour-blind way I was still seeing everything. During this part of the programme, that white norm, I had been conditioned to take for granted, began `breaking down` as I began to really see myself as a white person, with all the taken-for-granted power that comes with it.

Gandhi expressed his great regret that activists across India could not take part in training in the cause of gaining independence (17). Lacking this he foresaw violence. 1980s Britain saw truly staggering numbers of people taking part in anti-racist training, and, where it was done well, it created a different atmosphere at local level: one where black people were being responded to positively as users and as staff in a multitude of encounters with and within public services and community groups. Crucially white people were part of doing that too.

People like Basil, Tuku, Herman and many others were using their life experiences, education, skills, and personalities to mobilise others in a peaceful, non-violent manner. And it was being made clear to me that I could be part of that movement and so could untold others.

Focusing my job

In September 1982, I published my report about the first 6 months of my community development job. I went straight to the implications for public services claiming to genuinely provide services in a multi-racial area,

"In my view multi-cultural and multi-racial services are those where people of different cultures and races are employed at all levels. They are services where

a deliberate effort has been made to respond to the needs of different cultural and racial groups, as those needs have been expressed by the groups themselves." (18)

We have here this future oriented model of public service where users of services and local activists are actually part of the service. I argued for people inside 'the system' (to borrow Herman Ouseley's term) and from across the community, black and white, to come together to form a *network* to initiate and give wider access to programmes of 3-day anti-racism training. Hundreds of copies of my report went out, with a reply card in which people could say whether they wanted to discuss the report more fully with others. And over 50 people did.

Nobody from social services had ever done this kind of thing, on the issue of racism, in this area, ever before. That in itself got people's attention. The fact that I was being so transparent and making myself accountable well beyond the council's normal processes did not go unnoticed. After all I was appointed to work to an agenda within a population of 48,000: not to work to the agenda of a local authority!

'The Network' got agreed at a meeting of 70 people interested in my report (with 40 apologies). Overwhelmingly participants said it *must* happen. The report had really hit a nerve. The key word of the night's discussion was 'justice', meaning racial justice.

In particular the idea of holding organised meetings and activities away from one's employing organisation went down well. While an anti-racist network would have to be an organised and conscious venture, its location was as an amorphous network which could not be pinpointed, targeted and marginalised.

Make no mistake. While this story appears to be about public services, actually it is about a vibrant black and white network/community forming from among staff in these local public services *and* activists and staff in local community (civil society) organisations. This emerging community was working across the 'colour line' *and* across institutional boundaries. The spirit of the enterprise is captured in this passage from Michel de Certeau,

"...the goal is not to make clearer how the violence of order is transmuted into a disciplinary technology but rather to bring to light the clandestine forms taken by the dispersed, tactical, and makeshift creativity of groups or individuals clearly caught in the nets of discipline" (19)

Members of the network who were inside the public services were the ones who most felt 'the nets of discipline'. The network was enabling the clandestine to move into the light through 'dispersed, tactical, makeshift creativity', making it very hard for people with institutional authority to target it. The challenge was to shape responses using the resources available through the network.

Early in 1984 the first 'co-ordinating' group meeting of 'the network' was held and the room was packed out. We just had time to go round the room so each person could say what they thought 'the network' should focus on. No-one in the room had ever participated in anything like this. It felt brave, fresh, and really responsive to the times.

We started 3-day programmes with individuals from adult education, the youth service, local schools, social services, local churches and community groups. It was a perfect beginning to what would turn into a regular process year by year, over the next 10 years. 'The network' gradually involved more and more people, each of whom was turning that awareness into action.

'The network' was a completely new community in the making. As time went on, the potency of such an approach, to open up space for untold initiatives and developments, became immense. We were exploiting the power of 'the freedom to associate', inherent in British civil society. And at the same time, we were creating a new entity within civil society: the anti-racist network. It was the ultimate in autonomy.

Racism should not be a social service

The first service to change was a local resource centre, run by social services. The staff were two white men, two white women and two black women. The two white men thought they ran the centre and the four women felt totally unable to function. There seemed very little point running any kind of antiracist programme with this huge sexist blockage sitting there. So, one afternoon I facilitated a session in which each pair presented their feedback to the other two pairs and we simply continued doing this until the two white men agreed that they needed to change the way they operated.

The whole environment was extremely oppressive, inheriting grievances and incidents going back many years:

- poor communication internally;
- oppressive management practices;
- irrational decision making;
- high staff turnover/dissatisfaction;
- poor quality of services.

There was very little professionalism. Everything was far *too* personal. This was the dysfunctional bureaucracy. Later they would become a highly skilled, genuinely professional and effective operation.

Having cleared enough ground, the 3-day programme started by asking, *"When did you first become aware that colour made a difference?"* That got us off to a good start with lots of experiences being shared. In the afternoon, they worked in two groups, defining racial prejudice, racism and institutional racism.

They were particularly articulate in spelling out the way racism operated in education, through passports, in health, psychiatric and penal institutions, housing, in getting benefits, in industry and in the media. They knew how it worked!

Day one ended with an observation,

"...how was it that the first-time black children in care in the resource centre had a chance to talk about their racial identity, was when, quite by accident, the two black staff were away on a weekend with them...since they were the only staff with the group, it came up" *(18).*

Day two began with the whole group listening to a recording of a black person analysing racism. They went off in three pairs: a white middle-class group, a white working-class group and a black group to discuss the relevance of what they had just heard for their work.

The black group saw the issues as,

"-constant confrontation is necessary to get anything across
-moving on from past white retaliatory responses like `you've got a chip on your shoulder` or `aren't you being a bit sensitive` is not easy
-not being dependent on the white institutional hierarchy
-getting the necessary information to be able to challenge
-support black colleagues"

The white working-class group came back with,

"-do black workers collude in the inaction?
-how do we change collusion
-don't institutions permit change within a limited basis only?
-should I resign and let a black person be appointed?
-shouldn't there be a multi-racial monitoring board above us?
-as white workers how much do we allow black workers to be black?"

For the white middle-class group,

"-last weekend we had all white cover
-kids with parents of mixed race are giving black staff a very hard time
-domestic staff should have been here
-we don't know how to move forward,
-how do we take racism on when writing our reports?" *(18)*

It became clear that the resource centre staff's challenge was that structurally *all* the staff occupied a middle position in a white middle-class bureaucracy. But *society* has a hierarchy: the white middle class above the white working class who are above black people. Instead of being stuck in this conflict between white middle-class social work values and society's rigid hierarchy, the group decided to create a new option: to make *diversity the norm* within their working relationships with one another. This meant power spread horizontally, more than vertically. Thus, on gender, race and class issues, there is dialogue and negotiation.

In creating *that* working environment, the resource centre would then be worthy of being called a social service. Anything else was reproducing what happened in society with the additional burden of middle class white professional standards being imposed. And that was not really a *public* service.

The climax came when the whole staff group designed a subtly racist resource centre and then a resource centre acceptable to black people. The centre acceptable on black peoples' terms worked for white people better than the subtly racist one!!! That was the breakthrough: win-win. Staff then listed the blockages to making the transition. Looking at the list they decided it was better to face these challenges than carry on as they were and so began to plan the transition.

Here is one members of staff's comment,

"On the first day I thought, 'I've been here before', but then on the second day we really got to grips with it, and the third day has been really good, especially those two lists (blockages and the action plan), they are very relevant" (18)

A month later we held a one day follow up. One of the most telling statements was, *"Racism should not be a social service"*. From this point on, this group of staff grabbed their autonomy. They began to run a sought-after service. Their work became enjoyable.

Over the coming years this type of development took place in many groups of staff. There is no question in my mind that this veers towards the teal in that specific structures, processes and practices were created, by the people in the situation, to support a service acceptable to both black and white people. Staff want to come to work. Staff brought more of themselves to their work. As a community they evolved their own path forwards.

Constructing new internal landscapes

At the core of what Tuku brought to our discussions, planning, and interventions were power relationships based on a new kind of professionalism, appropriate to a black and white Britain. Within the dysfunctioning bureaucracies, the typical approach had degenerated to entirely personal relationships. Professionalism had gone out of the window (as the resource centre showed).

The official line in the professional roles created in the welfare state was that you were absolved of all personal responsibility: the bureaucracy would protect you if you screwed up. And the condition on which it would do this was that you *only* brought your professional self to work. You left yourself and your personal identity, at the office door. I think this has been responsible for public sector `cover ups` only now coming to see the light of day.

The conflict between having (officially) to work from a professional identity but actually finding this had degenerated into a sea of personal (and very dysfunctional) relationships, created quite a tension in staff. The resource centre showed this. This was a powerful contradiction which with the right handling did in fact turn into a source of immense energy for positive, humanistic change. Tuku really got this across,

"There is a continuum. No black man or woman ... .can ever walk away from the issue of race and racism. I am saying neither can white people walk away from it. You think you can. You think it doesn't affect you and I'm saying it does. That's the continuum on which there can be a commonality of experience provided we accept that it does in fact impinge on you. It cripples you" (18)

He was saying that by holding on to the old view of professionalism, white staff would continue to exclude black people, continue to suffer splitting of professional and personal selves, and would face increasingly dysfunctional work realities (like the resource centre staff). *This* is what we took `institutional racism` to mean.

As a network and as individuals in it we had to overcome considerable resistance from powerful senior staff. The network did, as was previously explained, create a new kind of politics at local level: agonistic politics. In each and every case we were able to eventually overcome that resistance. Each could have a book written about it. The overcoming of these very real attempts by powerful people in the system to sabotage our efforts, became *part* of the struggle to shift the way relationships between black and white constituted a racially just service. We were fighting against a system where power got invested in high up people with authority. We were becoming powerful people at the grass roots who were constituting racially just services. It was worth the struggle. In my local office there wasn't a single area of service delivery that did not make significant changes in how black and white people were engaging in this very human business of care: home care, childminding, fostering and adoption, mental health, social work practice, and so on. And one by one all the other local offices run by the department enacted their versions of these changes.

For example, the white head of the fostering and adoption unit had appointed a black deputy and several black staff. As a black and white staff group, like the resource centre staff, they had organised their structures, practices and processes to make them far more functional, inclusive and supportive of a genuine professionalism. As a result, the number of black foster parents increased substantially. And with that came the opportunity to place black children with black families. This was strongly resisted by their (all white) line management: those with power through authority. The newly appointed black deputy, and some very experienced black and white staff, developed effective interventions. They ran a one-day conference, at national level, in collaboration with similar teams elsewhere in the country exploring the way forward for placements that work better for both black and white. Their keynote speaker was a figure with acknowledged experience and knowledge in this whole area and was black. Holding this event publicly showed their peers elsewhere how they were developing. The speaker also was effectively saying to those in authority who were resisting back at base, leave them alone, this conference is setting the standards, not you! This event completely overpowered the resistance within the department.

The 5th newsletter of 'the network' published in January 1987 gives a sense of the scope of concerns and issues at that time:

- Details of the shocking consultation by the director of social services;
- Criteria for buying-in anti-racist trainers;
- A critique of care in the community;
- An article on housing associations and racism;
- Another critique of the re-organisation of an entire local authority;
- A piece on fostering;
- A list of 10 excuses white senior managers won't tackle racism;
- A very forensic piece on the work of educational pyschologists;
- Details of institutional racism in schools;
- An article on planning departments and racism;
- A piece about the benefit system;
- A scathing article about inner area programmes.

The network functioned like a giant autonomous team, with groupings forming within it to tackle specific issues as they arose. The network grew and grew. Locally we got the attention of the council's chief executive. He got the point. The services over which he presided would need to change in their mainstream operations. We started working in collaboration with other networks on national issues.

The power of communities and networks

These two stories, coming from radically different eras in the history of Britain show the power of networks and communities, when they get the support they need to truly realise potential. Their messages are as relevant today as they were in their eras. These experiences were truly liberating. More of these kinds of experience in today's contexts will also be liberating. Britain's inability today to foster these sorts of engaged communities, at the local level, is creating the soil for extremism. The tendency to polarisation is intensifying. When amber, orange, and green tend towards absolutism, they become shrill and dismissive. We need the unifying framework these sorts of developments can bring

With the right support, communities and networks can be extremely powerful at making, initially inconceivable changes, actually come about. In these two cases community development input was crucial. So too access to small sums, places to meet etc. The antiracist training was self-funding.

There is something else to learn from these two experiences. It is that initiatives by communities in civil society tend, as George Monbiot puts it,

"(to) proliferate, spawning further ventures and ideas that were not envisaged when they started. They then begin to develop a dense participatory culture that becomes attractive and relevant to everyone" (20).

This property of civil society to develop unexpectedly in this way is called 'thick networks'. This means a proliferation of developments, all created by the people in them, under no one central control. It is this dynamic that took hold on the Estate and in the anti-racist network. Monbiot gives the example of Rotterdam's Reading Room. The disused Turkish bath spawned restaurants, workshops, care co-ops, eco projects, and craft collectives. It became a cultural hub which inspired others to do something similar elsewhere in the city with new schemes starting every week. Empty shops found new uses, start-ups proliferated, care, literacy, mental health, and debt were just a few issues finding responses. Micro-funding and crowdsourcing supported initiatives. Longer established residents and incoming migrants got arenas and activities to do things together. The city council collaborated with community groups (21).

We saw what families, friends, and any resulting communities do, in their positive aspects, in the previous chapter. We can now add that networks and communities, in their positive aspect, also do integration, bonding, overcoming isolation, overcoming fragmentation, learning, developing, realising dreams, and supporting one another. The 'thick networks' process means networks and communities offer a really substantial repairing of the social fabric.

In Britain today, too little has been going into supporting this to happen. And this is an extremely powerful way in which Britain's potential is being stifled. Despite civil society being strong, the overall impact, if it were properly supported by government, could mean many more families, friends, networks and communities *actually* repairing the social fabric.

We are now moving on to look at organisations, followed by a look at politics. We are departing the 'ground of life' (families, friends, networks and communities) for things `man- made`! In some ways it feels like our way of doing organisations and politics in Britain has been hijacked by an alien way of thinking, certainly from the perspective of people for whom family and friends is very much their centre of gravity. When we enter the world of organisations and politics we enter far more complex territory, full of unfamiliar words and concepts, and complicated power dynamics. It was this that struck me so forcibly when I first became a full-time paid community worker employed by a local authority. It was a shock. So much so that I wonder how many `put up` with being in an organisation? This may be, in part, why so many want to be their own bosses as self-employed. We are about to encounter something very unexpected: it doesn't have to be like that. There is a next generation of organisations that feel much more like communities and who look after everyone much more like positive families.

5 - Better organisations

*Modern organisations have brought
about sensational progress for
humanity in less than two centuries
.... And yet many people sense that
the current way we run organisations
has been stretched to its limits.*
Frederic Laloux (1)

T he business approach so familiar today was a breakthrough from the bureaucracy that preceded it. Orange achieved results of an order of magnitude entirely impossible with paternalistic, amber bureaucracies,

"These organisations retain the pyramid as their basic structure but they drill holes into rigid functional and hierarchical boundaries with project groups, virtual teams, cross functional initiatives, expert staff functions, and internal consultants, to speed up communication and foster innovation" (2)

To get and maintain competitive advantage it is necessary for these organisations to tap into the intelligence of the many in the organisation. Top managers set an overall objective, leaving parts of the organisation to be `empowered` to think and act so as to move in that direction and achieve those targets. How those targets are met is much less important than that they are met,

Unfortunately, letting go of this control doesn't always happen. And groups of talented, capable people can feel stifled and undervalued (3).

This approach has given birth to a battery of management processes: strategic planning, budgeting cycles, key performance indicators, and balanced scorecards. Accompanying these are processes to 'incentivise' employees: performance appraisals, bonus schemes, quality awards, stock options etc,

"..people tend to wear a professional mask. One must always look the part: be busy but composed, competent, and in control of the situation"(4).

Success is purely about money and recognition. Growth is success. This can engender a certain kind of emptiness. It is these kinds of organisations which can degenerate into individual and collective greed.

From my own experience, I can say that orange leadership fails to appreciate that these managerial disciplines *re-constitute* the mental make-up and the actions of staff. Managerialists tend not to understand how social realities are constituted by the prevailing consciousness, the relationships, the structures, practices and processes. All these things shape the mindset of the employees. If we want something more human we have to find ways to constitute that. So what might the next generation of organisations, that do this, look like?

Drawing from Reinventing Organizations here are three examples of teal organisations. Firstly, we have a public service supporting older people in the community, then a blue-collar engineering company in the car industry, and lastly a third sector organisation providing homes and shelters for the mentally ill, the disabled, people with drug and alcohol addiction, and the homeless. These examples are followed by a fleshing out of the structures, practices, and processes that Laloux has found to be key to teal organisation. Finally, from my own experience, I bring in an example of a Buddhist organisation as well as three examples of public service autonomous teams.

Buurtzorg healthcare

The neighbourhood nurse is an essential part of the Dutch health care system. The state created small areas around which to organise community nursing support for older people. These self-employed nurses began to be grouped into organisations. Economies of scale meant 295 organisations merging to 86 in five years between 1990 and 1995. Orange business organisations were developed. These quickly moved to a format of call centres, standard visiting times, and planning the use of nurses: a system which clients and nurses hated. Patients lost the personal relationship with unknown faces constantly appearing and staff found the working conditions degrading. It reminds us of homecare in Britain today.

In 2006/7 Jos de Brock created Buurtzorg. It started with 4 other nurses using a self-managing approach. They re-integrated everything that the orange approach had separated out. The team members took full responsibility for every aspect of the service. Now Buurtzorg's teams tend to be 12 community nurses working with 50 people in a small, well defined neighbourhood. At the end of 2014 they had 800 such teams across the country. The team is in charge of everything: how many patients to work with; who to work with; where to rent an office; how to decorate it; how best to integrate with the local community; which doctors and pharmacies to work with; and how best to work with local hospitals. By 2014 Buurtzorg had 9000 staff and 80% of the market share, serving 70,000 patients a year. Have a look at Jos de Blok`s presentation to the RSA at the end of 2014 (5).

They are very good at teaching people how to operate without a boss. This includes how to run meetings, how to deal with conflict, different types of listening and different types of communication. The absence of rules and regulations imposed by an HQ creates a huge sense of freedom and responsibility throughout the organisation. Fluid `hierarchies` of recognition, influence and skill start up across and within teams. In 2014 they had an HQ of just 45.

Teams learn a group process for making decisions. It is very significant that this process does not rely on achieving consensus. It is enough that there is no principled objection. The solution can also be revisited. They can get an external facilitator in anytime. They can also ask other teams by using an internal social media platform.

Since nurses are scattered across the country, most will never meet face to face. The internal social network means they can locate specific expertises, then pick up the phone and talk. They can post questions on the platform in a facebook style stream. On average nurses log on once a day and there is a high level of engagement with the technology. Buurtzorg have made the web part of being self-managing.

Clients love it. At most they have 1-2 nurses working with them. They sit and drink coffee. Their whole objective is they want people to have rich, meaningful, autonomous lives. The older people only use 40% of the hours prescribed by GPs because they live their own lives, which saves the state a lot of money. For the nurses, self-development comes built-in,

"It's a journey of personal unfolding, in which true professionals are born. Many nurses report their surprise at how much energy and motivation they discovered in themselves..." (6).

The work naturally prompts teams to consider innovating and developing new services. Should teams work on prevention with physios coming in and teaching people how to move and change things in the home? The Buurtzorg CEO`s response to such questions is, *"how should I know if we should do it nationwide..lets see if the energy goes that way"*. Putting the suggestion out through social media and developing training has resulted in 90% of teams also now doing prevention. But some don't want to. The ethos is, *"let the reality decide."*

FAVI automotive supplier

This is a family owned French brass foundry which gets most of its income from gearbox forks for cars. It is physically demanding work. The competitors all moved to China for cheaper labour costs. Favi stayed put and is now the only manufacturer in Europe, but it commands 50% of the market. It has legendary product quality and on time delivery. Not a single order has been delivered late in 25 years. Favi has achieved high profit margins year-in year-out. There is *no* employee turnover. There are 500 employees in 21 teams called mini factories of 15-35 people. Teams are assigned to specific customers: there is a VW team etc. There are `upstream` production teams and support teams. Each team self-organises and there is no middle management. There are no rules or procedures except those each team decides for itself. Staff functions all disappeared as the tasks were taken over by individuals in the teams. The sales department has been disbanded too.

Previously a factory worker reported to a team manager, who reported to a workshop manager, who reported to a service manager, who reported to production manager who reported to the CEO. Previously when an order came into the sales department it would be passed to the planning department. They would give sales a predicted shipment date and allocate machine time. The day before production, scheduling would take place. A detailed plan of what to produce on which machines and when, would be made. Human resources would allocate workers. Basically, workers did what they were told. They were given no information or say in their work. As a consequence, it was `just a job`, and there was no real commitment. This was orange Favi.

Now when an order comes in, the team responsible for making parts for the car manufacturer set up a short meeting with the account manager for that company. They plan on the spot and agree a shipment date. All a sales person is there to do is to serve the client well. There are no sales targets. Account managers are motivated to feed their team work. All orders are discussed in terms of how many it gives work to rather than its money value.

There are no executive team meetings. No one meets at the top. All functions are in the teams. Typically, each team holds 3 kinds of meetings: a short tactical discussion at the beginning of every shift; a weekly meeting with the sales account manager to discuss orders; and monthly meetings with an open agenda. Cross team meetings take place if needed, say for `load balancing`.

Favi has an `ideas scout` who goes round the world looking for machines, materials, and suppliers and comes back to Favi roughly once a month. They hold a conference to share findings and the topic determines who shows up.

RHD human support

RHD started in 1970 with a $50k contract to provide community mental health services in Philadelphia. They now have 4,600 staff providing services worth $200 million to 10s of thousands of people in 14 states. RHD provide homes and shelters for the mentally ill, the disabled, people with drug and alcohol addiction, and the homeless. They have grown on average 30% a year over 40 years. Currently they have $2b in revenues and 200 units making autonomous decisions. The care they provide is extraordinary.

They have, like many teal organisations, explicit principles on which the whole thing is founded:

1) All people are of equal human worth;
2) People are essentially good unless proven otherwise;
3) There is no single way to manage corporate issues well.

Each programme is run by a self-managing team or `unit`. There are 20 -50 people running a unit who develop their own sense of identity, purpose and pride. There are no job descriptions. A unit is responsible for its entire operation. Central staff are kept to a minimum. Specialists can counsel units but the final decision is up to the unit. Units have directors but they can't impose decisions and can't hire or fire anybody. There are regional supporters, like Buurztorg, but responsibility for resolving problems rests with units. Hubs, which group units, have no business targets and are not responsible for their unit's financial results.

RHD manage status, power and money according to the three principles. Self-management is fundamental: people need the freedom to decide in the moment how to best meet the needs of the people they care for. There is a safe and open environment throughout the company, which, *"helps people tap into their deepest humanity to bring out their care for others"* (7). It also raises everybody's awareness of the words and actions that create or undermine a safe working environment.

Structures, practices and processes of teal organisations

These examples confront an easy and wildly incorrect assumption that if there is no command and control then anything goes. This clearly is not the case. Like Participles` circles and life programmes, family groups, the work on the Estate and the antiracist network, there are structures, practices and processes in place. However, they are developed with and are being freely entered into among those involved. There is psychological ownership. There are no bosses. In addition to being organisations these are, from another standpoint, *communities* with shared objectives who have developed ways to achieve their shared objectives. They have compelling collective purposes, and in that context, the individuals participating together, to achieve those purposes, flourish: they are part of something they really want to be part of.

In these three organisations, there is a striking similarity in their structures, practices and processes. Because amber and orange style organisations are so powerfully imprinted in us, I want to develop a forensic anatomy of these three examples from Laloux`s research. It is not just that the imprint is strong, it is that what command and control has been based on is a fundamental of human nature:

fear. Fear runs right through orange organisations, from sanctions and punishments for infringements, detailed instructions and codes, all the way to an obsession with competition and the very survival of the organisation. From the standpoint of control, and the fear of the loss of it, this is all reasonable because the environment cannot be controlled. Unless all the controls are in place the assumption is the organisation definitely will not be able to survive. Hence taking away all the control (in the form orange does it) becomes *incomprehensible*.

Generally, the inheritance within organisations in Britain has been rationalist. This means thinking and doing are separated and a tremendous amount of planning takes place. But the experience this kind of culture creates, within an organisation, is that the people at the top don't know what they are talking about. They are seen to be out of touch with realities on the ground. People on the ground feel powerless because they are not listened to by people at the top. What Laloux is showing us is a totally different organisational culture in which thinking, being, and doing are all in play for everybody as part of a hyper-active community of people sharing the running of the organisation.

So it is very difficult, without reading the above concrete examples of this completely different way of running organisations, to even comprehend how it is possible to survive without command and control. This is even more the case when you factor in the kinds of figures from Wilber for how many people in the population are likely to have these various consciousnesses: 70% amber/orange, 25% green, 5% teal (8).

Given all this, how does a teal organisation even begin to get going? For Laloux everything hinges on the consciousness of the CEO. If the board also shares this then a transition to teal can happen: the structures, practices, and processes can be created, and the workforce goes with it. It is managers in the old set up who tend to resist. But being teal, solutions for them appear. He argues for three steps in making a transition: self-organising, wholeness, and evolutionary purpose. The last two are relatively easy. The first is the really big challenge to get right (9). We need to also bear in mind that the organisations Laloux researched had been experimenting for between 10 and 40 years.

At the core of being self-organising is a CEO holding the space for teams to decide everything to do with fulfilling the purpose. This is a very different role for a CEO. They follow the same rules as everybody. They also have a second key role: they model this teal way of looking at things.

Everyone works in teams. Work is organised through team meetings and people talking with each other between teams. Virtually everything that would 'normally' be a specialist function in a pyramid structure, happens either in the teams doing the work or in support teams that work just like all the teams.

It is the working in teams *and* as a whole community that gives these organisations the ability to flexibly respond to anything that comes their way. Continually moving between teams and the whole sustains the kind of community that can do teal, as we will see.

So how do they make decisions? They use `the advice process`. If someone sees something needing to be done, like a new piece of machinery needing to be bought, a new way to work needing to be thought about etc they can just do it. They can use the advice process to put forward their proposal. They have to get the views of those with relevant knowledge/experience and those it affects. The broader the scope of the proposal or the more money is involved, the broader the advice process goes. They do not have to get consensus (this is crucial), they just need to have considered all views. This process can be used for an individual wanting to go on an external training course all the way to a substantial investment in a new piece of equipment. In AES, one of the organisations Laloux studied, a woman working on the west coast of America, in the early 90s, felt that offsetting CO_2 emissions was part of the organisation`s purpose. Through the advice process millions of trees were planted. This definitely was very different from a typical orange process of going for the cheapest or minimal contribution to sustainability to avoid a hit on `the bottom line`. In teal it's a question of what is the right thing to do.

The advice process is very much a living system with its own identity. It is a way for a resonance to be created. It is something for everyone collectively as a `we`. There is no single dominating voice or `I`. It is a case of listening and partnering with it.

In an orange organisation there are levels in a hierarchy with an executive committee at the top. There are endless meetings to transmit information up and down the structure. In a self-managing teal organisation there is no executive committee. There is no equivalent hierarchy needing information going up and down, so there are far fewer meetings. Things are resolved in teams. Even in a downturn they do not lay off staff. They use the advice process and work out a way to move forward together. It is not quite true to say teal has no hierarchies. It is rather that they have replaced the `dominator hierarchies` of orange with the `supportive hierarchies` of teal.

Everybody is different so some do more than others, people have different capabilities. Some have developed expertise that others can use. There are informal networks of influence, exchange, etc. No one has a job title or job description: they have roles. Roles are proposed/taken on using the advice process. Individuals can have a number of roles which may change. With regular team meetings it becomes easy to see the need for new roles. Teams can create new roles through someone stepping forward and bouncing the idea of a new role off relevant people or discussing it in a team meeting. No one has to be asked permission. If it is agreed the new role is created.

There is a peer or self-based salary, review and feedback system. If an individual feels they should be paid more they can propose this. Everyone knows how much everyone earns. It is peer based. Some get paid more but this is not a problem. Teal organisations do not replicate the huge disparities of orange organisations where a CEO can be paid 400 or 500 times the lowest paid. Once or twice a year there is feedback from peers about performance (because its useful). In Heiligenfeld the yearly appraisal asks two questions: Is my heart at work? Do I sense I'm at the right place? The organisation is helping individuals own growth process. Feedback and performance management, when coming from peers, is coming from care, whether they have been inspired, touched, or angered. In orange this is much more performance in terms of what the employee has done for the organisation. Individual incentives like bonuses get abandoned but the organisation will distribute, equally to all, a share of profits.

How do conflicts get resolved if there is no boss to try to deal with them? Conflicts are resolved among peers using a conflict resolution process which new staff are trained in. The teal organisations, which Laloux researched, have developed remarkably similar ways to handle conflict:

> Stage 1 one-to-one discussion;
> Stage 2 mediation with a trusted peer;
> Stage 3 mediation by panel.

There is a real intensity of relationships in teal. And this can bring up what Laloux calls 'shadows' (i.e. friction between people on the surface, 'stuff' inside individuals only they can deal with). Shadow work becomes opportunity for self-development (more later). Just listing three stages above really doesn't get to the guts of how to actually resolve conflicts. In a moment I will go into the depth to which the culture of teal gets created. It is a culture in which you really are able to bring the whole of yourself to work. There is no sense you might be branded a trouble maker or whistle-blower as with orange organisations. Nevertheless, in a teal culture you may feel you have to speak up, that a deeper truth needs to be heard, even if others might not want to hear it.

Teal organisations put a lot into recruiting staff who are right for teal as well as an enormous amount of initial and then ongoing training so a safe and productive working environment is sustained. Interviewing is by peers. It might start with an introduction to self-management and then move on to a succession of interviews by peers. There may be quite a number, which encourages questioning at a deeper level. They are all in the direction of are we meant to journey together? Will they work in this environment and towards the purpose we are trying to serve? They are, after all, hiring a whole person. They focus less on skills which can be picked up later. Applicants who prove to be ego-centred or low on 'self-reveal' get weeded out in this process.

Incoming employees get rights and responsibilities spelt out in a manual. These are rules staff have determined together to live by. They get extensive training in working in a team with no boss, conflict resolution, the advice process, wholeness etc. Employees are in charge of their own learning and can use the advice process.

Values in teal are not a slogan. They spell out in detail what they mean: behaviour that is encouraged, behaviour that is not. Teal organisations have got to create safe space and that includes things like not making judgments, not rolling ones eyes, and no sarcasm. How else is a space created in which you can authentically be who you are and vulnerable?

In one of the teal organisations, Heiligenfeld, every Tuesday, 350 employees meet for 45 minutes to reflect on a topic proposed by one of them on things like conflict resolution, failure, sustainability, technology, or personal health. The topic is presented for 5 minutes, individuals self-reflect, then discuss in small groups. Doing this weekly creates incredible trust and intimacy,

"In the confines of the small group, helped by their colleagues, people dare to dig deep and gain new insights about themselves and others" (10).

Following the small groups, there is open mic so those who wish to can share what came up for them. There is no scripted outcome and no expected end product. Everyone comes out with their own personal learning. Collective insights emerge. In this way the whole organisation grows its way through topics and in the process fosters community and a common language,

"Colleagues are exposed repeatedly every week to a space made safe by ground rules that invite them to truly be themselves. They learn to see each other in light of their deep humanity..the trust, empathy and compassion that build up in the meeting expand well beyond the confines of the meeting to permeate the whole organisation" (10)

Teal organisations create dedicated moments to re-visit their values with whole day events, surveys etc. All this is generating a common language and ground-rules.

A teal organisation wants people to bring the whole of themselves to work. Here are two examples of practices to support that.

Wholeness has been taken to a whole new level in the 5 mental health hospitals run by Heiligenfeld. The hospitals are spectacularly successful. They are explicitly setting out to support `the whole person`. Everyone is trained in active listening and non-violent communication. To put this into practice, every meeting room has hand cymbals. Meetings start with 1 minute's silence, then possibly some humour, all of which grounds everyone. Who has the hand cymbals today? Those who take these during a meeting have an additional role in the meeting. If someone is speaking from ego, the keeper of the cymbals rings them. While that is happening, everyone is silently reflecting on who they are trying to serve. They are all silent till the last sound has finished. Usually the keeper of the cymbals only has to make a move to pick them up. They are rarely used. The result is meetings without ego.

You would think a school with 500 adolescents might have some serious challenges and problems with attendance, behaviour, engagement with learning and being part of a community. Not so at ESBZ. ESBZ is a self-managing school which invites all their pupils to truly be themselves. It is daring them to speak what truly matters to them. They take the view that when going to school becomes wearing so many masks, students don't really learn.

One of the practices is the whole school gathering every Friday for 45 mins. They sing a song for 5 minutes (which settles the community) and then it's an open mic. There is one rule for everyone who takes the mic: we are here to praise and thank each other. What happens is that people tell stories about each other and reveal something about themselves. This erases the boundaries between students and teachers. Everyone may feel down or need support and everyone has the gift of empathy and of finding ways to offer support and friendship. Adolescents dare to be vulnerable and authentic in front of 500 people. The school has no violence problems. The school has an extraordinary spirit of learning, collaboration, and maturity.

In teal a lot of attention goes on self-development. Most of this happens in doing the work itself. The shadow work referred to earlier has been responded to practically. One of the organisations offers ten free counselling sessions per year to employees and their families. Another gives everyone $200 and a day off to get something special for someone and come back and tell the rest of us what happened! Teal encourages the sharing of beautiful stories. The power of storytelling is really used well. This grounds the culture in actual experiences. Sharing experiences creates gratitude and appreciation. These organisations also create reflective spaces like quiet rooms, yoga classes, group coaching, and they build in collective moments of self-reflection.

Teal is a living system which evolves. Survival is not a fixation. Competition is not even mentioned. It vanishes because if the purpose of the organisation truly matters, there is no competition. While the `for profit` teals make a profit, making the profit is not the point. It is a side effect of pursuing the purpose *really well*. Employees are coming together as a community to fulfil human needs and actualize their lives. Even the blue-collar engineering firm has expressed its purpose in deeply human terms. Favi is there to provide super meaningful work in a rural area and secondly to give and receive love from clients. They arrived at this through a Friday afternoon whole staff meeting, working in small groups. They were `listening in to the purpose of the living organisation called Favi`. Eventually they discover what is meaningful. These organisations are not just doing what they want. They embrace suppliers and customers in these processes of aligning with purpose.

We can get a sense in all this that a teal organisation cannot leave the culture to chance. In an orange organisation `culture` tends to be viewed as `soft`. What really matters in orange is `hard`, the complex organisational machinery. But in teal all four quadrants are fully engaged: a change in one quadrant ripples through to others: mindsets, behaviour, culture and systems are all in flow. Change mindset or behaviours and culture changes. Change systems and culture changes. It is eminently possible for a community, which is like a fast-flowing stream, to maintain a flourishing, ever developing, teal culture when the four quadrants are constantly in play.

SGI-UK: a teal of Buddhism

Frederic Laloux gives us such a clear picture of a teal organisation. When I first read it, it kept reminding me of the Buddhist organisation I have been a member of for over 40 years (11). It too has been evolving and innovating over this whole period. It is continuously finding the best way to express the state of life we members call Buddhahood (but which can equally well be described as teal).

As of 2018 SGI-UK had just under 15,000 members across the UK. Straight away it is a shock to go to any SGI-UK activity and see that it is by no means white and middle class. You ask yourself what such diverse people have in common. SGI fosters a kind of unity which is quite rare but which human beings yearn for and which Laloux shows being developed in teal organisations. It is known as `many in body, one in mind`. In other words, a unity built on the uniqueness of what each individual brings of themselves, combined with a profound spiritual unity of sharing the same profound purpose in life.

On the one hand SGI-UK clearly is an organisation. It is a registered charity. It has budgets, centres, staff, an IT system, an in-house magazine, runs courses etc. However, it sees its purpose as the happiness of each individual member. Laloux has used the metaphor of `shadow work` for the negativity individuals experience in themselves, drawn out by the intensity of relationships in teal organisations. In SGI-UK winning over this negative side we each have, *is* the purpose and it is expressed as individuals doing their own `human revolution`. The more the human revolution the less the hold the narrow egoistic self has, the free-er someone is from the hold their own negative tendencies have and the fuller, deeper, and more fulfilling life becomes. A bigger life develops.

Buddhist teaching is extraordinarily profound and includes the principle that a single moment of life is influencing the world around that life. It is shaping that self, their relationships in society as well as the environment (12). As an individual member I am not only changing my inner world and my behaviour, I am also impacting the wider world around me. For each individual member all `four quadrants` are in play. What is distinctive, as an organisation is that it is the upper left quadrant that is most the focus of individual attention: what is going on in my life, inside me. The organisation is there to support individuals to have that experience of their own self-motivated inner transformation. SGI-UK also has a framework for change in society, focusing its efforts, as an organisation, on peace, culture, and education. So not only are individual members contributing to change in society (through their work, volunteering, family, friends etc etc), but so too is the organisation. This is a socially engaged form of Buddhism.

What do SGI Buddhists believe? At the core is being able to get into rhythm with what an American scholar, Richard Seager researching the SGI movement, called, *"the awakened heart of the living universe"* (13). It is the teachings of Nichiren in the 1200's that provide the platform for the SGI movement. The core belief is that the universe is a compassionate intelligent life force or super-consciousness: a cosmic life force connecting all life throughout the universe and which has always existed. A key belief is that a human life comprises 9 consciousnesses: the 5 senses, the conscious mind, the sub conscious, and 8th consciousness in which all our causes and effects are stored (aka karma), and this 9th Buddha super-consciousness. We are an expression of life and therefore also have within us this connecting cosmic life force. Buddhist practice is about raising this depth inside us to be the state of life we are living from in daily life, and which is shaping the world around us. Because we can make causes from the 9th consciousness we are no longer shackled by our karma. From this standpoint negative life is also a manifestation of this 9th consciousness. SGI members learn how to use this 9th consciousness to win over their negative tendencies.

Although SGI-UK has all the practicality you would associate with an organisation, actually it is an ultra-active coming together of people sharing the purpose of raising their life condition as part of transforming the world. Because each individual member has the power to get the four quadrants working powerfully for themselves, collectively the experience is extraordinary. It literally is a movement powered by its membership who do everything to move it forward, because there is no separation between their activities in daily life and activities in SGI-UK. It is an organisation without walls.

To be in battle with `fundamental darkness` (the SGI-UK equivalent of shadow work) so directly, calls for a lot of support. Yes, the individual is learning to `stand alone`, but at the same time the compassionate thing is for there also to be support. There is a structure of leadership `in faith` who are not some second level of membership but are equally members, engaging in the same struggles in life and sharing their experiences alongside everybody else. SGI-UK is like a huge leadership training programme. Members can call on leaders at any time (within the bounds of common sense, and generally not after 9pm) for guidance. If you have become stuck, being able to talk with someone who can help you see the way forward is just great. There is also an enormous amount of one-to-one, be that visiting someone at home or in a public space.

There is a central structure or a supportive hierarchy. Everyone is in a local group. The local group is the bedrock of the whole thing. In the UK, as of 2018, there were 630 local groups. Each local group is autonomous and works together as a team and is part of a larger whole. Members of a local group learn to work together. The differences and difficulties between people in a local group are literally the fuel for its growth. This is the power of an underlying practice of 'human revolution' built-into this community. People focus on what they need to change or what they can do to strengthen their own lives for the positive, especially in difficult situations. There is fantastic support for others, especially at difficult times in life. Members come together once a month to share their experiences in discussion meetings which are open to all. There the discussion very much reflects the concerns, experiences, and lives of the people at the meeting. You can feel truly part of the human race, in its positive aspect, through discussion meetings. What each member is learning through experience is that when they change the responses from those around them changes. We are fuel for each other's growth.

Just as atoms are in molecules which are in cells which are in an organism, so local groups form together to create a larger group, which combines with other larger groups to form even larger groups until eventually it is a body of the entire membership. Each larger group has its leaders. Built into that structure of leadership, throughout the whole organisation and at every level, are youth. From this solid structure there are quite a number of spin-offs. The organisation comprises men, women, young men, young women, and children and young people. In effect this has become a men's movement, a women's movement supporting and being led by a youth movement.

To give an example, SGI-UK's youth in September 2017 proposed that three events be held in March 2018 to share the sense of realistic optimism that the youth of SGI-UK have developed. They wanted to respond to a sense that many young people in British society were not in a great place. The events were not for the people coming to them to start practising Buddhism, rather the aim was to share a profound kind of hope.

The SGI-UK youth were able to galvanise the support of the men and women across the country who held the space so that youth created the preparations for and running of the three events all held on the same day at the same time and with broadly the same mix of experiences, performance, video, emceeing and deejaying. On March 17th 2018 a total of 6,000 young people participated in three 'Generation Hope' events, one at the Passenger Shed in Bristol, one at the Manchester Conference Centre, and one at the Apollo in Hammersmith, London. Judging by the comments from people who came these events thoroughly achieved their purpose.

There are many other aspects to SGI-UK that members have developed, like having a Chorus, an educator's group, an LGBTQ group, and annual symposia involving academics studying the SGI movement's annual peace proposal to the UN and other bodies. The membership runs the four centres SGI-UK currently has. Staff provide the necessary infra-structuring of an information system, finance especially for booking community halls around the country, publications, etc. The financing of SGI-UK comes 100% from voluntary contribution by its members. To say SGI-UK`s activities spiral off in all directions is an understatement!

So is there an equivalent of a teal CEO? Yes there is. It is Daisaku Ikeda (14). Since the 60s he has been this global movements equivalent of a teal CEO. Daisaku Ikeda is a peacebuilder, Buddhist philosopher, educator, author and poet. As a peace-builder he is the founding president of SGI of which SGI-UK is a part. When the total number of monthly discussion meetings is added up in the 192 countries with an SGI organisation, it comes to the largest peace movement of ordinary people in the world. Ikeda has also founded several international institutions promoting peace, culture and education.

A core focus of Ikeda's peace activities has been the goal of nuclear disarmament. He has inspired grassroots efforts for a nuclear-weapons- free world over several decades and has continued to explore viable routes toward nuclear abolition in his peace proposals. He has published peace proposals annually since 1983.

As a Buddhist philosopher he has met with key leaders, cultural figures and scholars from every region of the world to discuss ways of resolving the common challenges facing humanity. He has published dialogues probing the crucial issues of our time with over 80 such individuals. The very first of these dialogues, Choose Life, was in the UK, in the 70s, with the historian Arnold Toynbee, shortly before he died (15).

As an educator he has founded a Soka (value creating) educational system of primary and secondary schools as well as Soka university in Japan and America (16). Ikeda may well be the person in history with highest number of honorary doctorates awarded by universities all over the world: 379 as of April 2018 (17)

As an author he has written The Human Revolution, and in 2018 finished the 30 volume New Human Revolution (18). These tell the inside story of the origins and growth of this movement across the world. The Human Revolution focuses on post-war Japan up to the end of the 50s. The New Human Revolution starts in the early sixties as the first pioneer members emerged on all the continents. At that time there were perhaps 8 members in the whole of Europe. Today there are, as of 2018, around 145,000 in 34 countries of Europe.

He has, more than anyone else, modelled the life of someone fully living the consciousness everyone in this movement is developing. SGI members find themselves receiving inspiring messages, the SGI country organisations do too. He is known by everyone in the movement. He simply inspires, encourages and guides. He literally holds the space in which this movement flourishes as a living entity.

By definition you bring your whole self to activities in SGI-UK at every level, in a local group, in any of its larger groupings, and in meetings by gender. By listening in to our purpose of human revolution and transforming the world through our transformation, we evolve activities which seem to resonate with this, like Generation Hope.

I could go into great detail about how the culture is maintained, what rules there are for keeping the space safe, how leaders get appointed, who decides how money is spent, how decisions get made, how communication happens etc., etc. Suffice to say SGI-UK has evolved structures, practices and processes appropriate to its culture of fostering fundamental respect for the dignity of life, both within its membership and out into the wider society.

SGI members experience one another's hearts and the organisation itself is transparently just ablaze with heartfelt interactions, friendship, and trust. This is a movement that has found a way, in the midst of the realities of daily life, to enable its members to go beyond the limited ego and just being stuck in the inherent negativity each of us has.

We are getting a sense here of a completely different way of doing ` organised religion`: one leading into transformation and helping to move humanity towards the next consciousness.

Three autonomous teams

In every decade of my work, when I look back, there were autonomous teams who completely outshone everything else around at the time. I didn't realise it at the time but they were teaching me a vital part of the jigsaw of what future public services in Britain, that work really well, need to be like. In chapter 8 I probe into teal public services but here, in this chapter about organisations, I feel compelled to include these three examples of autonomous teams. What is truly significant for me is that they each were able to function so freely whilst being surrounded by or embedded within decidedly unfree public service contexts. This is a theme I develop in chapter 8: that public sector teal development isn't necessarily going to follow the formula of a CEO and a board needing a teal consciousness. Laloux`s account of the origins of Buurtzorg is already suggesting this.

In chapter 4, I narrated the story of the Estate. There was a story missing: the story of the advice centre I was a team member of, along with my community work colleague, three social workers, two housing assistants, an administrator and a receptionist. We were based in two converted flats on the Estate. We took control of how we offered an advice service. How we responded and adapted by physically being on the estate and right on everyone`s doorstep, was under our control. I don't know where it came from but we were using the phrase, *"breaking down the distinction between the givers and takers of services"*. This operated as a source of direction and inspiration as we thought about how to develop the centre and its services. We were to provide information about various services and benefits. The team also had a mandate to bring people together for mutual self-help, to put pressure on the authorities for better services, and generally add to community life.

By the autumn of 1974 an average of 500 to 600 callers a month were coming into the advice centre. Bruce and I were working intensively with the community, but what the community didn't see were the equally intense discussions and involvements we were having with our colleagues, especially the 3 social workers. All the systems and procedures familiar to social workers were simply reproduced to surround these 3 workers. Their office started filling up with casefiles, just like they would in a conventional social work set-up. Bruce and I were filled with horror at this. It seemed to represent a huge missed opportunity for social work to challenge itself to offer something much more relevant to the lives of people on the Estate.

The three social workers we had started with, all left. This process was tough and took the time it needed to take until the three social workers themselves could finally accept that they needed to move on. Transitioning teams that inherit people with `baggage` will all face this heartache. But it has to be done. On June 1st 1976, the advice centre began its new way of operating with a line-up of 3 new social workers. The centre was open for 5 social work sessions a week.

Firstly, there was a system of review which made a definite decision about the future handling of each case. A limit was set on the number of cases 'allocated' to each of the social workers to ensure 50% of their time remained free for `group work`. Any work going on beyond 2 months had to have a particular objective in mind and when achieved the case was closed. The team leader monitored caseloads to make sure they stayed workable.

What did the new social workers do with the remaining 50% of their time? A group was started with primary school children trampolining at a leisure centre. Most of the children had brothers or sisters 'in trouble'. Another worker linked up with older people and started organised outings. Some work went on setting up a babysitting scheme. Another example was bringing together socially isolated people. Then there was work with adolescent girls, groupwork with some women on the estate, and a non-swimmers' group for boys.

As members of this team we talked with residents just like we talked with ourselves (a bit less jargon and definitely fewer acronyms) about how to develop the advice centre. We were re-shaping how we did things as we went along, taking stock of what was happening, in order that what we did with residents could get better and better. We constantly communicated with our hierarchy. We advocated for changes in how we did things or what needed to happen for the team. We were fully awake, conscious human beings, learning about the power we really had to make our own world of work change.

After a morning meeting in the town hall I remember walking back into the advice centre to be greeted by our receptionist, *"Jim, what should I say to Mr Holbrook about his claim to Social Security?"* It was our receptionist greeting me at the front door. All our rooms were fully occupied. Everyone was engaged in animated conversation. I asked Mr Holbrook if we could go and talk in his flat! I could see how radical the advice centre was becoming. Real people had a foothold on Council territory: a space normally defended by the administrators who wanted to keep their system clear of confusion and incursions by actual people!

This second team is working in what I would call the long shadow cast by institutional care. It is a story of how good use of IT can defend an autonomous team in an orange world. Erving Goffman's full frontal assault, in the 1950s, on total institutions had set in train a consciousness that total institutions are much more damaging to the self, the psyche, and to well-being than the condition people were incarcerated for (19)! The belief in total institutions never recovered. Indeed, subsequent decades brought fresh revelations of dire inhumanities perpetrated on inmates by the staff of total institutions both here and in America, reconfirming Goffman's message.

The outreach support team was a team of great characters with a manager, Steven, who did not have a care background. They were keeping substantial numbers of people with learning disabilities living independently in their own flats. They had escaped the institution. They had a hugely challenging and creative brief: *"on-going support of a practical nature to these users in every facet of their day to day living"*.

I knew, from going out and being with these workers, that this team were achieving great things. Stories poured out of them and the people they worked with. But they had no way to turn that into 'hard data' which could inform the department's senior managers. Spending hours writing reports for social workers didn't do that. I created a software rating tool with them.

Instead of having to take 2 days out of each month to write reports, it now took 2 hours a month and provided far better and much more systematic data. Of course, the social workers complained that they were not getting a 'picture' of the work, but this was over-ruled. The management really liked it and didn't want to go back to lengthy text.

Moreover, because all 5 workers were doing this every month, the outreach support team had instant and highly useable management information. Workloads could now be seen very clearly. Staff stopped going off sick! They grew their autonomy and expanded the scale of their work. More people escaped the institution.

The third team had been the worst day centre for people with physical disabilities. It was frankly not worthy of being called a public service. Service users were suffering an oppressive regime. The centre got contracted out to be run by a national charity with a track record in working well with people with disabilities. The fact of the contract wasn't what changed things. It was Donald, the new manager. He created a very autonomous day service run by staff and service users working together. This is the point of this example: leadership trumps contracting.

A member of staff under both managements captures the moment of change,

"Empowerment became a big word when the new contract began and the new national body took over. Christmas was coming. Something as emotive as Christmas. These are disabled people. We have to `do for` ..but actually the Christmas activities were the opening up of empowerment for all of us. What happened in the end was that users were preparing dishes. They didn't need us. In the end we had such a great Christmas."(20)

I asked Donald for his version of the story,

*"Service users said to me `What are you doing about Christmas?`, I replied , `You want a Christmas party, you sort one!` There was so much anger and bitterness among service users because, as they saw it, it was **my** job as manager (to sort the Christmas party). Before the contract service users would pay the Council price for lunch. But staff had **more** and without paying. I said, `There are no free lunches`. For a period of time I took control. Having lost control, power was returned for empowering use. I looked at the talents people had. At that time everyone had a perceived role...staff had accepted roles. . I think as a manager you are there to empower the employees around you. Why is it that whenever a user is asked by the manager to talk in the office they always say `what have I done wrong`. What have we done with the way we have used power!"(20)*

Who or what was the biggest threat to empowerment? The chef! Donald again,

"I wanted service users to be able to make their own teas and coffees. I waited until the chef was busy with lunch and then went into the kitchen. It is so easy to stop seeing the humanity in the work we do. If we don't keep seeing it the chef will start to dictate!" (20)

From this the service became outwardly focused, engaging with the youth of the area and engaging with agencies like the police for the first time. The centre became a site for trainee social workers, police officers and nurses to do placements. Service users who had become engaged with the staff and manager started engaging with the local health services and with social services. None of this was in the contract between the national charity and the local authority.

These three examples begin to show the power of autonomous, self-managing teams *in a public service context* (beyond the nursing of Buurtzorg). They show the need to enable those with baggage that doesn't fit with teal to move on, to develop really useful tech, and for leadership to trump contracting.

Later this notion of public services in Britain moving to autonomous teams is further developed.

There can be no question that teal organisations massively realise individual as well as organisational potential compared with their orange counterparts, not least because they set out to do just that. These are organisations in which this understanding of how social realities are constituted, is acted on to positive effect. Orange separates thinking and doing. With teal thinking, *being* and doing are all together for everyone involved, as a community. What we have from this chapter is a clear picture of what teal organisations look like.

6 – Politics

"…the great unresolved struggle of our time, that of ordinary people to gain control over their own lives to get out from under schemes imposed on them externally by powerful elites and to build a genuinely participatory culture" John Shotter (1)

There is something very central to power *when it is viewed as something at work in daily life.* That 'something' is that our social realities are constituted through our relationships in which we struggle to shape what is going to happen. The antiracist network in chapter 4 was all about this. John Shotter captures this underlying dynamic, that the teal organisations of chapter 5 also put into practice,

"For those within a situation feel required to conform to the 'things' within it… because we call upon each other morally to recognise and respect what exists between us. Thus as neither 'mine' nor 'yours' the situation itself constitutes something to which we can both contribute: it is 'ours' …… It is a situation in which I feel as if I have made my contribution, and in which you feel as if you have made yours. Unless this is the case, I may feel that I am having to live in your reality, or you may feel that you are having to live in mine, or both of us may feel as if we are having to live in a reality not our own. The opportunity to contribute or not to the construction of ones social realities is what there is in such situations to struggle over: if social realities are socially constructed, then it is important that we all have a voice in the process of their construction, and have our voice taken seriously, that is responded to practically" (2)

I think this dynamic is central to a kind of *living* politics which the ordinary person can feel connected with. This intensity of personal engagement I take to be central to a teal politics. The blunt truth is that, so far as current orange national politics is concerned, most of us feel that, in general, we are having to live with a politics defined by professional politicians: that our voices are not taken seriously.

Previous chapters have been able to compare orange and teal *actualities*. I can't do that here because I don't think we have teal political actualities currently functioning. However, we have *indications*, like the one above about the intensity of personal engagement. We also have a considerable number of developments going on which also point towards what teal politics looks like. I want to run through `orange/actuality-teal/indication` contrasts in three steps. This is because I want to be more forensic than simply focusing on national politics (parliament and the party-political system). I want to bring out some of the hidden aspects of our political system. I want to start locally, then move to the middle layer of social policy formation and then end with the national.

By doing this I am redefining politics as a contestation, experienced in daily life, between the three big aspects of the country: markets, the state and civil society. What is essential is grasping the consciousness that is powering the configuration of these three. I think that configuration plus the consciousness tells us more about the use of power in the country, in our daily lives, than simply focusing on parliament and the parties.

Orange local

Because of my background (see introduction) I know about the politics of daily life in Britain from the ground up. I know about the class politics of council estates. The anti-racist struggle I narrated in chapter 4 taught me about a very different kind of politics. My work with disability communities (which you will hear about later) taught me about the power of something, people with disabilities, have called the social model. This focuses on the humanity and normality of the person with disabilities and the inhumanity and abnormality of structures, practices and processes bearing down on them within society.

When you start at the local level the big thing to notice about Britain's orange politics is how much comes from central government. Secondly, trying to pin down just what local is, is like trying to nail jelly to the wall.

Writing in the 80s, John Stewart bemoaned the excessive concentration by local authorities on providing services (3). Pre-occupation with running departments tended to crowd out any broader or more political take on the local population and what a local authority could be doing. Also local authority powers to raise money and control spending started to be seriously eroded in the 80s and 90s (in part a response to the inflation of the 70s). A central government fully intent on converting Britain over to being run through markets rather than bureaucracy took on rebel authorities like Liverpool. Central government was determined to clamp down on continual rises in local taxation (through the then rates) as well as local authorities moving income from housing rent to pay for other things. Today we probably don't realise the significance of the centre `allowing` local authorities to raise money beyond the level agreed by central government, for example to put more money into social care. That `allowing` is still on the basis of all the other financial controls remaining tightly controlled, from the centre.

Apart from controlling money, central government's other means of controlling what local authorities do is through 'guidance'. It is a monster deluge of day by day instructions from civil servants about what can and cannot be done. In some respects, we have government by spreadsheet! Despite devolution through 'local assemblies' in Wales, Scotland and Northern Ireland, there is still a good deal of detailed direction coming from the centre. This is all very orange.

The fundamental of the NHS is for the centre to control it and for it *not* to be part of local government. Today there are groupings of GPs across the country (GP clinical commissioners) grappling with local spending decisions within the strict 'guidelines'. Their grapplings are similar to the grapplings of local councillors. Very often the geographical area covered by GP commissioners is broadly the same as the area covered by the local authority.

Clustering locally there will also be a criminal justice network shading into alcohol and drug addiction. So too a housing network. Many business networks will also cluster locally, very often coterminous with the above. In addition to any formally organised civil society assembly (yes there are quite a lot of these), civil society organisations and activists are to be found clustering around all this too.

This jelly of local clusterings is trying to respond to its local civil society which (as we saw in chapter 2) has poverty, malnutrition, homelessness, stress, mental illness, violence, and a torn social fabric. What orange tends to do is try to keep these clusterings in separate silos, each being dealt with directly through central government's 'guidance'. The local agencies of government and their staff are enmeshed within the crippling constraints of central control by 'guidance'. The message is that 'the centre' does not trust 'the local' to get on and run its own affairs in ways that are *locally originated*. This is a crucial way in which local politics feels like having to live in a reality determined by somebody else. What is constituted locally isn't fully constituted within 'the local'.

There is also an imbalance between urban and rural. In the countryside there are parish councils. This is the layer of elected local government below local authorities. They are responsible for services such as management of litter, verges, cemeteries, parks, ponds, allotments, war memorials, and community halls. In cities there are some neighbourhood councils, but it is very patchy. The main point is that these bodies have also been emasculated and starved of funds. There is no question that they have the potential to expand what they can do. Currently urban dwellers are disenfranchised relative to rural dwellers.

What I think we have locally, is a longstanding historical set up waiting to have new life breathed into it. The jelly can become something really solid, working much better for its local population. Teal leadership will, I believe, breathe that new life.

Teal local

Democracy starts with `the demos`. In Wendy Brown's word *this* is why democracy is important,

"There (in `the demos`) we realise and develop our distinctive capacities for association, speech, law, action, moral judgment, and ethics. Thus our political nature issues from the distinctly human capacities of, on the one hand, moral reflection, deliberation, and expression, and on the other of generating multiple forms of association. Moral reflection and association making- these are the qualities that generate our politicalness." (4)

David Marquand puts it this way,

"We learn by doing; we absorb the disciplines of self-government by governing ourselves; we enlarge our horizons to embrace the common good by taking part in collective action, first and foremost at the local level" (5)

These are the kinds of things people experienced in Participle's work, family groups, on the Estate, in `the network`, in Laloux's teal organisations, and in SGI-UK. In market-based Britain's politics, the space for the population to experience `the demos` is extremely restricted. So here is what I consider to be a teal vision of a future British politics: in a teal politics 90% is local. What remains in Whitehall has reduced and reduced. It is like Buurtzorg and the other teal organisations HQs being tiny. The centre is there to support the autonomy of the local. Teal means a self-governing Britain where sovereignty is experienced, primarily as local. This is trust in the people. Like all teal developments presented so far the process of getting there really matters because psychological ownership is key, and that takes time and the sheer experience of trying things out, learning to work together and finding ways forward.

The `teams` that make up a teal polity comprise local assemblies. However, they are in those geographical areas, across the country, currently defined by their jelly of local clusterings. They are not like the devolved assemblies. Government is in service to these local assemblies. The prime minister holds the space for the teams to decide. This is a massive shift of power and resources. It is a huge opening up of space for `the demos`.

I think the way the country wants to go is for civil society, local public services and local businesses to come together by forming local assemblies: for the current jelly to become integrated, stable and strong. The job of teal politics is, first and foremost, to establish a unifying framework, nationally, which legitimates the local.

Local assemblies have the job of understanding local need and getting these needs met. These assemblies then provide the basis for far more effective uses of government funds, charitable donations, and private money. Most importantly these kinds of assemblies become the basis for implementing the autonomous, self-managing model of responding to need that totally redefines our current public service idea (see chapter 8).

There are three, challenging integrations at issue here:

> 1 Bringing all the 5 social policy areas together *locally* (benefits, health, care, education, housing and criminal justice);
> 2 Bringing the local state, civil society and businesses together;
> 3 Bringing elected representatives together with officers and activists.

One of the many challenges in this is the availability of local teal leadership capable of making these integrated local assemblies a working reality. Is there any evidence that the country `wants to go this way?`

Civil society has been going in the direction of local assemblies of various kinds for some time.

What do Par Bay, NW Ipswich, Stoke North, Barrowcliff and Ewanrigg have in common? They are 5 of the 150 `Big Local` areas working across England (6). There used to be an organisation call The Community Development Foundation. It folded and gifted substantial sums to `Local Trust`. The Lottery has also put money into Big Local, the name of local groups operating under the umbrella of Local Trust. Here is what the website says about Big Local,

"Big Local is an exciting opportunity for residents in 150 areas around England to use at least £1m each to make a massive and lasting positive difference to their communities. Big Local brings together all the local talent, ambitions, skills and energy from individuals, groups and organisations who want to make their area an even better place to live." (6)

So this is local people, in an area, learning to work together and shaping the development of their area.

Secondly, the Transition Town movement has, as the name implies, also been a way for towns to develop a kind of civil society gathering and initiative: not quite an assembly but definitely diagnosing and responding to need, in far more sustainable ways, locally. As the website says,

"Transition is a quiet revolution unfolding around the world. People like you and I are seeing crisis as the opportunity for doing something different, something extraordinary. The guy sat next to you on the train this morning may well be setting up a community brewery. The woman opposite could be the director of a

community energy company. The driver could own shares in a local farm. It's everywhere." (7)

There were 2 transition initiatives in 2006 and by 2013 there were 1,107 in 43 countries. Currently there are 245 in the UK. This too is a great development initiated by local people in civil society.

A third kind of local assembly takes us to Saul Alinsky's thinking about peoples' organisations (8). An example is The East London Communities Organisation (TELCO for short). This is an organisation financially independent and rooted in a diverse membership: members of local churches, trade unions and schools. Through a democratic process this organisation identifies common issues and adopts them as an agenda for action. Over more than 20 years, TELCO alliances have spread to other parts of the UK using these principles.

All this is self-evidently strengthening the capacity of civil society as an independent force for change in Britain. If local public services and businesses were involved we would be close to the integrated assemblies argued for earlier. But there is a layer of political activity missing: locally elected representatives. Here too there are examples of re-thinking going on. Frome is an example. Independent councillors with no party affiliation run Frome town council. Here are their core values and their rationale for how they do local politics,

*"**Independence.** We will each make up our own mind about each decision without reference to a shared dogma or ideology.*
***Integrity.** Decisions will be made in an open and understandable manner. Information will be made available even when we make mistakes and everyone will have the opportunity to influence decisions.*
***Positivity.** We will look for solutions, involving others in the discussions, not just describe problems.*
***Creativity.** Use new, or borrowed, ideas from within the group and the wider community to refresh what we do and how we do it.*
***Respect.** Understand that everyone has an equal voice and is worth listening to. We will adhere to these values by challenging ourselves and each other to:*

- *Avoid identifying ourselves so personally with a particular position that this in itself excludes constructive debate.*
- *Being prepared to be swayed by the arguments of others and admitting mistakes.*
- *Be willing and able to participate in rational debate leading to a conclusion.*
- *Understand the value of constructive debate.*
- *Accept that you win some, you lose some; it's usually nothing personal and there's really no point in taking defeats to heart.*

- *Maintain confidentiality where requested and agree when it will be expected.*
- *Share leadership and responsibility and take time to communicate the intention of, and the approach to, the work we undertake.*
- *Have confidence in, and adhere to, the mechanisms and processes of decision-making that we establish, accepting that the decisions of the majority are paramount.*
- *Sustain an intention to involve each other and others rather than working in isolation.*
- *Trust and have confidence and optimism in other people's expertise, knowledge and intentions. Talk to each other not about each other." (9)*

Frome has direction and is thriving. There are other examples too like Devon United (10).

Why go to all this trouble of bringing elected reps, leading people across local public services, business people, and civil society people into one local assembly?

Local assemblies become the demos. They return the experience of running our own affairs back to local people: the very reason for having democracy in the first place. They also help restore the social fabric by being able to sense and respond to fast changing social realities. It is in assemblies that shifting and newly emerging needs are identified and the responses assessed and decided on. They become the legitimating force behind self-managing/autonomous teams potentially combining state employees, volunteers, sessionally-paid local people, and business people: a completely re-defined notion of public service. They are the way to transition out of the current dysfunctional public services (more in chapters 8).

It doesn't mean the NHS stops focusing on and making decisions on uses of resources that are strictly its concern. Ditto local authorities and other agencies. But it does mean a serious local political `will` shared locally across the sectors, to put assemblies at the centre as the way to get the available resource better focused and used. Local assemblies offer a way to focus in on something very local that is causing concern. Examples might be domestic violence, the state of the high street, homelessness, rural transport or violence. All this depends on teal leadership. A leadership with amber, orange or green consciousnesses will not be able to achieve this.

In terms of making such assemblies happen, relevant teal-like methods have been developed like those by the P2P foundation (11). They are especially effective at enabling complex realities and diverse agencies/groups to find common ground. The notion of `the commons` is key.

The commons is a general term for shared resources in which each stakeholder has an equal interest. More concretely the commons is a resource (land, knowledge, a city, software etc) over which a community has shared and equal rights. The commons is about a community of people organising themselves to manage and protect the resource, and the rules, systems and negotiations needed to sustain it. The commons is about protecting what is `inalienable` and should not be sold or given away.

In "Network Society and Future Scenarios for a Collaborative Economy" co-authored by Vasilis Kostakis and Michel Bauwens they develop the concept of the commons,

"It could be said that every Commons scheme basically has four interlinked components: a resource (material and/or immaterial; replenishable and/or depletable); the community which shares it (the users, administrators, producers and/or providers); the use value created through the social reproduction or preservation of these common goods; and the rules and the participatory property regimes that govern people's access to it." (11)

This kind of thinking has been used by city authorities like Bologna in Italy to draw up a `commons charter`, in order to protect the city in its public aspects. In this case, they have done it with civil society organisations in the city. (12).

Frankly there is a wealth now in Britain of methods, technologies, and experiences for creating, making decisions in, ensuring active participation in, and real accountability of such assemblies. Laloux gives a fictive but realistic account of a large scale event enabling hundreds of employees to re-work their organisation (13). The world café approach, appreciative enquiry, future search, or process design are just some of a multitude of techniques available. Art, video, internet conferencing, electronic voting, in short, myriad tools can all be used. What is most needed is teal leadership.

Orange middle

This is a very, very significant part of our political system. But it is almost completely hidden from view. This is why I wanted to take a more forensic view: to draw a boundary around what is political that includes the exercise of enormous political power but in ways that are outside the paraphernalia of elections and political parties. I am referring to the civil service or the sources of control by `guidance`. But most of all, by `middle layer` I am wanting to focus on social policy: specifically, what shapes benefits, health/care, housing, education and criminal justice. In chapter 8 I will deal in detail with these five areas. Here I want to explore the culture and thinking of the social policy side of these. This is inhibiting the state from effectively responding to the overwhelming demands of the torn social fabric.

When you hear the word 'modernism' you might think of a certain kind of architecture or a style of painting. But it is also a word used in social policy. It is the dominant way of thinking in Britain's civil service and in social policy. Significantly, in a modernist mind-set, the self does not figure.

It is a mindset among policy elites, national and local politicians, civil servants and managers. It is a way of thinking rooted in the enlightenment of seventeenth and eighteenth century, European philosophy. It is a highly sophisticated version of orange. The question is whether such ancient roots are now adequate.

When Tony Blair implemented health action zones, a researcher from the Manchester Business school, Su Maddock, had a look at how things were going. Because the policy, unusually, brought civil servants directly into contact with local practitioners, she found there was a kind of war of perspectives. How the two parties understood their worlds was completely different,

"Poor practitioner/policy maker relationships are not improved when practitioners and local managers are overworked and unable to reflect on their work, and are irritated by theoretical debate when struggling to manage staff, budgets and daily crises" (14)

And this is how she unpacked the `modernist mindset` of the policy makers and civil servants,

"Policy makers and advisers continue to come to government along the Oxbridge route which results in a cultural mindset and knowledge bank that is detached from personal complexities, process and people relationships. The dominant mindset within the civil service is the rationalist paradigm. This grips much of the civil service and undermines internal transformation processes largely because there is no shared philosophical underpinning for transforming relationships. The rational position relies on indisputable knowledge and logical argument and is often formulaic and detached from practical and emotional realities" (15)

As Maddock suggests, modernist thinking is not particularly interested in the inner workings of the people who are the target of social policy. It is easy to see how people with this perspective cannot understand that what *they do* has an impact on relationships between people. The relational aspect of life is no part of their vocabulary. Researchers with this perspective will see mental processes as needing to be studied in isolation: divorced from the social, historical, and cultural context of the person. Can this possibly provide an adequate foundation for policies to do with addiction, homelessness, education, care, health, benefits and criminal justice? These all rely on social, historical and cultural context. Crucially they also rely on personal relationships.

Further aggravating this subtle but devastating type of disconnect is the rationalist organisational culture social policy makers work in. It generally separates thinking and doing. This leads to action which comes from theoretical planning and cannot keep step with fast changing, and more is the point, *chaotic* realities. Cultures of thinking, being and doing provide far better organisational support for the making of social policies that are experienced as transformational by people in society.

A humane society needs to know how to translate issues and needs, raised within the population, into the rule of law, ways to regulate behaviour, enforce sanctions, and intelligently promote needed developments. Sadly, in Britain this process is now creating problems as social policies fail, sometimes spectacularly. Were the translating of needs and issues into regulations, sanctions, and developments working, the extent of suffering and dysfunction in all 5 main social policy areas that we see in Britain today (chapter 8), would not be happening.

I want to lead into a teal approach to social policy with this from Daisaku Ikeda,

Everything in our lives, far from being immovably determined, can be transformed for the better through our actions in this moment. In this way, ...a change in our inner determination (internal cause and effect) in this moment can change the present reality of our lives that produces future outcomes. At the same time, it emphasizes the critical importance of conditioning context (Jpn: en; relation) that can powerfully shape the interplay between (internal) cause and effect. In other words, depending on the context of the relations that are formed, the same cause can give rise to widely varying effects. (16)

Internal cause and effect probably needs some explanation. Let us take the example of a young person who goes home to spend the weekend with parents, there is a blazing row and they leave before the weekend is up. This is a very external account based on observable behaviour. It doesn't tell us what is happening inside the young person. Let's assume the young person doesn't realise that, unknown to themselves, *they despise their parents*. This suddenly takes us inside the life of the young person. This `internal cause` carries with it the related `internal effect` of pushing their life into a very low state in which it is impossible to have dialogue and there is only anger. But if they change their heart by overcoming their tendency to despise their parents, everything will change. The internal `magnet` will no longer be there for anger in their dealings with their parents.

But Ikeda also stresses the `importance of the conditioning context`. So, it is also open to the parents to change the way they are relating to their offspring: possibly more seeing the whole person, genuine compassion and care, and less judgemental and controlling.

Now substitute for the young person visiting their parents, someone doing drugs, or a young person working on their homework (despite a very unsupportive family) or the thief who has done time standing in front of a potential robbery. Now add to this, the innumerable policy enactments across these three longstanding and intractable areas of social policy: drug rehab, educational disadvantage, and re-offending. What I referred to earlier, as practices that engage the inner lives of the very targets of social policy, suddenly now become rather crucial to actual transformation. Of course, social policies are dealing with people for whom the inner change may well *not* come initially through personal realisation. In which cases the conditioning context becomes all important in leading to that happening.

The long and the short of orange social policy in Britain is that we tend to ban blazing rows! We go for the external and observable. Our market based social policies in educational disadvantage, drug addiction, re-offending etc overwhelmingly focus on externals and do little to recognise the importance of the conditioning context. It is hardly any wonder that we have such levels of exclusion, addiction, full prisons, etc.

Let us take educational disadvantage and look at it in more detail. We currently allocate to any primary school child, whose parent is eligible for free school meals, a sum of money to be spent on enabling *that child* to progress. The idea is to enable them to make up the lost ground of their lower starting point.

The statistical basis of this is itself the point I am making: free school meals *continue* to be a very good predictor of not being able to progress in life either in secondary school or after school. *The persistence of this correlation is the evidence of the failure of the best of social policy intentions.*

Unless the life of the person engages inwardly in some transforming way (supported by an appropriate conditioning context like a superbly skilled inspirational teacher), that correlation will grind on and the social policy will be fighting an uphill battle. In this example that 'uphill' may be years of living with parents where this kind of achievement is not valued and which gets internalised. The individual may also lack the comparable stimuli, socialisation, and experiences which in other children and their families supports achievement educationally.

A teal social policy will move on from the obsession with 'disadvantage' that has characterised British social policy for so long and become based on a fullness of life and trust in the inherent dignity of life.

Teal middle

If we take the insight from John Shotter that opened this chapter and translate it into a simple rule for social policy makers it would be: don't try to make policy using the market-based model of service implementation (chapter 2). Instead focus on how the struggle to created shared purpose and meaning between people in micro contexts can be supported to create social realities which work. It is from this shared reality that," *all the other socially significant dimensions of interpersonal interaction, with their associated modes of subjective or objective being originate and are formed" (17).* This shared meaning making has to include the people who are the targets of social policy. This is what Lalouxs` teal organisations do. It was the dynamic developed by Participle, family groups, on the Estate, in the Network, and within SGI-UK. What Shotter also gives us is an understanding of how community can be speedy in creating a complete change from what has gone before. Therefore, supporting communities, on the ground, in these key areas of social policy becomes vital. It is this dynamic of moving between community, where we can be inspired to change, then consolidation through one-to-one, that can enable genuine transformation.

What this offers the civil servants charged with formulating social policies is the creation of new shared worlds of meaning, which *they* are party to alongside people who are the targets of the social policy (as well as those who work with them). The logic of applying the teal advice process is that makers of social policy seek out and engage with experts as well as people affected. This will call for teal leadership from the makers of social policies.

I cannot stress enough what a dramatic shift of consciousness this represents for such core public institutions in Britain as the civil service. What we inherit is a culture in which people focus on getting the policy changed or getting the practices changed and then they feel frustrated when they don't change or the results are not what was intended. What they are not yet focusing on is the consciousness powering these policies and practices. This is the price paid for neglecting to be party to the body of shared meanings and understandings powering *everything* in that context. The world which needs to be entered is not restricted to thinking. Transformational social policies will not have arisen from mere ideas and think tanks. Transformational social policy has thinking, doing, and becoming all together. This is teal policy making.

Orange national

Despite the dramas of UKIP, the formation of the Lib-Dems, the Green Party, and parties representing Wales, Northern Ireland and Scotland, in my view the dynamic of British politics still orbits around two parties. There are still two *main* contenders slugging it out in the boxing ring of Britain`s political culture: the blue (conservative) corner and the red (socialist) corner. Their domination is creating a kind of stalemate. Why is this?

The blue corner believes we need to build a society from the freedom of the individual to have enough money and property so that they don't need the state to help them. They are 'independent' and can 'look after themselves'. The word for this way of looking at how politics should steer the country is `liberalism`.

Now this can get confusing because most people think `liberal` means being willing to respect or accept behaviour or opinions different from one's own. The word liberalism here is about freedoms resulting from being able to buy or sell in a market. Unlike the use of the word in America, I am using the word liberalism here to mean a political perspective that puts the highest value on freely trading. When trade is going on freely, it is believed this, in turn, leads to political freedom. So, liberalism sees the freedom to trade and have markets, as trumping all other kinds of freedom. And this kind of political thinking wants the state to play a minimal role because the state is equated with loss of freedom. Liberalism is a particularly British way of thinking politically which goes back to John Locke in the 1690s. It has a long history. It is truly ancient.

The red corner is a relative newcomer in that it has come from Karl Marx in the 1840s-80s analysing the antagonism between labour and capital in the industrial revolution. Developed by the labour movement into socialist politics, this thinking is the mirror image of liberalism. In this thinking individuals cannot be free unless they unite. Indeed, being forced to buy and sell for profit in a market is a kind of 'slavery'. The role of politics is to liberate the mass of working people from enslavement to capitalism. The red corner have viewed markets with deep suspicion, as the very epicentre of human exploitation and degradation. Historically the red corner has replaced markets with state planning, and then grudgingly returned state planning back to markets as state planning fails spectacularly.

The red corner has a simplistic view of human life. It`s focus is on economic exploitation and how this colours the whole of society. Collective effort is one thing, but the inability to anchor the red corner in solid understandings of the inner lives of individuals is a substantial limitation. The red corner comes across as naively optimistic.

Equally the blue corner, while it does have a view of human life, takes a too negative view: that people are fundamentally bad, and need to be controlled and disciplined. It too is not interested in the inner lives of people: just how their negative behaviour can be controlled. It is also a perspective that is relatively uninterested in `society`. The blue corner thinks inequality of all kinds is inevitable and good (providing the impetus for people to better themselves). And it tends to be pragmatic, which, although popular with an electorate, is not a solid enough basis for governing.

We have to acknowledge that both the blue and the red have great strengths. Together they hold important truths. The red corner has put up the most incredible fight to get social justice, in terms of class. This has been a decade after decade after decade struggle, which still goes on. The blue corner has secured the place of markets as fundamental to us having any chance of prosperity. It seems obvious, but don't we need both markets and social justice working together? But it is literally inconceivable that the blue and red corners would *ever* go into power together! Hence the stuck politics.

Both these political perspectives are fundamentally materialistic. This may go some way to explain how, in Britain, we seem to have a democracy that is in some sense profoundly heartless. In today's Britain neither the blue nor the red seem to me to really address the desires and needs of Britain's population. It is as if they are more interested in arguing with each other than understanding fully and then addressing the populations needs: arguing over which way the house will burn and rather than putting out the fire. It is amber and orange in a fight to dominate, both of whom consider their way the only way. That is the nature of these consciousnesses: they think they are right and theirs is the only way. With British politics it seems to me to be a case of, `if the premise is problematic, so too will be the results`.

There is another uncomfortable truth in all this: this stuck politics reflects the voting public! If we want a different politics, we, the voters, had better change our consciousness. On the other hand, the appearance of teal consciousness on the national political stage would be capable of appealing to a population of majority amber/orange. That is the great virtue of teal leadership as the teal organisations of chapter 5 show.

A teal political philosophy, guiding national, middle and local

Perhaps we can start with a thought experiment where I boil things down to simple essentials. On the one hand liberalism will say I can only be free through markets. What I do with the results from trading in a market is my affair. The collective dimension is very weak. On the other hand, the socialist response is that freedom comes from the collective dimension. The individual dimension is weak.

I am fully aware that these over-simplified essentials have been compromised as the real world has gone and embedded itself so that what is said by politicians has now moved some way from all this. But I think it is worth getting back to this simplistic thought realm because it shows that how freedom is understood has never really been looked at from a teal standpoint. I think the teal viewpoint is the missing dimension that people want to see: a politics with *all four quadrants working together*. I would like to explore this.

Orange/amber political thinking (albeit with the numerous green add-ons) is either-or: one is essentially collective in approach while the other is about the individual. Neither really concerns itself with inner lives: "*the subjective realm is fundamentally set apart from the objective realm*". (18)

From a teal standpoint the individual is there and the collective is there. Inner is there as well as outer. Teal freedom has the four quadrants working together. Is there anyone who has done the political thinking which makes these connections? Searching widely, I have concluded that Carol Gould has set the teal freedom ball rolling (19). She has spent a lifetime developing thinking about democracy designed to,

"...overcome the deficiencies and inconsistencies of the two alternative theories of liberal individualism or holistic socialism" (20).

Her life's work has been about the major problem of contemporary political practice: liberal democracies do not yet provide the conditions for both full individual freedom *and* social co-operation. The elements making up the torn social fabric are telling us this. But the previous chapter has shown how teal organisations are already doing this. Even so I think Gould's clarity of thought might even help teal organisations. Putting her thinking into practice will certainly help foster much greater participation within organisations, across the board.

Her definition of freedom adds something quite crucial: in exercising freedom the individual is *undertaking an activity of self-development*. Freedom inherently is about self-development. That is why it is so important. Societies in which freedom is restricted are societies in which individuals lack the ability to develop themselves *in ways of their own choosing*. There is something contradictory about being directed in the ways you will be able to develop yourself. What Gould also brings into this is that *social co-operation is necessary for self-development.* It is through doing things with others that we develop ourselves. As we pursue her train of thought we will see she is not denying that people obviously do develop themselves, under their own steam.

We have a start point which brings individual freedom, self-development, and social co-operation together,

"Thus it will be seen that freedom understood as self-development requires equality and social co-operation...... *Conversely social co-operation among equals requires their individual freedom......, since otherwise it would be a form of domination or coercion of some by others" (21)*

We can understand equality in the teal sense of people having different capabilities, interests etc but coming *equally* from a shared purpose, or unifying framework, which unites them. Their very differences become harmonised for some shared purpose. This is quite a different kind of equality from the very crude kind of literal equality-as-sameness which history tells us is unworkable and dehumanising. Equally teal is not sanctioning ridiculous inequalities like CEO salaries at 400 or 500 times the lowest paid.

The rest of Gould's thinking unpacks and clarifies the implications of this starting point. What about conflict and antagonism? What Gould is saying is that social co-operation and the exercise of individual freedom will bring conflict to the surface. But that in itself is not a reason for saying that we should not seek for individual freedom and social co-operation to work together. All it means is that as we develop social co-operation, we build in ways conflict can be mediated.

The teal organisations we looked at in the previous chapter all did this. SGI-UK has it built-in as human revolution. I think the way the conflict between the playscheme group and the tenant`s association on the Estate resolved, is also a good illustration of the workability of this in practice. Teal doesn't ban the results of deep-seated conflict as orange does. It works with it.

The mutual realisation of freedom and social co-operation cannot be `top down`. It cannot arise through an increase in state power, centralised authority, or coercion to increase social co-operation. To do this would inhibit individual's self-determination. Such a change must arise from our lives, from the sovereignty of the people in the specific context. This does not mean political authority is compromised and the country descends into a state in which no political decisions can be made. But it probably does mean Britain`s ways of making decisions needs developing so that, like teal organisations, there is, for example, the equivalent of an advice process. On the basis of a teal consciousness we will need new structures, practices and processes through which to truly govern ourselves. I have already made some local and social policy suggestions.

The bedrock for Gould is not isolated individuals, as it is in liberal theory. Rather she concentrates on our nature as social beings. She talks about `individuals-in-relations` whose mode of being is fundamentally in and through social relations. Individuals are obviously primary but the relations between us are *also* fundamental aspects of our *being*. A human beings' world shrinks dramatically if they only have themselves all the time. It was with individuals-in-relations in mind that I proposed the ecology of support for realising potential.

These relations between us are not of isolated abstract egos standing in external relations to each other. Neither is there some overarching totality of which individuals are mere parts or functions (with these two we are back to the polar opposites of liberalism and socialism). It also does not mean individuals are wholly constituted by their `relations` (a totalitarian nightmare!).

Rather individuals choose which of the many possible relations they could enter into. We have an original capacity for freely choosing purposeful activity. I believe this is much more the model of Britain as it is today and that this is a Britain bursting to find a way to do politics where this is built in. A teal politics is one which has policies designed to foster this widely across society *and* which models it in the very workings of the political process. We are a long way from that at present. However, as I hope readers will see by the end of the book, there are innumerable micro contexts in organisations, project etc, where this *is* the reality. Perhaps this is telling us we are not so far away from constituting a very different politics as we may think.

Shared involvement through activities means many individuals acting together with a shared or common purpose. This common purpose is distinct from the individual activity of individuals acting to realise their own separate purposes. Common activity is not simply an aggregation of individual activities: common activity is defined by a shared aim and joint activity to realise that aim.

The autonomy of *individuals-in-relations* is different from *individual's* autonomy exercised in pursuit of his or her own ends. Individuals-in-relations choose to form relations to pursue shared objectives. These are voluntarily chosen. Individuals in the group are free to choose and to act on these shared objectives. There is a kind of shared autonomy arising from their mutual decision to act together towards some shared end. Civil society in Britain in my experience, tends to do this *as the norm*. Teal organisations do this with, for example the proposing of roles. Getting this shared autonomy into the political culture is part of teal politics. Individuals-in-relations are binding themselves to their decisions freely and in this way they are giving what they are doing an authority stemming from their own mutual self-determination, not from an external or imposed authority,

"Where members of a group make decisions by such shared authority, they obligate themselves to abide by these decisions" (22).

This is one reason why I argued earlier that a teal politics would be 90% local.

The `self-development` aspect of politics I would connect with integral`s phrase `shadow work` and the SGI practice of human revolution. In a very basic sense, unless individuals-in-relations change, especially their consciousness, nothing fundamentally will alter in politics. This is the dynamic engine of a teal politics. New structures, practices or processes which do not grow out of *this* earth will not work.

Resonant elsewhere?

In Macron`s France I think the really interesting bit of it has happened. It is easier there for a completely new political party to form. For many it was more a social movement with meetings in cafes after work (23). People previously alienated from politics got involved, in some cases becoming MPs. Whether this enacts a teal-like consciousness remains to be seen.

In 2016 in the run up to the US presidential elections, Bernie Sanders went from 3% name recognition to winning 22 states. He developed a way of amplifying the person-to-person communications way beyond just having paid staff. There were 4-5 volunteers for each staff member. This created a politics of belonging and community. The volunteers were from the same community. The connection was instant.

With Macron and Sanders, we have indications of teal-like ways to mobilise political support and create a new political constituency. In the UK we do have a new political party in formation during 2018, Renew (24). A major challenge for them will be to unite people across the tribalisms and stuck divides that the existing parties seem to have added to rather than addressed. The power of teal to unify needs to be seen at a very early stage.

What about the quality of political leadership once in power?

Anne Mette Fisker Nielson teaches at Soka University of Japan and is a world expert on the Komeito party (25). On 17th March 2018 she gave a talk in London which offered a rare glimpse inside Japanese politics. Komeito means clean government. It was a party, formed in the 50s, aiming to do just that: create a politics free of corruption. Komeito is Japan's third party after its equivalent of the blue and red corners. Actually, the blue corner has virtually held power throughout the period, with rare exceptions. Because Komeito has appealed to a substantial body of the electorate it has been able to be the second party in coalition. What is interesting here is that this third party has brought dialogue to otherwise entrenched positions. Its stance has become to work with the complexity so that better policies and laws can result. Perhaps a third party can be a way of creating transition to a teal-like politics nationally? At the very least it can act as a force unifying apparently irreconcilable forces.

Justin Trudeau of Canada has made a very deliberate effort to try to unify and not get stuck in just more tribalism. On gaining power the first thing he talked about was bringing Canadians together despite their differences. He wanted to re-build relations with indigenous people and for government to be open, ethical and transparent. The Trudeau government invested in public transport, rural communities and northern regions, green infrastructure, and affordable housing. Religious freedom and women's rights have been strengthened. No doubt there are reasons to be critical but generally we can say this is a political leadership steering clear of deliberately fomenting greater rigidity in and extremes of tribal divisions.

Finally, Spain gives us an example of a political party which has created structures, practices and processes to get issues experienced locally to become a national political agenda. They have connected local and national. I am talking about Podemos (26). Circles were formed in towns, cities and rural areas all over Spain creating a political agenda (amplified by social media) inside Podemos which was the basis for them to fight the national elections in November 2015. Podemos secured 66 elected MPs. It is not just that the local and the national became connected, the circles provided exactly the sort of direct, face to face environment in which people experience the demos and feel party to creating a reality.

Despite the somewhat old fashioned and bumbling appearance of the house of commons debating, a quick look at Parliament's website shows what an efficiency oriented, orange 'legislation factory' it has become (27). Merely adding on 'citizen's assemblies' or the use of technology to broaden participation or clustering referenda like Switzerland will not have the desired effect of creating psychological ownership of our national politics in the population (28). The orange consciousness will prevent this. Such developments would be seen as token affairs, bolted on to a thoroughly orange politics, to make it look like it is involving people, when it really is not.

How to summarise the core of the change needed across social, cultural, and eventually political realities in Britain? The seismic shift in thinking achieved by Einstein with the theory of relativity connected the micro (quantum matter, things like electrons etc) with the macro (space and time and the universe at large). $E=mc^2$ relates the micro and the macro. Einstein also created a dramatic shift in thinking away from a linear understanding of the natural world (that Newton had established). With Einstein *matter bends space and time*.

We need a similar dramatic shift in thinking about society, culture, politics, organisations, community and social realities. It is this direct connecting of the inner life of the individual and broader societal change that is at the heart of the new kind of social action we are now seeing in Britain. We similarly need to embed in politics this relating of the individual life (micro), with the social realities (macro). And we need to break out of linear, modernist thinking to something that better appreciates and supports a genuinely participatory culture.

A teal politics is not so much about better representation, or more deliberative processes. Neither is it just the agonistic politics of Chantal Mouffe. It is a coming together of a unifying consciousness capable of leading that reconfiguration of the state, markets and civil society into becoming a unifying framework. Specifically, it is about a reconfiguration that has civil society at the centre and being actively supported by both markets and the state. As the next chapter clearly shows, all other configurations have been tried and shown themselves unable to provide that unifying framework. Civil society Britain is the one remaining configuration. As I show in chapter 9 (and as has already been indicated) this is where a substantial element of the country is already headed. That is the macro vision in which, I am arguing, individuals' micro ecologies of support for realising potential will most flourish. No liberal democracy has yet done this. To transition to teal as the leading consciousness has no historical precedent. I believe we are in the midst of such a change. Ultimately it is this that accounts for the unprecedented turbulence in today`s politics. That is a Britain *really* leading the way in the world. I take up that teal vision in chapters 9.

7 - The historical dimension

*"Past, present and future are not three
different things. We should use the past
as a model for examining the present
and illuminating the future"*

Daisaku Ikeda and Sarah Wider (1)

H istory matters. The changing configurations of power between the state, markets and civil society, from the industrial revolution on, give us valuable insight into what configuration will make Britain`s realisation of potential really sing. We can also identify the types of consciousness powering each configuration more precisely. So, what was the configuration/type of consciousness in the industrial revolution?

Industrial revolution Britain

Here markets were at the centre: industry, commerce and trade all expanded dramatically. If we are looking for a key symbol of the age it might be the steam engine. Why? Because it broke being chained to the seasons and the natural order in order to ensure power. Manufacturing could now be 24 by 7. Age old limitations on production were swept away.

The rapidly expanding middle class created a consumer revolution which further drove the industrial revolution. So, for example, Wedgewood pottery was part of a shopping revolution. Oxford Street had 153 shops with a huge range of goods. Advertising, marketing and the creation and management of consumer demand began (2). The biggest empire the world had ever seen, was feeding industrial production at home and providing markets for Britain`s manufacturing. Machinery was exported to the colonies to boost productivity, under the protection of the navy. The explosion of wealth led to the establishment of London banks and the stock exchange. There was a dramatically improved lifestyle for middle and upper levels of society. GDP *doubled* in the 18th century.

We can symbolise the central place of rapidly expanding markets with this diagram:

Figure 2

Expanding markets and trade

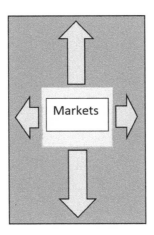

The small box represents markets at the start of the industrial revolution and the arrows and the larger box, the ever-expanding industry, commerce and trade.

The state was right there, alongside this expansion, making sure everything was done to support it. Here are some examples. Far better roads were needed and so parliament legislated to support trade through turnpike roads. 300 miles of useable road, 17 years later, had become 15,000 miles! Decreasing journey time meant more time for production. The canals halved the cost of transport: 1 canal barge versus 100 pack horses! Parliament wanted improved trade so companies were set up to dig canals, creating incredible engineering feats. The state spent on the navy to protect traders exporting machinery and goods to the colonies and returning with raw materials: Britannia became a naval superpower (3).

We can expand our schematic diagram:

Figure 3

Expanding markets/trade supported by the state

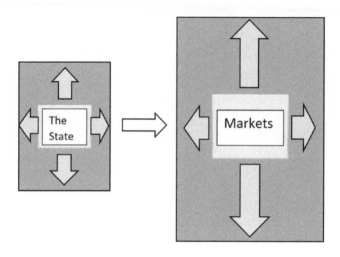

The scope, size, and spending by the state increased exactly at the time that markets expanded. Much of that expansion supported market expansion.

Civil society, at the very same time, dramatically expanded its repertoire. Britain was a very class divided society. On the working-class front, the first truly civic activist organisations emerged, trying to address poverty. The Friendly Societies were formed. By 1815 they had a membership of just under a million working people helping each other in times of need. By 1870 they had 4 million members. The co-operative movement was launched. You can palpably feel the working class organising so their ecology of support for realising their potential was in place.

The middle class produced renowned social activists. There was reform of child labour. Anti-slavery societies emerged. Public torture began to be abolished. An enormous number of 'good causes' were catered for: stray dogs, stray children, 'fallen women', drunken men and many others. Surveying London charities in 1861, a total of 640 were found. Their income exceeded what was spent through the Poor Law. Virtually every religious denomination had its own 'benevolent' society. There were housing charities, ragged schools, and housing settlements. Many charities we are familiar with, date from this period: RSPCA, YMCA, Dr Barnardos, The Salvation Army, and the RNLI. We can see how the Victorian era shaped Britain's civil society today.

At the top of the tree our civil society fostered free exchange of ideas. Civil society provided the open culture within which invention and free thinking happened. Without this, inventors and capitalists would not have found it so easy to join forces. Free thinking industrialists and scientists presented theories and experiments to eager audiences. An example was the `Lunar society` which was about thinking the unthinkable and producing astonishing ideas. Practical knowledge intermingled with `men of ideas`. Self-taught scientists came together with men with money from industry. Travelling lecturers fed the curiosity of the public. The British at that time were at the cutting edge of knowledge. All this `freedom of association` was happening within civil society. This was the `age of reason` in full flight. We are beginning to get a sense of the consciousness powering the industrial revolution.

We now have all three parts of the industrial revolution operating system (OS) in place schematically: markets dominated but were supported by the state and civil society. All three were `expanding` together at the same time.

Figure 4

The Industrial Revolution configuration

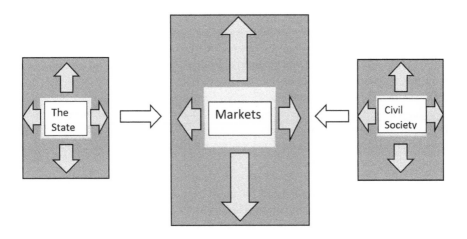

So, what was the consciousness powering all this? It was the consciousness of the age of reason.

In the face of medieval dogma, there was a questioning by a few brave individuals. They began investigating for themselves how nature worked. This began the movement we now call 'the enlightenment'. Across Europe, the enlightenment fostered the creative capacities of individuals. It fostered scientific reasoning and experimentation (and spawned multiple science related fields). There was also freedom of thought, one manifestation of which was philosophy. With philosophical thinking, nothing was exempt from critical scrutiny. By the time of the industrial revolution, the intellectual climate in Britain was of free exchange, not censored by church or state. Newton explained gravity. The Christian view had been challenged by evidence. Market dominance during the industrial revolution was made possible by a whole new way of managing factories (which became 'scientific management'). The belief was that wealth could grow infinitely. Human beings were acquisitive by nature and material advance equated to progress. Rationalism and reason were the watchwords. The metaphor of the age was the machine. If we think back to Wilber's colours (chapter 1): this is orange, very orange.

The transition to welfare state Britain

Although orange was very much the dominating consciousness, this is Britain we are talking about. It was not and still is not a mono culture. Freedom of thought and association brought a totally different consciousness to prominence: the romantic movement.

The romantic movement challenged the rationalistic spirit of the times. This is an insufficiently recognised humanising episode in our history. The romantic movement arose from sheer human distaste at such excessive emphasis on rationality and its consequences. Jeremy Rifkin comments,

"The Romantic movement was a reaction to the Enlightenment fixation on reason. It became a powerful counterforce that deeply affected every convention and social institution, from marriage relations and the rearing of children to ideas about justice and governance" (4)

The romantic movement challenged the spirit of the times. Romantics looked out on the world as a living organism and saw human beings as deeply affectionate and social. Progress, for romantics, was the power of imagination, self-fulfilment and a sense of community. In essence, the romantic movement promoted a belief that at the core of every being there is an authentic self that is pure in nature but corruptible by society. This consciousness powered the friendly societies, the co-operative movement, reform of child labour, anti-slavery societies and the abolition of public torture. With the romantic movement, we see a puncturing of the dominance of the Victorian status quo.

Nevertheless, Victorian belief in the power of reason and enterprise were strong. In upper and middle class circles it was believed that scientific, social and legislative improvements could raise the entire working class above the poverty line. While the political rhetoric of the 1800s was about free trade and a small state, actually the state took on more and more. Central government maintained 'paupers', limited the employment of women and children, regulated emigration, controlled pollution, financed schools, prisons, and police forces, and enforced nuisance removal, vaccination and the civil registry of births, marriages and deaths. Sixteen central administrative departments were created between 1825 and 1850 (5). The country was giving birth to the centralised administrative state we know today. Town councils were busy too with public wash houses, libraries and parks.

By the turn of the century the famous 1906 liberal government implemented welfare policies for the old, the young and working people. Pensions were introduced for the over 70s. For the young, there were free school meals. Legislation on children's welfare meant severe penalties for child neglect or cruelty. Juvenile courts were set up and young people now went to borstal rather than prison. Labour exchanges were established and the National Insurance Act was passed ensuring free medical treatment and sick pay for 26 weeks. 13 million workers came under this scheme. Asquith and Lloyd George saw the state, not as an obstacle to freedom, but as a way to expand it for more people through social insurance and pensions.

There were 29 labour MPs in the 1906 parliament. Having a small minority of MPs conferred considerable power on them because they represented a very substantial body in the population whose parliamentary representation would only grow. The industrial revolution is synonymous with class oppression. Intense class conflict was at the heart of the society. For example, in the late 1800s, in the industrial cities of Britain, between *a quarter and a third* of the population were living below the poverty line. Victorians were pragmatic. This was reflected in their initial attitude to class: the more the working class gained from capitalism, the less likely they would be to overthrow it. Derek Fraser puts it like this,

"There were still many who foresaw that society must be radically altered by social revolution of the masses, but others came to the view that the working class was safe and could be trusted with the vote. The millions of members of friendly societies, the hundreds of thousands of co-operators, Sunday school teachers, and trade unionists and thousands of investors in savings banks and building societies- these men could not be dangerous" (6)

Based on contributory principles, Lloyd George's 1909 'Peoples Budget' successfully redistributed income by taxing the wealthy to pay for measures for the poor. For the first time, government money was available to use in the interests of the poor. The budget became a tool of social policy.

The 1909 People's Budget sparked a battle royal within the elite. This was one of the key strands preceding the establishment of the welfare state. Opinions about how to use the funds generated by the People's Budget were voiced through a Royal Commission on the Poor Law of 1905-9. It split into two groups, a majority group and a minority group, who produced their own reports.

The majority report put blame on 'weak morals' as a cause of poverty. The minority report argued it was caused by the organisation of the economy. So, one group put the responsibility squarely on individuals, the other took a structural view.

The majority report wanted public assistance committees of local authorities to replace the Poor Law. The minority report wanted specialist education, health, and pension departments of central government. It also wanted a powerful new national ministry of labour with labour exchanges and retraining. During times of cyclical depression, the minority report argued for such a ministry to embark on great schemes of public works. The whole of the minority report anticipated much of the modern welfare state. Much of the vision contained in it materialised.

Civil society activists, Beatrice and Sydney Webb, were behind the minority report. It was they who introduced a young economist called William Beveridge to the Liberal government. Winston Churchill was, at that time, working alongside Lloyd George. Beveridge became his advisor.

It was Beveridge who was behind labour exchanges and the legislation for parting company with the Poor Law. It was breaking the entanglement with Victorian Britain that was going on for the liberal government at this time. Beveridge became the director of the new service: a state run nationally financed system of labour exchanges, to be used on a voluntary basis. This was quite an innovation in a free market economy. And, of course, it was Beveridge who eventually introduced the welfare state.

But things were about to take a downward spiral.

From 1920 to 1940 unemployment never went below 1 million. During the Great Depression it reached over 3 million. Contributory principles groaned under the weight of so many people in need and so began the 'dole'. Whilst government continued trying to make the insurance approach work, benefit payments became completely disconnected from insurance, instead being funded by the treasury.

Working class collective action during the 1920s and 1930s increased. The government response was to cut the dole and balance the books. Harsh means-testing led to 53% of claimants having their claims disallowed or reduced. This further entrenched class tension. By the end of 1931 some 400,000 people, previously entitled to benefit, either no longer were or got less. Vincent analyses the impact,

"The terms of exclusion of the poor from society were redefined to meet the conventions of the modern state. In place of disenfranchisement and the workhouse, there was the means test and the inspecting officer policing the

management of the family economy. In theory, the bureaucratisation of welfare promoted access and justice, in practice it engendered alienation and fear" (7)

If we wonder about the harsh sanctions of today's benefit system, it has precedents.

By 1939 pensions, health insurance, unemployment insurance, long term unemployment relief, housing subsidies and an embryonic hospital service were available to a large proportion of people. Spending by government on these had grown, from 2.4% of GDP in 1918, to nearly 12% by 1938.

The changeover to welfare state Britain

It was world war two, however, that created the real impetus to depart from Victorian Britain and establish a profound change in the operating system. Things were already moving in this direction as Fraser explains,

"British imperial pride had received a jolt when it proved so difficult to subjugate the Boers...and this was compounded by the revelation that so many volunteers had been rejected on health grounds......an atmosphere of international Darwinism plus an arms race in Europe gave a novel importance to social questions......the realisation by some businessmen that competition in the international market place could make welfare provision an asset" (8)

In this way, an informed public opinion was created which viewed welfare legislation as in the national interest. Business played a key role in supporting this change in Britain's operating system. Fraser again,

"These three factors-electoral advantage, new liberal ideology, and national efficiency- combined with humanitarian concern, bureaucratic initiative, social investigation and popular demand, produced a comprehensive programme" (9)

The middle classes in Britain also supported a movement towards less inequality. During the war, evacuation brought the state into social affairs, and the children of the urban poor were visibly experienced by rural families. These first-hand experiences of the condition of working class children became powerful engines for change. The working class had to be offered a new deal if the war was to be won.

This was the deal offered by Churchill: fight the second world war in return for a more enlightened and more open post-war society. The welfare of the whole society was part of the total war effort. The powers of the state went much further than in the first world war and paved the way for the state taking the leading role in welfare state Britain. The idea was popularised that the state could solve social problems.

The economist Keynes returned to Britain from America and was based in the Treasury (10). The austerity imposed by the economic conservatives during the great depression was completely eclipsed. Increased state stimulus and planning seemed to demonstrate the validity of Keynesianism (investment in state services as a stimulus to the economy). Perhaps what applied in war could be done in peace-time too.

All this, powerfully shifted markets out of central position to be replaced by the state, itself in turn influencing markets and civil society:

Figure 5

Welfare state configuration

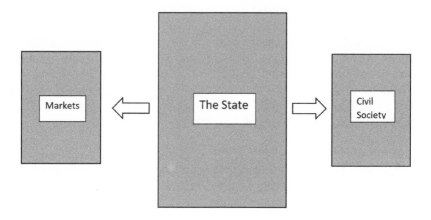

The hopes for the post war reconstruction were on a far grander scale than during the first world war. Rather than attempting to revert to the pre-war situation as soon as possible, the aim became an overwhelming desire to build a better future, using the possibilities Keynes presented of state investment.

Much larger numbers of children were eating at school and drinking milk by 1945, paid for by the state and affecting the children of the rich and poor alike. It became universal provision. Similarly, the National Assistance Board by 1948 had become a universal welfare agency.

But it was the 1942 Beveridge report which opened the way to the welfare state proper (11). It was an immediate best seller. It argued for revolutionary change, not just building on past experience, but improving on it (a very British revolution). It put the case for adopting family allowances, creating a comprehensive health service, and maintaining full employment. It promised universal social security without a means test. Systems were put in place to tackle the great `evils`.

What really captured popular imagination was that society could organise itself so that want, disease, ignorance, squalor and idleness could become things of the past. This really caught on. Whereas Britain had had the freedom to speak, write and vote, now it was getting freedom from these five 'giants' as Beveridge called them. The vision was enormous and compelling. The working class really felt their voice had been responded to.

And what of the consciousness powering all this?

The values powering this were about faith in administrative procedures to enable large scale organisation that was effective in eradicating the 5 giants. Right at the centre was a faith in bureaucracy, coming, in part, from industry practices crystallised by Frederic Taylor (12). Taylorism has 4 rules:

1. Replace rule-of-thumb work methods with methods based on a scientific study of the tasks;

2. Scientifically select, train, and develop each employee rather than passively leaving them to train themselves;

3. Provide detailed instruction and supervision of each worker in the performance of that worker's discrete task;

4. Divide work nearly equally between managers and workers, so that the managers apply scientific management principles to planning the work and the workers actually perform the tasks.

In these we see the beginning of `scientific management` principles (which underpinned the managerialising of public services in the 1990s).

As a backdrop, the success of the American approach to the depression had hinged around the ability to create state organisations capable of `making things happen` on a mass scale. So, it did not seem unreasonable that industrial scale bureaucratic organisations could be the glue to hold together the new universal or collective provisions of the welfare state. It made it conceivable that the 5 giants could be slain.

From Max Weber came the notion of rational-legal authority (in contrast to traditional and charismatic authority). Weber considered bureaucratic authority structures superior because in them the choice of who should be given authority was determined by rules and legally binding procedures. It was possible, in theory, to make large scale bureaucracies accountable to political direction and control (13).

Rational-legal authority enabled continuity after a leader stepped down. Society had an endless supply of people because it could, theoretically, choose successors on the basis of superior leadership/technical ability.

Henry Fayol specified administrative principles (14):

1. The span of control (the maximum number of employees that can be managed by one manager);
2. Exceptions to routines (workers do the routine, managers do the exceptions);
3. Unity of command (each worker reports to one boss);
4. Hierarchy (the organisation as a pyramid).

Luther Gulick worked for Roosevelt. He took Fayol's administrative principles further (15):

1. Organisations are more efficient if they divide work into small specialised segments;
2. Work is allotted to those with skills to do it in each segment;
3. Work should be co-ordinated through supervision;
4. Tasks should be clearly defined and instructions and direction clear.

He saw technical competence as crucial to efficient government. Gulick promoted the professionalising of business management and public administration. Along with universal services came universal rules and principles which could be applied to *any* organisation, be it a business, a hospital, government department, prison or a school (we also see this being claimed in the 90s in the managerialising of public services).

Underpinned by these ideas, the British government could develop state funded organisational structures covering the whole country. The 50s and 60s saw year in year out growth in spending on these services. It seemed that professionals could operate from and function fairly well within very stable bureaucracies operating public administration principles and employing considerable numbers of administrators. All this was profoundly different to Victorian Industrial revolution Britain. In this welfare state operating system, the state was entirely central, influencing markets and civil society. This remained the emphasis in Britain even into the 80s.

What kind of consciousness is this? It is distinctly amber. It appears Britain's driving consciousness took a giant backward step from the standpoint of those committed to orange. At the time it seemed a step forward in terms of stability, regulation, prosperity and full employment. Fundamentally it was Britain's response to class oppression.

The response: market-based Britain

In the 50s and 60s the welfare state got going. So too the green consciousness of 60s flower power era. And so too the elite thinkers who wanted to put markets back in central position. It is their efforts, rather than the results of 60s green consciousness that later shaped British politics. Green consciousness has remained more a cultural than political phenomenon.

During the whole post-war period, off at the very margins of society, a very different consciousness was developing, totally unlike and at odds with everything the post war period stood for. They had no time for the culturally based self-help and swinging sixties versions of personal freedom. They wanted markets to be the central force providing personal freedom. And, crucially, they got organised.

Between 1943 and 1980 a web of institutions and people grew up to spread and popularise market ideas so that they eventually seemed the natural alternative to the failing bureaucracy of the welfare state. It was these think tanks and their ideas that propelled Margaret Thatcher to power and started Britain down today's market-based road.

Daniel Stedman Jones work on this post-war movement comes up with a good definition. He sees it as a movement focused on developing a,

"free-market ideology based on individual liberty and limited government that connected human freedom to the actions of rational, self-interested actors in the competitive market place" (16).

This movement was a reaction to a large interventionist state, which involved regulation of markets and industry, high taxes for the rich, and an extensive welfare programme for all.

This group saw the interventionist state as 'creeping totalitarianism'. Here was a body of thinkers and activists who did not believe in bureaucracy at all. For them large scale liberal democracies *had* to use markets, right across the society as the most efficient means of distributing resources.

A leading proponent was Friedrich Hayek with his 1944 publication *The Road to Serfdom* (17). For Hayek the price mechanism was supreme. The undistorted price mechanism served to share and synchronise local and personal knowledge so individual members of society achieved diverse ends without state interference. Hayek defined freedom as a condition of men in which "*coercion of some by others is reduced as much as possible*" (18).

For Hayek, this kind of economic freedom was also the basis for a fuller political freedom. It was a profound political and moral force shaping *all* aspects of a free, open society. Hayek vigorously opposed any attempt to put planning at the centre of government. Since human capacities in no way could match the price mechanism, planning would always produce interference and inferior results.

Hayek also clearly articulated a view that people are fundamentally unequal and society *should* have substantive inequality. Any notion of redistribution is contested and seen as engendering dependency. It is the individual, in the market, that is sacrosanct.

A body of people formed around Hayek who shared his values and thinking. In 1947 the Mont Pelerin Society was formed. In 1949 Hayek wrote a paper which argued that individual liberty within free markets could only be protected by an elite-driven and an elite-directed strategy of opinion formation. The key in all this was to change the minds of the 'second hand dealers in ideas', the intellectuals,

"The strategy was clear : ... target the wider intelligentsia, journalists, experts, politicians, and policymakers. This was done through a transatlantic network of sympathetic business funders and ideological entrepreneurs who ran think tanks, and through the popularisation of (market) ideas by journalists and politicians" (19)

Hayek took the view that,

"It is no exaggeration to say that, once the more active part of the intellectuals has been converted to a set of beliefs, the process by which these become generally accepted is almost automatic and irresistible" (20)

The Mont Pelerin post-war network opened up new bridges between the academy and politics and a new form of political organisation was born: the think tank. Significantly, two of them, the IEA (Institute for Economic Affairs) and the AEI (American Enterprise Institute) argued that social and economic inequality are necessary for social and economic progress.

Transition to market-based Britain

World war two and the formation of the welfare state had acted as a kind of sleeping pill to the slumbering beast of class oppression. The pill had lasted into the 50s and 60s. By the 70s however, the welfare state could no longer be funded with year on year increases in government spending. The economic realities of the loss of empire had hit home. Industry declined while union power increased. All this re-awakened the slumbering beast of class conflict. In the 70s the post war `settlement` with the working class broke down. The 70s was the decade of a colossal upsurge in class politics. And with it came the buzzword of the decade: militancy. This is Daniel Stedman Jones take on the 70s,

"(The 70s) were a rare moment when the pieces of the political and economic jigsaw were strewn all over the place, in need of painstaking re-arrangement" (21)

The `painstaking re-arrangement` was actually a major shift of power back to the dominance of markets, that the welfare state had interrupted. It began at the end of the decade when Margaret Thatcher was elected prime minister.

The road to that point was heavy going. Industry was full of politicised unions. Socialist thinking was everywhere. There was an escalating trade union power struggle with the government, centred around the miners, and continual strikes. There was unemployment. Companies were closing. The economy was in tatters. Governments changed like traffic lights. All this was the backdrop to my work on the Estate (chapter 4).

The two political ideologies, the blue and the red, were fighting over the soul of Britain. The blue corner were saying, `We have a new approach`. Keynesian economics was patently failing. And waiting in the wings with a totally different economic policy was Milton Friedman. He argued that Keynes had forgotten about controlling the supply of money going into the economy. The best way to bring down inflation, according to Friedman, was by controlling the supply of money: monetarism and economic policies on the supply side of the economy began to be implemented. The lengthy preparations by the Mont Pelerin free marketeers were now paying off. Their policies were entering the mainstream of British politics, starting with economic policy.

Friedman provided the most significant, consistent and systematic alternative to Keynes. His technical analysis of the failures of demand management convinced policy makers in 1970s: the error in Keynes was underestimation of the importance of a stable supply of money. Governments should make monetarism a guarantor of stable markets, rather than using fiscal measures to try to get full employment.

The 70s was characterised by class politics nationally *and* locally. The 80s were schizophrenic: market-oriented politics nationally, and anti-racism locally. The nation went market. The government used the force of law to re-orientate society. But, just as, in the 70s, class erupted from within the bedrock of British society, in the 80s it was the turn of race and racism.

Nationally all forms of social solidarity considered to be in the way of markets, were dismantled. What market policies required was a flexible labour market. Nationalised industries were privatised. There was considerable de-regulation. National wage bargaining was broken up and dispersed around individual employers and local parts of the country. This decade saw further decline in the country's manufacturing base and greater priority being given to 'the city'.

The Thatcher government targeted the unions. At a national level some of the early 80s felt like an intensification of the class conflicts of the 70s. By 1982,

3 million were unemployed. For the whole of 1984, the government and the miners, were locked in a do-or-die struggle. Nevertheless, in 1987 Margaret Thatcher got a third term of office with a majority of 101. *This* was the `elite` agenda at work, at national level. The efforts of Hayek, the Mont Pelerin Society and the think tanks were spreading a new, broad policy package going much further than economic policy.

While all this was going on, black people took to the streets. In 1979 Blair Peach, a teacher, was knocked unconscious during a demo against a national front election meeting in Southall and later died. In 1980 St Paul's in Bristol saw racial violence. This was quickly followed in 1981 with uprisings in London (Brixton), Birmingham (Handsworth), Leeds (Chapeltown), and Liverpool (Toxteth). In April 1981 police lost control of the streets of Brixton. The Brixton uprising became the subject of the famous Scarman report which denied institutional racism in the police force, arguing instead that racism was down to a few `bad apples` (22). 70 black people were caught up in the New Cross fire of January 1981. 56 survived and 14 died. The cause was never made clear.

All this was the backdrop to my work during the 80s with the anti-racist network. The uprisings gave the first ever black officers in local public services real power. Anti-racist training, engaging white staff as well as black, within local public services right across the country started a process which lasted throughout the 80s. It was only to be eclipsed by market policies pouring into local public services throughout the nineties,

"The government goes in for private ownership, because assets in private hands are cared for and used efficiently, while assets in public hands too often have been allowed to decay and stagnate and become a burden on the community... ... .We need (elected) members and officials who are not wedded to the power base of a large department; who do not believe that success is measured by the number of staff they employ and the amount of money they spend... ... ...Their task is first and foremost to serve the public, the consumer" (23)

This was the brave new world that began to be implemented locally during the 90s. Performance indicators, quality initiatives, purchaser-provider and much more were transferred from the private sector across all the main social policy areas in benefits, health, care, education, housing and criminal justice.

Schools could opt out of local authority control. Housing revenue accounts were ring fenced so that they could not subsidise spending on other things. There was a far-reaching NHS white paper. There was Compulsory Competitive Tendering (CCT) for refuse collection, cleaning buildings, catering, maintenance and repairs. There was `next steps`, the civil service managerialisation programme. Councils were to regulate and monitor a multitude of services provided by contractors.

You would have expected, the political figure at the centre of all this, Margaret Thatcher, to preside over the implementation of all this throughout the 90s. But in a telling episode of political `blindness` she was forced to resign. The poll tax was a deeply unpopular measure. It became an open invitation to civil disobedience. By 1990 there were *18 million* non-payers. Unrest grew and resulted in a number of Poll Tax Riots. It is very significant that Thatcher believed in the market thinking *more* than the realities on the ground or on any political advice from those around her. To those wedded to an ideology, with so much at stake, it is an early example of `nothing counts as evidence` or, as it later became, `there is no alternative` (TINA). It was a supreme irony for her to be defeated by a cornerstone of market thinking: the poll tax.

After this dramatic start to the national politics of the decade, John Major was elected with a narrow majority in 1992. In 1997 New Labour, under Tony Blair, got a majority of 179, such was the unpopularity then of the `blue corner`. However, for local public services it was as if very little had changed: New Labour stood for managerialism and market policies (although with a bit more of a human face).

As the 90s wore on the market-based policies did not just focus on housing, education, or social care, but focused on *the very system itself* that was providing services locally: this made it an operating system change for public services (but one with a continued bureaucracy inherent in it). What nobody banked on was just how tenaciously the old order (based on decades of bureaucratic thinking and practice) just kept on going underneath the market and managerial reforms. All over the country, at the local level, new senior staff came forward, enthusiastic to take up these new initiatives. To give a sense of the scale of this, there were 10,000 senior general managers in the NHS in 1986. By 1995 there were 26,000 (24). Like it or not a market-based version of the welfare state was being born *and* the country`s operating system was being changed into the current configuration of the state, markets and civil society. We have already had a look at this in chapter 2. Here is reminder,

Figure 6

Today's market-centred configuration

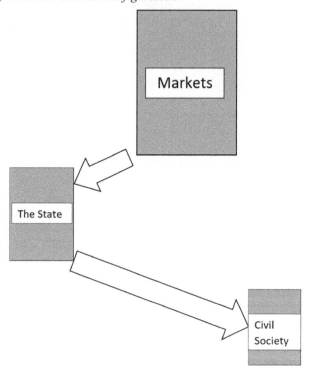

In this diagram of today`s operating system, markets/ businesses are centre stage. But the state is off to the side, but subjecting *itself* to market-oriented policies. The state influences civil society, which is in the most subordinate position within the country. Chapter 2 has already presented the consciousness powering the country in this configuration.

During the 2000s the impact of market thinking, implemented throughout the public services, turned market thinking from being a broad policy package to being part of the very culture of the country: becoming the air we breathe. In the next chapter we will see just how powerful a force, for creating change in the culture, our public services are. In this sense, the apostles of market thinking have shown us something very valuable for shifting the operating system of Britain today to its next configuration

What has all this got to do with Britain fulfilling more of its potential? Firstly, the consciousnesses powering these configurations was either amber or orange. These bring with them limitations on the potential that can be realised. Let us be clear, while the consciousnesses that Ken Wilber has colour coded are moving in an upward, progressive direction, that doesn't mean that nation states and their politicians are necessarily reflecting that progressive trend.

Secondly, the changing configurations of power between the state, markets and civil society, from the industrial revolution, to the welfare state, to market-based Britain, shows us that in none of these configurations has there been any real attention paid to the ecology of support for realising potential. The two market-centred OS of the industrial revolution and its attempted re-run with today's OS, actually erode that ecology in the mass of the population. You would have thought the welfare state OS would have offered greater support. Unfortunately, that massive flow of resources went into professionals and administrators and didn't really get through to the mass of ordinary people.

The argument here is that how markets, the state, and civil society are relating, that *these* relationships are crucial for whether or not the right synergies are there for individuals realising potential. So where will Britain go next? The next most logical configuration would appear to be a civil society centred Britain where the state and markets support civil society. We will probe into this in chapter 9.

8 - The decisive role of the public services

*"Something that should serve us
somehow comes alive, gains its own logic
and starts to work against us"*

Thomas Sedlacek (1)

Gains its own logic and starts to work against us", reminded me of a French TV detective series, screened on UK TV called `Engrenage` (Spiral). I take engrenage to mean being caught up in a system which locks everyone into a fixed way of responding. Just like those cringe-making moments, occurring far too frequently, when something awful has happened at the hands of a public service and the hapless spokesperson is hauled in front of the TV cameras. All they say is, "lessons will be learnt". I want to throw something at the TV, because I know they won't. The decisive role of our public services is to break this vicious stuckness. This chapter explains why orange public services create `engrenage`. We will start by understanding how local public services were managerialised in the 90s. Secondly, I will be going through the services in the 5 main social policy areas contrasting orange with teal (yes there is some). I want to end with a teal model of public service together with examples of how *any* public service can start that transition now.

How local public services were managerialised in the 90s

I directly experienced, as an insider, the transformation of public services in the 90s. The intention was for public services to become market-based. However, no one tried to get rid of the underlying bureaucracy. Bureaucracy is built to continue, no matter what the circumstances. As a result, UK public services have now become *both* bureaucracies and organisations based on market thinking: in other words, hybrids.

The public service organisation I worked in in the 90s thoroughly grabbed hold of all the government's market-oriented initiatives (below). That organisation only lasted 10 years before a new generation of leaders had to come in and completely re-work it. That public service, newly born from the plethora of market initiatives, could not handle the complexity that had built up placing unforeseen demands on it. By the 10th year, they had reached such a point that the whole 'new public management' edifice was torn down and something with far more solid foundations, in what would really work, began to be constructed.

Working in social care, at the time, it was bizarre to be grappling with initiatives straight out of a previous era in manufacturing. The 'new' repertoire we were being required to make integral to what we did encompassed service level agreements (SLAs), contracting, quality, performance, audit and IT. These were the market thinking fundamentals for the orange version of a public service.

If a service could not easily be contracted out, the new approach was to specify the service, set up the contracting process, with tender documents, follow a tendering process, take the options to a committee, and then set up the service monitoring process with the successful provider. This was time-consuming, generated a lot of paperwork, and severed the two-way flows of talk between staff that had hitherto ensured human intelligence. The contracting process of itself did not ensure better services. Only leadership can really do that.

'Quality' was an early part of the 90s 'new public management' revolution. Two private sector approaches to quality were shoved into the public services: BS5750 (basically kite mark your service), and total quality management or TQM. Even though BS5750 was designed primarily for very tangible kinds of services, it was amazing how many services, like social care, tried to use it. TQM turns a standard organisation on its head and puts the 'customer' at the top: management is there to serve customers. This ignores the reality that the hybrid public sector organisation is still a top down bureaucracy.

In July 1991 John Major introduced his Citizen's Charter: a method of requiring all public services to produce information for 'citizens' (2). By 1992 the Audit Commission had a duty to set out what data best indicated the performance of a local authority. This created a culture of 'performance indicators' (PIs) and targets, which other kinds of public service quickly incorporated. PIs became the new thing. With them you could (theoretically) compare different services, unit costs, and output measures, and draw conclusions (managerially) as to which was more efficient.

Specifications, standards, contracts, quality, all lent themselves to being measured (turned into targets and PIs). They were all also things to be inspected/audited. And this is where a real change of culture was being experienced: *the audit didn't really need to find out the substantive reality of the service and how effective it was*. Rather it was necessary to audit whether the PIs were being met, whether the quality was as specified, whether the contract was being adhered to. None of this tells anybody whether the service is working well for its users. I think this quote says it all,

"What's really distressing...is that though my sister is surrounded by people spouting the 'rhetoric of care', no one seems to give a damn about her personally " (3)

Audit was a very powerful way for market thinking to take hold. The very process of audit further entrenched this sense of the managerial processes mattering more than the substance of the service. Michael Power with his `The Audit Society: Rituals of Verification` really illuminated this,

"The audit society is a society that endangers itself because it invests too heavily in shallow rituals of verification at the expense of other forms of organisational intelligence. In providing a lens for regulatory thought and action, audit threatens to become a form of learned ignorance" (4)

Power was arguing that excessive reliance on audit and inspection actually *transforms* what is audited and inspected,

"Audit is never purely neutral in its operations; it will operationalise accountability relations in distinctive ways, not all of which may be desired or intended. New motivational structures emerge as auditees develop strategies to cope with being audited" (5)

And something else further entrenched this kind of culture: IT. What did new public managers value most? It was information. They did *not* value human intelligence, conversations and relationships. We can appreciate what a shock this was for services in which relationships are fundamental.

We are beginning to see where engrenage comes from.

The benefit system

In November 2015, the chancellor announced that £217 billion was allocated to the benefit system. So, what do we get for our money? Is it still the historical legacy of class warfare and the oppression of the poor, that we saw in the last chapter? Over the long term this system has definitely staved off poverty and hardship in very many lives (6).

However, all is not well.

The current system is punitive. It is based on the assumption that reducing benefits is an incentive for claimants to seek work (`reverse incentivising`). `Sanctions`, which are serious reductions of benefits for a fixed period, are done on the basis that they are necessary to bring about a positive change in someone's behaviour.

The University of York led a research study involving researchers from six universities. They interviewed 480 users of benefits between 2014-15. They found a third had experienced sanctions, but found hardly any evidence of any positive change in behaviour. In fact, the opposite was the case: sanctions had severely detrimental effects on health, emotions, finances, debt, rent arrears and fostered increased reliance on foodbanks. What the research did point to was that *support, rather than sanctions, was more effective* (7). In 2014 20% of people on job seeker`s allowance were `sanctioned`, often for trivial reasons like missing a bus or a family crisis (8).

Work capability reassessments create a wasteful and expensive cycle of:

- a claimant losing benefit or having it reduced;
- having to appeal;
- the tribunal re-instating benefit;
- the claimant being paid backdated benefit.

All of this is unbelievably stressful.

Form ESA50 has 6 pages of questions about physical capability and 4 pages of questions about mental, cognitive, and intellectual capabilities. Underlying this is a managerial pre-occupation with measurement.

On the physical side, the form is demanding to know, answers to such questions as can I...

Pick up a pound coin?
Communicate a simple message to other people?
See to cross the road on your own?

On the mental side, can I....

Use a washing machine?
Meet people without feeling anxious or scared?
Get food and drink to my mouth without being helped? (9)

The answers to these and similar questions will be scored. Above a certain score you will stay on benefit, under that score you will lose benefit and it will be assumed you can work. Your only recourse is to appeal. This standardised or `one size fits all` approach misses the true impact of the disability on the person. You can`t *measure*, in a standardised way, whether a person with disabilities can work or not, especially using these questions.

If a person has, for example, a long-term condition like Chronic Fatigue Syndrome they might answer that they can do everything on the form, but can`t work because they have very limited energy. For every effort expended, there is a cost. Every single day is a calculation about what you will be able to do and the costs of making those exertions. The form simply does not capture this evident reality.

The current benefit system is continuing the legacy of oppression going back to the Victorians. It is a major way that potential in Britain is being squashed: a clear example of the British state oppressing its own population.

This is not the end of the story.

Market thinking is supposed to boost efficiency. Yet the benefits system is unbelievably inefficient. On 23rd December 2015, the DWP announced underpayments and delays in payments amounted to £1.5 billion! No sanctions were imposed on the DWP for this. Delays in paying claimants, force people to use food banks. In 2016 more than 154,000 people waited for more than 10 days for their initial job seekers allowance claim to be processed, 44,000 of whom waited at least 17 days. When you have no money, every day is torture (10).

In 2016, Concentrix, the contracted `provider` charged with policing benefit fraud, had its contract removed because of the sheer weight of complaints. The complaints included one from a single parent accused of cohabiting but whose partner had died! The Concentrix contract was worth between £55 and £75 million over three years (11).

What can we say about the teal in this extraordinarily orange context? We have to go abroad for any actualities. The leadership of the Belgian federal government's social security department has gone teal. Paul Verhaeghe says of this department,

"For over ten years now, Frank Van Massenhove has headed the Belgian federal government's social security department, using an entirely novel approach: `Our staff control their own lives. People work wherever, whenever, and however they want...But because they have so much freedom, we do need to know exactly what we can expect of everybody. This is the crux of the new approach to work`. The results are stunning. The social security department is Belgium's best functioning public service....his department is seen by federal officials as the best workplace in the country" (12)

But what kind of system might teal leadership create? We have had a glimpse of it in the work by Participle with Angela and other `troubled families` (chapter 3). An *actual* benefit system would adapt itself to the needs of individual claimants and *support them* to move forward in their lives. It is, after all, your life, not the life of the benefit system that is at issue.

It is highly significant that it was a civil society organisation, Participle that imaginatively, and effectively, organised around how the person concerned had defined a path forward. Being a civil society organisation, it could engage fully with claimants using the benefit system. It enabled people, over its ten years, to stand on their own two feet, many of whom came off benefits. This kind of active, intelligent support through a human network, *as well as* support through money, seems to me to have more chance of enabling people to move on and would constitute a genuine benefit system.

What are the `metrics` of a benefit system worthy of a 21st century Britain? Firstly, it does not oppress its own citizens, but is a liberating experience. You become free to live your own life again, bearing in mind for some people they are never going to go back to where they were before. It certainly does not mean everybody on benefits getting back to work. The ability to put money, agreed by `the benefits system`, into stuck situations imaginatively (without audit sections screaming!) would mean people, until now seen as `claimants`, creating new social enterprises, new self-employment opportunities, gaining new educational qualifications taking less medication and needing fewer or no visits to GPs. For people for whom work just is not viable, extending the circle of friends, having a social life, being able to contribute to others and not just passively receive, are hallmarks of a life with dignity. For some, whether they work or not, personal care is extremely important.

Discussions about state benefits invariably bring up the topic of universal basic income (UBI). It means *all* citizens of a country regularly receive an unconditional sum of money. For some this takes away the pressure to have to work. A number of pilots were under way at the time of writing. UBI has its supporters *across* the political spectrum. Would *just* having a guaranteed income provide enough money for many current users of the benefits system, especially people with disabilities? In the UK is it more important to change the benefit system's long history of oppression? Meanwhile we await the results of the numerous UBI pilots.

Health and social care

In 2015–16, the UK public sector spent £140.6 billion on health and £29.9 billion on social care (13). 18% of that combined spend going on social care is not a lot. It is even less when you focus just on *adult* social care. In 2015-16 this was just 16.8 billion or 10% (14).

In terms of how these two services are organised, when the welfare state was set up, the NHS became a central government service. As social care evolved, social services became part of local government. The NHS is a national government organisation, funded centrally, and its ethos, as is well known, has been to provide health care for all, free at the point of delivery. Social care comes through departments of the local council, funded through the local authority and offering means tested services. Care and health staff are on completely different contracts, with different line managers, and in organisations with radically different cultures, priorities and working practices. And yet an ordinary person needing care, in many cases, will need to draw on both services. A&E ambulance queues in winter and elderly people on trolleys in corridors, are the conspicuous tip of a huge iceberg that has been going on for decades.

`The market` has done nothing to improve this situation. The bureaucratic heritage is still there in both cases. The NHS especially has a directness of control by ministers and the civil service. Market values are what now dominate the service. But money alone is not really the whole story. It is the culture of market thinking that alienates and oppresses capable staff. Ex- consultant neurologist, Henry Marsh, gives us a sense of working in this market thinking,

"....working as a doctor felt increasingly like being an unimportant employee in a huge corporation....I felt less and less trusted. I had to spend more and more time at meetings stipulated by the latest government edicts that I felt were often

of little benefit to patients. We spent more time talking about the work rather than actually working... "(15)

Such people need to be trusted and given the autonomy to get on and fully bring themselves to the tasks in hand. A practising nurse Jean Mathews had this to say,

"The secondary care organisation is slowly being engulfed...conformity through control based discourses... perpetuating organisational hierarchy and eradicating autonomy, ownership and intellect from the front line...drastically threatening an environment of trust, motivation and collaboration"(16)

There are perverse impacts when you bring profit into a public service like the NHS, Marsh again,

"(Manager)`I`m afraid that this last year we made one million pounds profit for the Trust whereas the year before we made four million, even though we did not do any more work`.
(Surgeon)`But where on earth did the three million go?`
(Manager)`We spent a lot on agency nurses. And you`re spending a lot more on putting metalwork into peoples spines and you`re doing too many emergencies - we only get thirty per cent payment if you exceed the target for emergency work`
(Surgeon)`What would the public say if they knew we got penalized for saving too many lives?`"(17)

There is a GP and nursing recruitment crisis (18). In 2017 the Care Quality Commission found that 68% of hospitals needed to improve. We are seeing the highest rates of cancellation of urgent operations. In social care the media tell us, almost daily, of the closing of care homes. A third of nursing homes provide poor care (19).

Home care has been particularly badly hit by `the market`. Workers, normally on zero hours' contracts, often earn the minimum wage or less (after they pay their own travel costs). Never knowing who will come through the door is the most frequent complaint. Visits are too short, and because the home carer has too many visits to do, service users often don`t know when the carer will turn up (which can cause stress and anxiety). Working within this regime, home carers all too often become uninterested in the person. Some appalling practices take place. Home carers can be sacked if they turn whistle-blower. Equally, users of home care fear they will lose the service if they complain. This is industrialised `care`. It is in this context that many home carers have to deal with very challenging behaviour: such as people with dementia. Markets are supposed to drive up standards, but in the home-care market the opposite is happening. But let us remember this kind of dehumanised system was the springboard for Buurtzorg (chapter 5).

For another layer of insight into how hybrid public services end up in a state of `engrenage`, I think it is Paula Hyde who has most accurately pinpointed the abuse engendered by rational managerial regimes inside care organisations. How can this be, we might ask, on hearing the words `rational` and `managerial`? She has articulated subtleties of this hybrid public sector world with its indirect forms of control (all quotes note 20),

"...staff who start working with good intentions, in organisations established for positive ends, find themselves causing physical and emotional harm to those they are entrusted to care for".

The consequences of the belief that managers can control care-giving are portrayed,

"Each poor report and review led to attempts to increase managerial control over workers activities..these task oriented processes emphasised physical care whilst devaluing the conversation and social contact that may have emphasised the humanity of the patient. More experienced staff were occupied with managerial tasks, requiring the most qualified and experienced staff to become office bound, leaving the care of patients to untrained, unsupervised, poorly paid, bullied and humiliated staff. In these circumstances, bullying and mistreatment of patients mirrored the bullying and neglect experienced by staff ".

The rational managerial belief here is that,

"abuse will not occur if the system is well designed, monitored and managed...in return staff are protected from any criticism.........were procedures and practices followed properly (hospitals-or any public service) would be able to prevent death and suffering.....These encourage staff to suspend thinking and follow procedure...this has dehumanising effects on patients and opens the door to systematic abuse of individuals in the proper conduct of business"

Thus, rational managerial systems aimed at preventing abuse are *self-defeating*.

A friend of mine, who manages a prison, told me of the time he put a prisoner `in segregation` because of the fear the person would kill himself. However, my friend went further and spent time talking with the prisoner. Other staff were also asked to check on the prisoner more frequently than procedure would otherwise have them do. But despite all this, tragically, the prisoner ended his life. Within a week the police were intending to charge my friend with corporate manslaughter. His departure from set procedure had actually triggered their intervention. He robustly defended his conduct and the police relented.

Is there anything going in the direction of teal? In the UK I don't think we yet have *a* Buurtzorg, but there are the beginnings of moves in that direction (21).

What is most definitely happening are three ways that teal is developing in health and social care: 1 new types of organisation; 2 networks of practitioners contesting within their places of work; 3 practitioners going independent.

The option to create a form of social enterprise called a Community Interest Company (CIC) offers a viable mechanism for integrating health and social care. With this it is possible to develop a third entity, with social objectives, different from both the NHS and the local authority and bring all the staff of the NHS and the local authority that need to be integrated, into that one body. A CIC seems a perfect option given its identity as a social enterprise, meaning it can work well with other social enterprises and communities.

Mount Gould is an example,

"Mount Gould is not, strictly speaking, an NHS hospital – nor a private one. It is run by Plymouth community healthcare, which believes it is the UK's largest social enterprise providing NHS services. As a community interest company (CIC), it has no shareholders and pays no dividends. It has recently taken over Plymouth's social care under a £71m deal, making it a pioneer in health and social care integration." (22)

Mount Gould is already:

- o offering alternatives to hospital;
- o working with job centres;
- o providing paid placements and volunteering (on the basis that people who work are healthier);
- o working with employers to make workplaces healthier;
- o buying in supplies from local providers (especially other social enterprises).

Let us hope that being under one roof they can remove historical boundaries, not fit people into boxes, and find more creative solutions that work better for people they are working with? Just because it is a CIC does not, of itself, mean there will develop a teal culture with all the structures, practices and processes necessary to make it work.

Bournemouth University lies at the centre of substantial networks of health and social care practitioners who are literally humanising services they work in. The inspiration for this comes from Caring and Well-being by Kathleen Galvin and Les Todres and especially their 8 point framework for humanising,

Forms of humanisation	Form of dehumanisation
Insiderness	Objectification
Agency	Passivity
Uniqueness	Homogenisation
Togetherness	Isolation
Sense-making	Loss of meaning
Sense of place	Dislocation
Embodiment	Reductionist body (23).

The left-hand side is their version of teal care: humanising. In June 2017, they ran the third conference on this theme of humanising services from within. We heard of NHS rehabilitation from stroke having fast `throughput`.

"45 minutes of each relevant therapy should be provided to patients deemed appropriate. Therapy time is now being measured and reported on in a national audit, with hospitals receiving scores for their delivery............Patients were rarely offered choices, or involved in decisions about their care. In interviews patients expressed the importance of their individual histories and experiences being listened to, but they were rarely given the opportunity to tell their stories" *(24)*

An entire multi-disciplinary team, operating in this managerialised context, was learning to `make pauses` to connect with patients or team members. In this way, they developed the relationships around the patient, working to widen them out. This energised practitioners, because it was why they came into the service. They were learning to see the same realities in a different way, which didn't take any more time, and to be a person not a role. Practitioners were carrying out what limited autonomy they could within a coercive system, and finding they could harness enough to humanise their work.

Similar stories were narrated by practitioners in this valuable network, with the local university acting as a hub (25). It is a model that can be taken up more widely. The LIFE programme at the University of the West of Scotland is another example (26)

The third route for teal is independent practice. Independent midwives are an example. (27). Acquired Brian Injury (ABI) provides another (28). There are other independent groupings, like doctors, occupational therapists, nurses, physio-therapists etc. Paul Verhaeghe gives us an example of a wake-up call for any specialist psychiatric services in the NHS working with young people. Therapists for Young People (TEJO), is a voluntary organisation in Antwerp set up in 2009. The people who set it up were the very professionals frustrated with their day jobs which were full of gap analyses, benchmarks, and key performance indicators,

"It's ironic that ....(their day job), full of highly qualified psychiatric professionals, is organised in a way that conflicts with every single finding of psychological studies of innovation" .(29)

TEJO offers free anonymous frontline services. They assume the youngsters they are working with know what they want to achieve. There is no registration, minimal admin, and almost no management. The overriding aim is that the therapists can do their work. It is staffed entirely by volunteers providing their services for free,

"Three years on, there are over 60 of them, and their ranks are swelling. ....their working method ties in perfectly with everything that promotes motivation: having autonomy, a say over one's work, self-management social control by fellow professionals, and a common objective..........many of its staff have regular jobs in the over-managed mental health system, but have lost motivation in their work. TEJO is the place where they recharge their batteries" (30)

None of the work in health and social care is easy. We are confronted by the fundamental vulnerability of the human being and our institutions and staff face severe challenges to actually respond to the extent and nature of those vulnerabilities. How Merseycare respond to suicide is incredible (31).

They have rejected any idea that suicide can be at a level in the background of the work they do. They have adopted the experience from Detroit: zero suicide. They learnt from Detroit that in 4 years they stopped 75% of suicides. The possibility of stopping *all* suicides became real.

The biggest killer of men under 45 in Britain is suicide. 75% of deaths by suicide are by men. In 2015 Merseycare adopted an approach of not seeing suicide as inevitable. The key tool they developed was training which can rapidly shift large numbers of peoples' attitudes. At the start of this training they find 70-80% think suicide is a selfish act and inevitable. 45 minutes later, this drops to 10%. Not only have they turned their 5,000 staff on to the zero message (mandatory training across the trust), they have taken it out into local banks, construction companies, councils, and taxi firms. They are shifting whole organisations internal conversations. They are a state organisation directly empowering people and families in their local civil society. People with suicidal thoughts are not being closed down. How did they develop this training? Only with the input of people who had tried to take their lives or had close relations who had. This is yet another example of people who use services coming inside and taking on roles inside the public service.

Housing

Housing is an absolute necessity. The housing crisis is right up there in holding back this country fulfilling its potential. For a longstanding liberal democracy to have a housing shortage, on the scale of ours, is incredible. Housing is central to the health of society. It achieves stability and creates jobs.

In 1980 40% of the population lived in council houses. In 2012 this had reduced to 11%. That's a massive marketisation of housing in Britain. So, council housing is not able to provide much of a response to the considerable housing crisis. Government policy has been for private companies to build houses to be purchased on the market. In 2015/16 there were around 150,000 'new builds' when it is reckoned between 225,000 and 275,000 *a year* are needed. In the *real* market in properties, the ratio of income to house prices has moved against buyers. In England and Wales, the average house price passed £300,000 in March 2016. Newly built homes were unaffordable for 4 out of 5 of families in work and privately renting. So how were they going to be bought? The £8.3 billion Help to Buy scheme, designed to help cash strapped buyers, is now helping people with much higher incomes. Many young people are turning to the bank of mum and dad, with £6 billion a year of support for 315,000 house purchases (32).

34% of the population are either in precarious work or the service sector (33). In the absence of capital and reliable income, renting is their only option. Rents are often unaffordable and the availability of social housing has reduced considerably. In contrast, by August 2016 private landlords were getting £9 billion through housing benefit: double the amount 10 years before (34). And this is with a considerable proportion of people, seeking tenancies, being refused by landlords, simply because they are on housing benefit!

We can begin to see why based on orange thinking there is the extent of homelessness we saw in chapter 2. So where are the teal options?

Late in 2016 an ex-homeless man on the Isle of Wight bought of bus with £7,000 of his own money (35). He fundraised £35k to convert it to have 18 beds, a kitchen and a seating area. The agencies on the island rallied around and work with the homeless people during the day to keep the people using the bus moving on and freeing up the beds. At 5.30 pm everybody sleeping on the bus that night gets a hot meal which is cooked in the bus by volunteers. The bus has a post office address meaning people on the bus can give this to a GP and get medical attention. It also means they can claim benefit. The bus goes round the island during the day finding homeless people. Having volunteers as staff means homeless people feel they can talk with them. It has a community feel. It is yet another classic case of civil society activists and organisations, as well as people inside local state institutions, working together.

Citizens UK has been pro-active and formed the capital's first community land trust. Through this new housing became available,

"Citizens UK's campaign for a radical form of genuinely and permanently affordable homes started over a decade ago. Now, after years of hard work and campaigning from Londoners, people can apply for London's first community land trust homes. Building at St Clements is nearing completion and you are now invited to apply for one of the 23 homes (36)".

Walter Segal was an architect who developed a system of self-build housing: the Segal self-build method (37). Kevin McCloud has long championed this community self-build method. He has featured Hedgehog Co-Op at Hogs Edge. In ten years, no one has moved away. Why do they stay, *"because of the community"* (38).

In 2016 the UK news covered a co-housing project that had taken a group of 25 women 18 years to turn from idea to actually moving in. As one of them said, *"There are 25 doors I can knock on….it is very confidence boosting to know `I'll be alright`. There's a communal area and we can see if anyone is not up and about" (39).* They are much less dependent on care services or their families. There are innovative housing co-ops and associations, offering involvement and creating additional value for communities. For example, Adactus, in 2015/16, spent £191,620 from their neighbourhood fund on 308 community projects (40). Housing can come from a family throwing open its doors. Tobias Jones has written a book about life at Windsor Hill where his family share their house with others, *"Most people arrive because of a desperate need-bereavement, depression, addiction or homelessness-while others come simply because they are dismayed by modern life" (41).* And this becomes, not retreating from the world, but a deeper engagement with it. A state supporting civil society would get behind such developments so they operated on a far larger scale.

On a more industrial scale commercial investors have begun to move away from investing in properties to buy. They are finding the long-term return on investment is higher when properties are built for *rent* because a community forms and the properties are looked after. In January 2016, the Guardian was reporting,

"British insurer Legal & General has teamed up with a Dutch pension fund manager to construct 3,000 apartments across the UK under a £600m "build-to-rent" plan. L&G and PGGM will initially build 650 flats in Bristol, Salford and Walthamstow, to help tackle the housing crisis. The UK private rental market has traditionally been dominated by individual buy-to-let landlords, but in the past few years, big institutional investors and developers such as Berkeley Homes have entered the market to build blocks of rental homes." (42)

Britain cannot swing back and forth between `build-to-buy` and `council-housing-for-rent`. We can do better for all generations by crafting, with organisations experienced in the field, like the National Housing Federation, a mixture of housing options for people at different stages in life (43). To be really effective we need to go local and get specific. There are three sources of new homes: the private sector, housing associations/not for profits, and council housing. Who is going to supply how much in any particular area? These three sectors working together at postcode level is surely the way to go?

Education

Education is the public service that should excel at fulfilling potential. Let us see.

At the inception of the welfare state, local authorities had control of education. But recently Government has created free schools and academies and funded them centrally. In effect Britain has two state funded education systems! This reflects the values of market thinking: existing provision needs to be challenged by offering alternatives or `challengers`. In 2010/11 there were 465 academies and free schools. By the end of the academic year 2013/14 the total stood at 4,548 (44). A dramatic expansion had taken place.

What they bring is the ability of central government to get its values reflected directly into schools. Academisation has been developed to keep the money and numbers in control. It promotes a business model in education. Academies are managed.

This is the driver,

"A high-performing education system is critical to national economic prosperity and to staying ahead of our competitors. Standards of academic achievement must be as high as possible, and schools must give priority to subjects and methods of teaching that promote these standards. Given the growth of the knowledge economy, it's essential that as many people as possible go on to higher education..... Because these matters are too important to be left to the discretion of schools, government needs to take control of education by setting the standards, specifying the content of the curriculum, testing students systematically to check that standards are being met, and making education more efficient through increased accountability and competition" (45) (my emphasis)

What this effectively does is take away pedagogy from the entire system. Or rather it is a cognitive pedagogy consistent with PISA that is being assumed as appropriate for everybody. And as the behaviour problems of many of our secondary schools show, a cognitive pedagogy does not suit all. What is PISA?

The UK approach reflects a world-wide `standards movement`,

"Since 2000, the standards movement has been turbocharged by the league tables of the Program for International Student Assessment (PISA). These tables are based on student performance in standardised tests in mathematics, reading

and science... ...PISA runs the tests every three years with groups of fifteen year olds in countries around the world. The number of countries taking part has increased from thirty-two in 2000 to sixty-five in 2012, and the number of students being tested has almost doubled from 265,000 in 2000 to 510,000" (46)

South Korea has been at the top. But when three Welsh teenagers tried learning in South Korean schools it was clear that their Korean counterparts have no life outside cramming for exams. The whole of family life centres around them achieving high exam results. It isn't just that the students arrive very early in the morning. They carry on until late at night in supplementary schools. It is crazy. The levels of teenage suicide confirm this. The South Korean government is now trying to create a more balanced approach (47).

The 2015 Education and Adoption Bill sharpened the dividing line between local authority schools and central government ones. One way it did this was to force all schools found inadequate and in special measures, to academise. This was intended to force such schools to leave the control of local authorities. The use of the law to go further and 'automate' academisation was resisted, especially when it was proposed that all schools become academies by 2022. In May 2016, the resistance was such that government had to abandon plans to force all schools to become academies (48). Actually, there are weak academies and strong local authority schools. Indeed, all schools are different. The format or structure of the school is not really the primary criterion: it is leadership and the quality of teaching that matters. Because leadership is key there are examples of academisation which have worked well for local clusters. These are people who know how to play the system to achieve what they believe is best for their young people/parents.

Inevitably, education in Britain's schools, from the central government perspective, amounts to achieving academic standards at all levels. The sole focus is on academic attainment as measured through testing and exam performance.

How are the staff bearing up? According to government figures, in 6 years, the number of newly qualified teachers who complete their training but never enter the classroom, has risen from 3,600 in 2006 to 10,800 in 2011(49). Those that do make it into the classroom, are leaving in substantial numbers within their first year. 40% are leaving in the first 5 years (50).

Schools have a choice, if their leadership is up for it. There are plenty of schools with teal leadership who are having to tick the boxes for the orange government system but actually are then developing a lot more besides on their own terms. They are doing their version of the humanising in health and social care (above).

It is the summer of 2015 and I am on the campus of Exeter University, in Devon participating with 150 other members of SGI-UK (chapter 5). *"Why are you here in Ashburton, Devon?"* I ask. He is from Italy. She is from Spain. *"It's the school"*. And then I get introduced to the concept of democratic education as

Sands does it (51) . No uniform, no bells, no silly, petty rules: freedom to be yourself, go at your own pace and make your own choices. Everyone has an equal say. Students and staff decide things together. And what did Ofsted say, "*Outstanding personal development because of the exceptional impact of the democratic principles*" (52). It's a community where teachers and pupils run the school.

Values based education is another non-Pisa approach. It has been developed under the leadership of an ex-head teacher, Neil Hawkes. They estimate around 3,000 schools in England and Wales are embedding this approach (53). Ken Robinson provides numerous examples of innovations within the system, where teachers and students have developed something exciting and totally engrossing. The most rebellious students have then become captivated. Their maths, English, etc. have improved. Here is one example. Grange Primary School in central England created Grangetown: a working `town` within the school. Every `job` was done by students. It created extraordinary engagement and they learnt the core disciplines. Grangetown harnessed their natural learning ability through role play and experiential learning. The town had TV and radio stations. The experience wrapped together teamwork, resilience, self-confidence and community responsibility.

In 2010, Feversham primary in Bradford went into special measures. When a new music teacher appeared, the school moved from 30 minutes a week music to 6 *hours* a week music! He brought with him the Kodaly method of children learning to play music. This makes it fun and involves games. With such a diverse group of children the music helps bring everyone together. Because the school became a far better place in which to learn, the school went into the top 10% for pupil progress (54).

Education is so central to Britain achieving more of its potential. Dig away at the realities going on in our primary and secondary schools and it is surprising how much progressive, relationship centred work is going on. I have just identified a few developments. The point really is that in education a *lot* is possible within the existing framework. However, it does take leadership. If that leadership has a teal conscious a *lot* more potential can be realised.

Criminal Justice

It was my privilege in 2007 to listen to David Weir talk about his research with the police. Wittily he had titled his presentation "The Shudda Brigade" (55). In other words, those in management positions hearing what their subordinates have done saying, "But you *should have* done this……". The police sergeant stands between the managerial hierarchy and the front line. They were reporting an intensification of demand for *information* from above. The setting of targets and the reporting of statistics, of every type, had become the very fabric of police work. Police sergeant's work became far more complex. They became subject to greater scrutiny, with more conflicts and contradictions needing to be resolved. This quote gives a sense of what Weir found,

"….if you've got a burglar, the majority of offenders are not well off, and they're travelling in stolen vehicles. We knew…..you've got a good idea if anybody is stealing vehicles, they're burglars……………But now, because he's got the directives from HQ that our autocrime figures are going through the roof, we're being targeted with autocrime"(55)

So forget theft from people's homes! In other words, it is no longer the substance of the work that is of interest to the hierarchy. It has become target and information driven, overriding intelligent, experienced based understandings. What the police sargeants said to Weir about the very interventions that *do* make a difference was: *"there is no way of measuring them"*.

By March 2017 newspapers were reporting the police being in a 'potentially perilous' state with ….

1. an acute shortage of detectives;
2. falling numbers of arrests;
3. victims being let down;
4. emergency calls downgraded;
5. investigations shelved;
6. not following up investigations;
7. suspects left untracked.

Since 2010 staff posts have reduced by 15,500 (19.5%)(56). Over the last 4 years the numbers leaving have doubled (57).

People accused of crime are taken to court, from prison or police stations, by two contracted companies Serco and GEOAmey. It is claimed that so-called, 'court custody' is *"an accident waiting to happen"* (58). Filthy cells, lack of appropriate supervision, are just some of the issues. This is not the 'safe and secure' custodial environment for detainees that Serco and GEOAmey are contracted to provide.

In the crown courts, two thirds of trials were delayed or did not proceed. As of September 2015, there was a backlog of 51,830 cases waiting for a crown court hearing (59).

As of September 2015, the UK had over 95,000 prisoners. The 120 prisons of the UK are pretty well full *and* there is a *50%* reoffending rate (where are they going to go?)! There are about 21,000 mentally ill in prison (higher than the 17,000 NHS beds available to mentally ill patients) (60).

The number of prison officers in the UK has been cut by an average of 41% per prison in less than 4 years. Officer grade staff working in prison stood at 24,000 at the end of August 2010. At the end of June 2014 there were 14,170.

(61). The bill to government for compensation payments paid to inmates is considerable.

Last, we come to the Probation Service. The cost to society of reoffending, has been estimated to be £15bn a year. Government's approach has been to contract probation services out, 'to shake things up'. The service was split up on the basis of risk. New, private, inexperienced community rehabilitation companies have been contracted to work with low and medium risk offenders. What remains of the original probation service 'specialises' in working with high risk offenders. In the old service, staff could mix the levels of risk of the offenders they worked with. This made for a manageable workload. Offenders could change risk level and *still have the same member of staff.*

Having only high risk as a workload has been found to create a relentless, urgent and intense workload. The chances of serious re-offending are now much higher. But to be low or medium risk is not a fixed categorisation. Many in this category live chaotic lives and may need emergency support at short notice through crises such as losing their home or returning to drink or drug addiction. These offenders still could commit serious offences and have to be carefully monitored.

To change them to high risk is complicated. Ditto for high risk to move to medium or low. Different organisations work with different risk people. The process is time consuming. They can be passed 'from pillar to post' and things can be missed on the way because the in-depth knowledge is no longer built up. The danger to the public has increased. In July 2018 probation contracts were ended 2 years early at a cost of £120 million. But I sense more 'engrenage' since the stated aim was simply that future contracts would have 'tougher standards'!

Is there *any* positive teal-like movement in this dismal scene?

In April 2015 the documentary film-maker Rex Bloomstein took the voice recorder into HMP Whatton in Nottinghamshire, the largest sex offender prison in Europe, to investigate how its inmates are rehabilitated for release (62). Sex offenders are 11,000 of the total prison population. Whatton has 841 inmates. They are all men. The prison governor is a woman. What runs centrally through the experience is non-judgmental groupwork. It costs £27,000 per man per year. But 68% don't re-offend compared with the 50% for the total prison population. Treating prisoners with humanity seems, literally, to pay.

There is just one UK prison calling itself therapeutic: Grendon. A visiting journalist found,

".....an unexpected camaraderie between inmates and prison staff. They chat about forthcoming events in the prison; they call each other by their first names; there is a mutual respect. The prisoners seem relaxed, the atmosphere is calm. There is none of the edgy us-and-them atmosphere that pervades other prisons - there is no sense of imminent danger. It is more like a student hall of residence than a category B prison." (63)

How does it work?

"The prison is divided into therapeutic wings. Each wing is a democratised community that selects its own officials and sets its own rules. There are three key policies that everyone is expected to observe - no drugs, no sex, no violence. If you breach any of the three, your peers can decide whether you should be allowed a second chance or be kicked out." (63)

You have to volunteer to go to Grendon. So they are dealing with a motivated population who want to change. Here is a view from `one of the team`,

"I can't do with having the victims on my conscience any more. Before I could not see the victims. Now I can. I feel when I'm in other prisons that it's just reinforcing my old behaviour - me against the system. In other prisons I feel like I'm an inmate. Here I feel I'm part of a team who are working towards my progress."(63)

Does it work?

"The reconviction rates are encouraging. For prisoners serving life sentences elsewhere, there is a 24% reoffending rate; at Grendon it is 8%. For non-lifers the reoffending rate is 10% lower at Grendon than elsewhere, and if prisoners complete the therapy, which ideally runs for at least 18 months, reoffending is slashed by 20-25%." (63)

Grendon has a waiting list of 200. The prison system hopes the newly opened Dovegate, with its 200 place, therapeutic community will take this waiting list. Could we have more confidence in humanity and make faster progress towards these changes?

Can the courts keep people out of prison?

In October 2015, the then UK minister for Justice was reported widely in UK media as he visited Texas. This was prompted by Ian Burrell`s research into how, counter- intuitively, the lone star state was keeping people out of prison *and* reducing re-offending. On TV we are shown Judge Bobby eliciting the grim truth from someone who came out of prison and slipped backwards (64). This is happening in a court full of addicts and alcoholics. The judge goes through it all in front of everyone like a father who really cares. And there`s a whole team whirring into action to support the detail of what the court decides. Only a half go on to re-offend.

Agencies focused on `offending` now have restorative justice. The perpetrator is a human being having to live with what they have done to the victim. The victim and the perpetrator can help heal each other's wounds.

Restorative justice puts in place facilitators and processes which bring the victim and the perpetrator together to 'repair harm'. John Braithwaite and Gerry Johnstone have both written about restorative justice. (65)

A teal model of public service

It is clear that market-based services have created a nightmare: 'maximum-effort-for- minimum-results' is an understatement. We cannot go back to the past of the old freedoms of professionals cosseted by hordes of administrators. So as a country we need to come clean and admit that we still have not cracked how to run public services that really work.

Jos de Blok, in his presentation at the RSA, talked about Buurtzorg's approach being a generic model and that he was working with the police and teachers. He saw the generic approach operating from three principles,

1 Do what is needed;
2 Reflect on what you are doing;
3 Use common sense.

He goes on to encourage us to build organisations that are created out of meaningful, trusting relationships, that create value for the community, create happiness and health for staff, and that avoid complexity (66).

Autonomous teams such as we saw in Buurtzorg, RDH, and from my three examples (chapter 5) are, without doubt, the future for Britain. As those experiences show, they simultaneously stop bureaucracy in its tracks *and* transform market thinking. This is exactly what we need in Britain with the hybrids we have.

Autonomous teams are the best way to get the focus on effectively solving complex problems through actual capability, skill, wisdom and sound action (including well placed collaboration). Autonomous teams can work to well defined briefs. They can be directed towards tackling complex needs in communities, exercising full responsibility in how this is done as well as being directly accountable to the very community they are serving. They can account for their work to public bodies like local assemblies (chapter 6).

What will really make for a whole new model of public service is bringing people together in teams in completely different ways that ignore institutional boundaries and concentrate on the capabilities needed for the tasks in hand. Staff could come from qualified (sometimes just by experience) workers *irrespective of employing agency*, activists, volunteers, sessionally paid local people (like family group leaders), as well as from local businesses. These are teams of staff without baggage, able to flexibly adapt to local needs, becoming very effective. Nimble, passionate people with enough training appropriate to the tasks at hand, and who can work well with others, can be very effective. These are teams using technology, training, and money in support of the shared purposes agreed locally as needed.

Frankly decades of being 'market driven' has created hybrids where staff have experienced re-structuring and re-organisations *all the time*. Staff have had to live with change, on pretty well every level, all the time. So UK public service staff will find shifting over to having autonomy a breeze! Practitioners are already headed in that direction, despite management.

Local *network*s of teams will form a living entity, sharing information and finding just the ways to respond to shifting vulnerabilities and suffering in the population. We will be seeing training in how to make team decisions, in keeping working relationships safe and clear, and in resolving conflicts, as we saw in Laloux's research.

We will be seeing these teams get together and use the repertoire of large group meetings, the use of open mic, small groups etc to continue to consistently create the open and safe culture needed to do genuine public service.

IT, finance, HR need a revolution in working together for the benefit of autonomous teams: genuinely being supportive rather than controlling and coercive. Laloux's researches are so helpful here. Support functions get taken on by the autonomous teams and if anything is left they too operate alongside and use exactly the types of structures, practices and processes as autonomous teams use. They are autonomous teams. This is the future of British teal public service.

Doing teal within orange

The next chapter will show business and especially civil society in Britain are on the road to teal. It is the state, and especially the 5 social policy areas that are lagging. Although it makes this chapter a little on the long side, I want to encourage staff inside public services to be bold by sharing three examples, from my own experience, of doing teal right smack bang in the middle of extremely orange set ups. (Chapter 4 already provided two examples, the Estate and the anti-racist network).

Laloux's approach of the CEO and the board having a teal consciousness, as the *condition* for transition to teal, needs qualifying when it comes to the hybrid public services in Britain. The reason I say this is because in my experience enormous transformation can take place within discrete units, teams, and whole services that may, in terms of the management structure, be within a larger body like a department or division. Where the top managers of that department or division have also turned themselves into teal leaders there is enormous potential for change. But even where top managers are holding the managerial and market oriented line there are *still* opportunities for real change. I would like to use three mini case studies to illustrate this.

The first is a discrete, self-contained learning disability service operating in a 90s managerial and market oriented wider organisation. The second is anti-racist project work carried out by two external consultants in two NHS trusts that were rapidly employing more and more managerialists. The third is a whole adult social services department moving from ignoring family carers of service users to actually responding extremely meaningfully. What these all show is the power of an operationally focused piece of work, undertaken within orange, to move a whole body of staff in a teal direction. The power of the work to do this lies in it just being self-evidently a far better way to work!

Learning disabilities learning to `do with`

The service had been bussing over 300 people with learning disabilities into and out of six day centres. They were classified as students and had a bewildering array of things to do once inside a centre. In the 90s that model began to be seriously questioned among people with learning disabilities. They were taking on the disability movement's `social model` which put the emphasis on changing structures and processes in society to give people with disabilities the kind of access in society the non-disabled took for granted.

One day I sat down with Roger (the overall manager) and the 6 managers of the day centres and the discussion `took off`. Roger was a genuine leader who was going far beyond the limitations of managerialism. We discussed the differences between planning and learning in their context: that in fast changing situations, planning might be aiming to get ambiguity clearer and remove too much uncertainty. While this might be what was intended, actually the ambiguity and uncertainty are inevitable in significant change so why try to remove them? Rather these sorts of hard to handle realities in the service were conducive to complex learning. This was a real `ping` moment for them because learning was central to the service. They twigged that a learning disability service itself had to major on complex learning as it transformed.

From here it was a short step to see that rational planning assumed you could always get an identifiable link between an action and an outcome. But with the impending scale and nature of the change that was just not going to be possible. They wouldn't be able to control it. The second ping moment was when they realised that they needed processes and systems which assumed complexity. Also they needed as much feedback as they could handle. What was deeply subversive about these discussions was that they were happening in a managerial culture which insisted on rational planning and control.

What was the concrete piece of work which catalysed a whole service change? We went for a survey. It wasn't supposed to be a research process. Rather it was getting `good enough` information (with some important safeguards) in order to get change started. Gould`s definition of freedom amounts to having a capacity for free choice. The managers and staff of this service, in the way they were going to do this survey and the kinds of questions it was asking, were going to great lengths to ensure freedom of choice among this body of service users and their carers/parents. A long history of paternalism had meant `doing to` was the norm. The survey was them starting to `do with`.

I developed some software they would be able to use to collect, `cannot be argued with` data direct from people using the centres *and* their parents/carers. It was a tool managerialists would understand. I could use the same software to interrogate the data.

I began to mock up forms which used questions in the first person: Things I like; Where I live; People in my life. And this was just the first section which was boldly headed `ABOUT ME`. Against each question there were multiple choice answers. All that was needed was a cross in a big box against what the service user wanted to say. The other three sections covered `THINGS I DO`, `WHAT I WANT TO DO`; and `MAKING IT HAPPEN`.

There were clearly dangers in asking staff to do it. However, the reality was that there was little choice. Safeguards were built into the surveying and it was decided that while some responses certainly might be `led` by the staff, we would proceed.

One of the biggest pieces of learning from efforts to change similar services elsewhere was that they had been blocked by the carers/parents. They had put their foot down and refused to entertain any real change in the day centres and certainly no closures of centres. We had to be extremely clear that this information collection was just that: information collection. Nobody was making decisions but change definitely had to come and it was surely better to base that on as much detailed information straight from the body of people using the day centres as well as their carers?

There was a simple two-page questionnaire produced for carers/parents which allowed them to say what they thought of what their son or daughter had said to their keyworker. In other words, we had to give the questionnaire completed by the service user to their parents/carers.

This decision was arrived at after lengthy consideration. We understood that some service users would be prevented from being as forthright as they would otherwise have been, knowing it was going to be seen by their parents/carers. However, if we didn't include them there was a serious risk that parents and carers would block any real change.

It took 514 hours of staff time to get 305 assessments done, which was more or less the whole day centre population. The assessment contained ways of tracking down unreliable information so, for example, assessments where the service user just says yes or no in a fairly random manner. Or where they change their mind from day to day. Another response was just saying yes to what they think will please the staff member. Another difficulty was the member of staff being able to judge how much he or she understood. These unreliable questionnaires totalled 12% of the assessments and were flagged up in the survey.

We got 232 carer forms back. They had taken this exercise very seriously. Staggeringly 80% of carers agreed with the assessments. This was a green light to get on and take action, based on the assessments. Many of the carers expressed surprise at how well the keyworker knew their son or daughter. This was a confidence and morale boost for staff. As one manager put it,

"....the two pages that gave parents the opportunity to comment on what their son or daughter had said, some staggering similarities came out of that. People who haven't spoken to us for years came forward. It triggered a more intense advocacy" (67).

Service users wanted to do more relevant and useful things inside the centres *and* they wanted more real-world engagement outside centres of their choosing. About 200 people with learning disabilities wanted to make new friends and wanted more opportunities to meet people. Very large numbers wanted better general fitness (140) and to lose weight (100). But substantial numbers said they were having problems with their eyesight, hearing, sleeping, their feet and teeth. A health improvement programme was definitely being suggested. Epilepsy and well women clinics were being requested.

The results were presented to staff, carers and service users, centre by centre. Roger produced a laminated card of the 9 goals which would guide the changes in the service. Right at the top of the list was membership of a centre being guaranteed and no reduction in the level of service. A key commitment was that the service would demonstrate that older and more severely disabled people were benefiting from the new developments in the service.

Towards the end of 1998 an extremely self-confident, and strangely un-managerial report, went from the ultra-managerial director to the committee arguing the service be given three years to evolve into something different,

"the approach to service change should evolve from the existing services...part of the change will be to ensure that services respond to the individual needs of service users to develop lives of their own choosing with appropriate support"(67).

Over those three years I 'measured' the change. The changes were evident as the 3 years progressed and were exactly in line with what the service users had said, and the 9 goals. Staff were learning to work more effectively in teams, especially how to engage *with* people with learning disabilities. Theatre and ceramics workshops started up, led by former staff who had gone freelance. There were shorter journey times, more continuity of drivers and pick up times, and better use of the bus fleet. The transport service had greatly improved. More were using public buses and trains.

Today there are no centres left, just small community hubs. There is no more large-scale bussing. This service became one of the Cabinet Office mutuals, getting 'spun out' of its public service department, to become a stand-alone organisation run by its staff: they have secured their autonomy. People with learning disabilities are living lives much more to their own choosing. Staff love their work. Younger carers especially really appreciate the change.

NHS managers and staff learn how to stop doing institutional racism

This is a three-stage piece of work that I think could be adapted for many other issues. The process created much needed autonomy in front line staff and new understandings in their managers. In 1994 I became a consultant to two members of the anti-racist network (chapter 4) doing a `health access project` with two NHS trusts. Black patients were being sent home too early, and their families/carers were not brought into the conversation about care/discharge *at all*.

The three stages were firstly to start at the top getting to understand how the managers saw the issues. We interviewed 53 managers spread across the two trusts. Secondly, because managers were denying there was a problem, we did a mini action-research project shadowing 30 black patients going through the system. The evidence was overwhelmingly negative: there was a problem. This opened the way for the third stage with the managers and the practitioners to be in 6 self-learning groups with a total of 100 practitioners and managers across the two trusts. This created the change that was needed.

Why start with the managers? Well they didn't seem to think there was a problem. They had a defensive list of things they thought were OK. There was a belief that the system itself was fine, if black people could just be communicated with and linked into it. Here are examples of their perceptions,

"The reason why we don't get Asians is because the burden is on the family"
"If they could speak English it would not be such a problem"
"Self-referrals can be made. However few people know this. There is a reluctance to publicise because of being overburdened with referrals"
"Why don't they come as they know we are here, I spoke to a group myself" (67)

Another assumption by the managers was that increasing practitioner's knowledge and understanding of lifestyles, values and cultural norms, would result in improved access to and quality of service delivery. This communicated an inability to accept responsibility for practice interactions in the moment, the embodied constructed realities, which very much *are* under the control of staff. Attention was being deflected away from these practice interactions. In the NHS it is easy to hide behind the mantra of `we treat everyone the same`, when actually staff were not. We made these assumptions and views of managers public with the practitioners and among all the managers (with the manager's agreement).

We next ran a mini action-research project with us as the project workers. We were referred black patients as they entered and passed through the system. We kept detailed records about each patient, their illness, treatment details, and the practitioners involved. In our conversations with patients we were trying to understand what they had been asked, what they had been told, their feelings of involvement with the process, what they understood, what was explained, whether they asked questions and how far they felt they were understood.

We had to be persistent with patients. To begin with they would not really open up but when it was clear to them that we understood what they were experiencing, a dramatic change took place and they talked much more openly. We found weaknesses in the referral systems, which led to significant difficulties for black and racial minority patients. There was a continual stream of black and racial minority elders admitted, discharged and re-admitted within a short period, who would have benefited from access to community health services and improved discharge arrangements.

Of the 30, 20 had been in hospital in the previous 12 months and had no referral from GPs to community health services. These 20 patients had no awareness of the option to refer themselves to district nurse care, speech therapy, physiotherapy, dietetics or podiatry services, despite potentially benefiting from at least one of these services. For many elders their hospital stay was psychologically traumatic due to minimal interaction with staff, poor information and negotiation about their illness or treatment resulting in inappropriate care. Carers were overloaded and excluded. Information given to patients and carers about their illness, treatment and care during and after hospital, was either irregular or non-existent.

After these results were shared, for the first-time, front line practitioners showed a genuine willingness to reconsider their practices, as they accepted our accounts of black people's experiences. The evidence was overwhelming. We argued for and got agreement to the self-learning groups.

All 6 self-learning groups (three in each trust) went through a threefold process of:

       1 Unblocking resistance to learning;

       2 Doing the learning;

       3 Turning the learning into action.

In each group one or two practitioners led the change. One practitioner narrated her experience of an angry African patient. The practitioner had also become angry with the patient and tried to ignore her. This had been going on for some time. The practitioner was now beginning to question her own actions and consider what different action she should be taking. In the self-learning group she revealed her own assumptions, *"I felt she did not like white people and that her family, although pleasant, intimidated me..."* In the next group meeting this practitioner talked about how she had approached the family differently and had had a 'good discussion' with the patient. What made this a 'good discussion' was that the patient had expressed herself and her concerns, resulting in a different and more appropriate service being made available. As she put it in the group, *"My inability to recognise these assumptions seriously affected the relationship".*

This experience had a powerful effect on all members of this group, leading on to more questioning of assumptions by people in the group.

Here are some statements from practitioners across the 6 self-learning groups,

- *"I will think about how I communicate to patients/ carers and whether I am really getting across"*
- *"I realise how much of a `professional` I become often to the detriment of my own culture".*
- *"I will try not to make assumptions that the family will manage but explore the reasons why they do not want services."*
- *"It was good to be able to talk freely about what it feels like to be black and working for the organisation. "*
- *"At first I couldn't see that we would achieve anything but after much discussion I have got more than I expected."*
- *"The input from other staffs experience and perspective was invaluable and it gave me insight into how other staff approach situations."*
- *"Our values and ways of working are also shaped by our organisation`s expectations. Have we questioned enough the culture of our organisation and its impact on our communication? " (67)*

This piece of work offers ways to work which go far beyond issues of race and racism. It shows us how much more lies behind today's headlines about the failures of the NHS. It suggests ways to humanise *any* service where practice is parting company with the lives of people on the receiving end. Not only that, it is a method for changing things while keeping the show on the road.

Social workers learning to respond to carers

For a long time in this department, social workers only focused on carers in their caring role and ignored everything else. But with another, very different, three stage process, imaginatively executed, social workers supported carers in their own right. It may not sound like much, but this is a huge change.

The three stage process was:

1 find out what social workers were actually doing;
2 find out carers experiences of seeing social workers;
3 bring staff and carers together to make the changes necessary for there to be really good `carers assessments` and effective support of carers.

Three of us, Sian, Emily and myself, with developmental roles inside the department brought it to reality. But the people who really made it all happen were a group of family carers recruited with the brief to work with us to make this change.

Stage 1 confirmed what we knew but gave it substance that could not be argued with. All the workers were very wary of engaging with carers because they felt they had nothing to offer. So, the insistent task focus coming from well over a decade of managerial reforms meant they were no longer willing to provide even emotional support.

Some social workers *did* put a lot of time and effort into talking with the carer but felt the systems back at base had nowhere to capture it. Since it wasn't being recorded or captured, it wasn't part of their work!

The department had developed a carers self-assessment form years before. Some social workers were treating this as the carers assessment and simply putting it on file when completed. *Nothing actually happened*. The intention of the legislation was failing miserably: the self-assessment forms were getting in the way of the relationship. There was a lack of information. Social workers were only seeing carers in their caring role.

Stage 2 kicked off with an opportunity to work with the department widely advertised among carers locally, and which resulted in a very strong group of 12 coming forward. The aim was being presented as, "*to develop guidelines ....on how carers want their needs assessed*". In November 2007, this group of 12 carers did a three-day preparation course. The idea was to prepare them to go out and find out about carers experiences of seeing a social worker. The course was run by two external trainers. The paperwork about it was shared around the department and it was creating a buzz.

Day one had carers interviewing each other. Day two focused on listening skills. Day three was about asking the right questions. On day four they simulated a real live interview situation with a panel and also tried to make sense of all the information. We also had two members of staff do the course alongside the carers. Sian was one of the members of staff on the course, and she already knew a lot directly from carers and had read all the research Emily and I had done for stage 1. Even so by the end of day two her comment is very telling,

"*realising that we in the department have such a long way to go in meeting carers needs, despite all the work that has been done already*" (67).

She hadn't realised how she was perceived by carers and how powerful an organisation like an adult social services department is for them. A week later a social worker who had also been on the course sent me this,

"..when they first began to care it started with just having to make minor adjustments to their own life. Their role as carer built slowly and it was only when they looked back, they could see how much they were doing and how their life had changed. ...They had all experienced being stressed, exhausted and not knowing where to turn. They all felt that when they reached the point of exhaustion that they did not have the energy to find out what and where help was available. ...by the time they had reached this point, letting go of their caring role or even a small part of the role, had become very difficult and they were often resistant to others taking over.....everyone complained about the process (of getting help) and how long and repetitive it was. If they had the energy to find out how to ask for help, they were met by a barrage of questions and no answers. It then took ages before anyone came back to them and by then they were thinking, `why bother`...when they tried to speak to a social worker they were not sure if the message had got through." (67)

From the course they posted out a very simple survey headed up with,

"We are a small group of carers and ex-carers. We want to know your experiences, good or bad, of talking with adult social services. Has this made a difference to your life? How? We will then be meeting with Adult Social Services with our findings, so that together we can make things better. Talk to the experts. We are also carers. We understand how you feel." (67)

These carers engaged with about 70 carers, from which came 4 key priorities:
1. Helping with caring so I can have a break;
2. Planning for an emergency;
3. Giving me information I'll find helpful;
4. Talking with me; not filling out a form.

The group then divided into teams. Team A took the first two themes and team B the second two. They used material they had had back from carers, plus their own experiences, to illustrate what they wanted to say. They prepared a 40-minute presentation to the departments 40 managers including all the senior managers and the director. Despite none of them having done anything like this, in those 40 minutes *they totally changed the willingness to make change happen in this organisation.* When the carers had finished, for about 45 minutes the managers presented their feedback and asked questions of the teams. This created a sense of being party to a rare openness of dialogue and engagement among all present. Some managers had been moved to tears listening to the carers. It had been one of the more powerful experiences of their professional lives. Towards the end of the workshop, the director, clearly emotional, said that some of what had been said had been very hard to hear, but they *had* to hear it and more important, from today, things would change. And they did. Writing about the experience one of the carers said about the last session of the workshop, "*I feel that this robust exchange was very satisfying for us and an ideal way to end the workshop*".

One week later a carers reference group was convened by the two new senior managers, Ron and Alan. Denise had asked them to ensure the whole agenda tackled through the workshop the previous week, *would* be implemented. Stage 3 was formally begun! The engine of change was a piloting with the 12 carers paired up with social workers doing new style assessments. One of the 12 carers then discussed how the experience had been with the carer experiencing the new assessment. They got very positive feedback from the carers who really appreciated the focus on themselves both in their caring role and in them having a life outside of caring. Carers really appreciated having one to one discussion. It felt very different to filling in forms: "*At last someone is listening to me*". Carers talked about being understood and feeling satisfied.

To get the infrastructure and services in place Emily and Sian worked flat out. Emily got an emergency support service up and running. Sian got carers grants in place. Direct payments were made available to carers. The electronic systems now held a new kind of carer's assessment for workers to complete. Carers worked with us on good public information and effective training. Sian was telling me that, "*We are seeing the first signs of workers beginning to think more creatively beyond the usual ways of responding*".

These three experiences demonstrate that a large public service organisation *can* completely change how it does something. It doesn't actually take much money to do it. What is crucial is to have the experiences of people on the receiving end coming into the status quo as part of a process geared to making effective change. All it takes is teal consciousnesses at the centre of the work.

What we are seeing with these three examples is that an organisational culture of thinking, being and doing is taking form within a larger context which continues to separate thinking and doing.

As suggested above I think Frederic Laloux's thesis that if the CEO and the board are teal then a teal organisation can develop needs modifying in light of UK public services complexities of accountability, structures, leadership, and a long history of professional discretion. In UK public services, teal can develop in the midst of orange.

I used Ralph Stacey's thinking about complex learning in all three (68). He argues that *any* operational set up in an organisation will throw up complex issues that it proves impossible to sort out in that operational mode. Organisations also need to develop a 'mode B' or learning mode where the self-same operational people create arenas in which they learn how to move forward with the complex issues. Laloux' teal organisations do this as the norm. I hope these examples show how making an orange organisation healthier or even verge on teal in certain aspects of its work, is not just worthwhile but also do-able.

The welfare state experience so far can be summed up as the lesson that we cannot *administer* human sufferings away. We do not spend over £700 billion a year as a nation to simply *manage* the pain and human vulnerability. Fundamentally we do it out of humanity. However, the way we do it in no way matches that humanity. With some notable exceptions we have degenerated into administering and managing it. It is time for the exceptions to become the mainstream. And that would mean Britain`s public services become exceptionally good. Generally, UK public services have been driven in the direction of `nothing`. We have seen uncaring, procedurally driven, fettered working environments that alienate staff and oppress service users across public services. The tantalizing prospect exists, that out of this the UK`s public services that begin making that kind of transition, will become incredible.

9 - Civil society Britain

"The environment we operate in determines how much of our innate potential we can manifest"

Frederic Laloux (1)

AND

"......many of the conditions of my life began to change when I got less offended by the truth: some of my problems are mine to solve. The new frontier for individuals and movements who want to radically change society is to first recognise the need for radical change within ourselves"

Darren McGarvey(2)

I have been arguing that a Britain realising more of its potential comes from a new configuration of power where both markets and the state support a very central civil society. This OS is about a shift in the purposes of each of these three. This is the focus of this final chapter. This civil society configuration is the one that brings the ecology of support for realising potential most fully to life. The amber and orange configurations haven't even come close in this respect. As the first quote above suggests, the big picture or the macro environment, matters.

While the macro matters, as the second quote suggests, we are at the same time *free* to develop ourselves, as it were 'from within'. Many of us have been fashioning something completely different from what our orange macro world would have us think, become and do. More and more people in Britain are seizing that freedom. It is taking the form of both an existential freedom pursued by individuals to become who they can be, *and* a leadership freedom shaping new ways of doing things (explored further in this chapter).

Chapter 2, and all the subsequent orange examples, show us that market thinking simply is not fit for purpose. It is now clear that it never was, but what else was Britain to do faced with the disaster of the 70s? I think we can say that Hayek`s experiment in running a liberal democracy through markets, has gone on for too long! This form of orange consciousness is no longer serving the people of this country. On a positive note, dissatisfaction with orange consciousness is providing immense energy powering innumerable micro changes in the direction of teal. The tide is turning.

What is fuelling that energy is that in longstanding democracies like Britain we desperately want something new to appear, which really helps people across the country better fulfil their potential. This, in turn, helps the country better fulfil its potential. New ways of doing things together, widely lived and experienced in the population, are benefiting from this energy. We are developing *in the body of the society,* islands of micro activity which work better, which have heart, and where individuals fulfil their potential better. These become the support for the new and better within areas of life that lie *on the surface of society,* like politics. As these islands increase in number, they will eventually usher in, not just a very different kind of politics, but the next consciousness, and with that, better ways to live our daily lives together in Britain.

At the core of the consciousness we are moving into is this view of life that inner lives, social, cultural and political realities, as well as the environment are one integral whole or a living universe where,

`..... life is neither a single unit entity nor a mere assembly of parts that work independently of each other. It is something that consists of multiple components functioning in perfect unity, smaller lives combining to form a greater life` (3)

None of the preceding configurations of Britain's OS have been powered by this kind of consciousness. So, let us now turn to the three elements of a civil society centred Britain: 1) business supporting civil society; 2) the state supporting civil society; 3) people in civil society creating teal initiatives. Let us start with business.

But before that, among the examples in this (and previous) chapters, how do we know they are in the direction of teal? My rule of thumb in selecting them has been that they are bringing into being a community, there is leadership, and together they are evolving supportive structures, practices and processes (especially autonomous teams). Also, that they are recognising the spiritual side of life and creating what could be called a humanistic development.

Some of the projects and developments you will read about in this chapter may well turn out to be more green than teal. But this is the point of teal, it actively wants to see good green. If not teal then the best of other consciousnesses is better than degenerate versions of them. Ken Wilber calls this way of bringing recognition and place for the best of the other consciousnesses as enfoldment. This is one way in which teal is a unifying consciousness.

I am not suggesting any of the people leading the various initiatives below have heard about teal. That's the beauty of it. I would say most people with a teal consciousness *don't know it's teal.* Creating things in the world that express teal does not depend on that leadership explicitly knowing they are teal. However, finding out about teal, all the other colour coded consciousnesses, the four quadrants, the ecology of support for realising potential and the civil society centred operating system, may well help these initiatives further consolidate and expand their efforts to embrace yet more people in more places more humanistically.

Because ecology, sustainability, and the arts are fully `out there` many of the initiatives detailed below seem, on the surface, to be triggered solely by those kinds of concerns. Some seem entirely technical, others pragmatic. However, dig a little deeper and the four quadrants are in play. The examples in this (and previous) chapters are where the potential for teal, in Britain today, is at its greatest.

Markets/businesses supportive of civil society

Figure 7

Markets supporting civil society

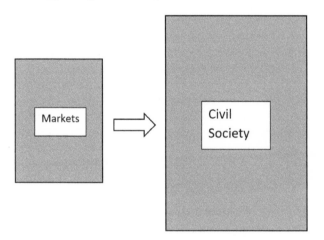

Markets, in the end are human constructs, operating for social and community benefit. Left alone markets invariably drift away from this. In an operating system supporting civil society, markets are regulated for social and community benefit. In such an operating system, individual businesses support civil society through the way they treat staff and the social and community benefit that accompanies what they build or provide. This is a business culture fully aware that certain resources must remain in `the commons` and be `inalienable`. Civil society orientated markets and businesses are there to responsibly generate and *circulate* wealth as a by-product of producing something well, that is really needed. These are businesses and markets that recognise they are part of a larger whole where that larger whole orbits around the bedrock of individuals, families, friends, networks, communities, and all the organisations and activities in civil society. Hence the willingness to be involved in integrated local assemblies (chapter 8).

By its very nature business is geared to economic efficiency and the pursuit of profit. But if the control of business is by those *only* seeking financial reward, then the logic of capital will operate unrestrained. What we must surely see is greater leadership in business able to temper the logic of capital with the logic of humanity? This is the whole point of teal leadership.

Imagine a Greek style yogurt producer who is Muslim and comes from Turkey, giving 10% of the company to employees. OK it is Chobani and is based in America, but the message is clear (4): temper the logic of capital with the logic of humanity. David Pike and Karin Sode, using crowd funding, are creating an energy company to rival Britain`s `big-six`by giving back 75% of profits to customers and putting customer reps on the board. They are looking to bring democracy and transparency to the UK`s energy market (5). They are tempering the logic of capital with the logic of humanity.

The `logic of humanity` can come from ecological impact and sustainability. These are changing car production towards electric vehicles, hybrids etc. But the industry has not been as bold as Riversimple. Here is their purpose, *"To pursue, systematically, the elimination of the environmental impact of personal transport"* (6). Note the key word `elimination`. They follow this with, *"Everything we do – the design of the car, the structure of the business, the people we work with – is in pursuit of this goal".* They are literally seeking to offer mobility at zero cost to the planet. What they have in development is a hydrogen car, with hydrogen filling points, and where you don't buy the car, but buy mobility. When you look at their team it is clear they have a community in formation. By the very nature of the challenge they have taken on, the path they take can only evolve.

I hadn't expected to hear a children's cycle manufacturer completely re-imagining the child`s bike experience, but Isla Bikes have,

"Her frustration with the cheap, heavy, poorly designed, uncomfortable children's bikes that her sister's children were struggling to enjoy gave her the Eureka moment she needed and Islabikes rolled into action in 2006... ... With a homemade desk, a £5 special offer phone/pen pot/stapler/ruler set and a single workstand for bike assembly, she set about changing the future of children's bikes and the expectations and enjoyment of junior riders everywhere." (7)

Here a bike is built for the individual child, sustainably and growing community in the process.

What very commercial businesses can now do is use a tried and tested methodology to move to autonomous, self-managing teams: holacracy, developed by Brian Robertson (8). It was developed at Ternary Software, in Pennsylvania (founded by Robertson). The company was noted for experimenting with more democratic forms of organisational governance. Robertson distilled the best practices into a system that became known as holacracy in 2007. Robertson then developed the holacracy constitution in 2010, which lays out the core principles and practices of holacracy, and has supported companies in adopting it.

The term holacracy is derived from the term holarchy, coined by Arthur Koestler in his 1967 book *The Ghost in the Machine*. A holarchy is composed of holons (Greek: holos "whole") or units that are autonomous and self-reliant, but also dependent on the greater whole of which they are part. Thus, a holarchy is a group of self-managing holons that function both as autonomous wholes and as dependent parts,

"A holarchy looks like a series of nested circles. Each circle (i.e. team) is made up of a set of roles, grouped together around a specific function—whether it be a specific project team, a department, a support function, or a business line. Some circles will contain sub-circles, and all are contained within the largest super-circle, usually called the "General Company Circle." (8)

Through the constitution, power shifts from being in the hands of a person to it being used generally within a process which the constitution defines in detail: this is constitutionally derived power. The CEO effectively hands power over to the constitution as a key step in the transition. It is a generic document available to any organisation wishing to move in this direction (9).

Britain leads the way with social enterprises. There are now 70,000 in Britain. It is estimated they contribute something in the region of £74 billion to the economy (10). In 2005 it became even easier to set up a social enterprise: the community interest company was born. This new type of company was introduced by the government in 2005 under the "Companies (Audit, Investigations and Community Enterprise) Act 2004" (11). Designed for social enterprises that want to use their profits and assets for the public good, CICs are intended to be easy to set up. They have all the flexibility and certainty of the company form, but with some special features to ensure they are working for the benefit of the community. They have proved popular and as of May 2016 there were more than 12,000 CICs on the Regulators register (12),

"......two areas where CICs have been most relevant: smaller, local enterprises and large spin-outs from the public sector.....especially from the NHS but also from local authorities. ...The CIC structure can also be suitable for charity

trading subsidiaries, particularly if the trading activities have a community interest element" (13)

We saw an example of a CIC, Mount Gould, in the previous chapter. Community Shop claims to be the country`s first *social* supermarket chain,

"Community Shop is a social enterprise that is empowering individuals and building stronger communities, by realising the social potential of surplus food....Members of Community Shop can shop for good food at great prices – easing pressure on family budgets – but also gain access to professional, personal development programmes, to kick-start positive change in their own lives. We call this The Success Plan." (14)

People sign up for a year if they are on means tested benefit. They learn to cook and get help with their CV. From being on benefit, 67% go back to work. They are already putting into practice the teal approach to a benefit system I argued for in the previous chapter.

There are many many other ways business can be supportive of civil society and not just be biased towards the logic of capital.

Britain has an outstanding legacy of co-operative ventures. There are many thousands of registered co-operative businesses operating in the UK. Alongside consumer and retail co-operatives, there exist many prominent agricultural co-operatives, co-operatively run community energy projects, football supporters' trusts, credit unions and worker-owned businesses. Co-operatives UK is the central membership organisation for co-operative enterprise throughout the UK. This is a co-operative of co-operatives: a co-operative federation (15).

Small and medium enterprises (SMEs) are 99.3% of all private businesses. So less than 1% are the large corporates employing 40% of the workforce. A big change in a small number of these companies can shift things.

Perhaps the business structure with the greatest potential for teal is employee ownership. The John Lewis Partnership is the best known, but there are others (16*).* Since 2010, employee ownership has seen growth of around 60%; there are now more than 320 employee-owned businesses in the UK, with more than 210,000 employees. Half that growth has been since 2014, when the government introduced Employee Ownership Trust tax incentives (17).

In the end it is teal businesses who really look after their staff and have a supportive eye to their families. Taking responsibility for sustainability and the environment comes as built-in. The greatest way to temper the logic of capital is through the kinds of teal business presented in chapter 5. These only show signs of increasing: Enlivening Edge is a website of the community taking Laloux`s research forward (18). There is a rapidly growing presence here.

The state as supportive of civil society

Figure 8

The state supporting civil society

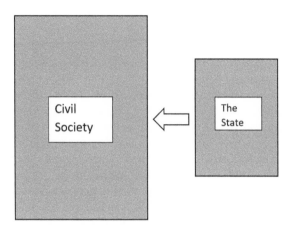

If we liken Britain to a room, the role of government can be likened to keeping it at the right temperature. Public spending, since world war two, has been one way that government has tried to regulate the temperature. The walls of the room used to be the welfare state bureaucracies. They could be relied on to provide services to a professional standard (which of course also had problems). But now with the attempt to turn the welfare state into something managerial and market based, something very unexpected is going on: the insulating property of the walls is degrading. No matter how many logs you put on the fire, the temperature keeps dropping.

Actually, government is burning *fewer and fewer logs* (austerity- budget cuts) *and the walls are degrading* (GPs and teachers leaving, demotivated staff, procedure driven cultures, dysfunctional organisations etc., etc.) There are many other examples of the insulating properties degrading. The benefit system now *creates* poverty. High levels of exclusion from schools is not consistent with a healthy functioning education system. Operations are being postponed. Pills are being given 'automatically'. Home 'care' is making older peoples' lives miserable. Reforming probation has unleashed a higher level of danger to the public.

Nationally the way the state interacts with markets and civil society is very crucial. After the great depression, the central political goal for government became reducing unemployment. After the stagflation of the 70s it shifted to reducing inflation. In a civil society OS, for Britain's potential to be realised, a core government goal needs to be maintaining a good social fabric. Getting the insulating properties of the walls to work is key to this and this is achievable through unleashing the autonomy of public sector staff (and all those others who will be working with them). It is achievable by creating Buurtzorg style freedoms across the board with exactly the right kinds of structures, practices and processes.

The part played by the state in this OS is to create exceptionally well run, enterprising, responsive, completely autonomous teams, across the board, with very clear mandates/purposes that are agreed. This is a state that infrastructures self-development first and foremost. It is a state in which community people, users of services and local activists are seen as integral to such services. This is 'the state' as an employer that people *want* to work for (bearing in mind this state won't all be 'professionals'-this is a state unleashing the 'non-professionals'). People want to work for the state because it offers meaningful work exploding with self-development possibilities and where 'staff' (bearing in mind this broad definition) feel they are part of something important for society, which helps others, *and* enriches their own lives. They want to get out of bed in the morning. They love their work. The British state fosters existential freedom. I can become who I can be. It stops oppressing its own population. This is a state actively supported by its people.

This is a state where the notion of the old welfare state and local authority departments and mega structures has atrophied in favour of living, continually adapting, configurations of autonomous teams. It is a state in which social policy is transformative. Indeed, policy making goes further with national government explicitly adopting civil society supporting policies, for example, to support community, voluntary organisations, and people with disabilities. Whitehall has been 'hollowed out': government and parliament are serving the local assemblies. These in turn have statutory powers to be party to the formation of new legislation and to provide feedback on existing legislation.

The political test of teal nationally is a vibrant, growing *unity* among politicians, able to bring together the 'tribes' of Britain (left, right, and centre ground, Muslims and Christians, black and white, feminists, LGBTQ, political greens, leavers and remainers etc., etc.) This is a political leadership committed to engaging in ordinary language on everyday issues that matter. This is doing far better than amber or orange ever have: a genuinely new politics centred on supporting civil society to flourish and hence Britain as a whole to flourish.

Such a state is one which *can* articulate the public interest, foster a *good* social fabric (especially through public services), and advance a *positive* identity of Britain and its people, which genuinely connects in the lives of people. Hopefully we are at last understanding that Britain's social fabric cannot be taken for granted, left to fend for itself or indeed plundered in the name of economic growth. When we go down that road, we are all threatened.

This is a state with sufficient intelligence to genuinely know how to harness the better insight that members of the public have, especially when those members of the public have taken the trouble to express that intelligence by forming an organisation. Currently, market thinking keeps civil society activists and front-line staff of public services apart: very far apart. This breeds distrust. It takes away the ability of front line staff to know that what they are doing is what people in their local civil society need.

But when civil society activists are working *among* front line staff and the two are communicating face to face, this frequent interaction means they come to understand each other and can establish what needs doing. In this OS competent leaders of effective local public services, dealing with a local crisis, will find themselves articulating and organising *to meet the wishes of their civil society activists*. Without even knowing it, that is what they find themselves doing. This is a re-defined concept of public service.

Currently it is just not there. In some cases, the divide is so great it has some of the characteristics of sectarianism. Things have become that bad. With the experiments in communism we know the state cannot replace markets. We *now* know market thinking is not good for state services. Mostly the experience in today's civil society is one of being ignored by the state. There are plenty of examples of civil society stepping forward, but not being adequately and positively engaged with by the state.

To take one example, journalist Jacques Perreti reported on a group of commuters (civil society) bidding to take over Southern Rail (train franchises are awarded by the state). This group succinctly and quickly diagnosed the problems, and what needed to be done, in ways no rail company had. Civil servants took their ideas but refused them a franchise on what seemed to be questionable grounds (19). In a state which supported civil society, imaginative ways to bring civil society activists into the very heart of such processes would be the norm. In a civil society OS, civil society activists are *in* the operation of state services.

In community development there is a long history of participatory budgeting. This might take the form of a local authority structuring ways for local communities to make decisions about the priorities for spending the local authority budget. In his RSA talk, George Monbiot made getting people involved in financial decisions one of his key ways for Britain to get to a better place. Rekyavik calls for ideas for improving the city and the spend on infrastructure,

"......*astonishingly 70,000 of the city's 120,000 people have taken part. Anyone can propose an improvement; anyone can vote for or against it. The fifteen most popular ideas each month are passed to the city council to consider. During the first six years of the programme, 1,000 ideas were submitted, of which 200 were adopted. The results seem to have been a major enhancement of both civil life and city's amenities" (20)*

Reviewing on a monthly basis builds trust. Good reasons are given for rejecting proposals. People can see there is point to their involvement. This is what a state supporting civil society looks like: representative democracy has direct democracy fused within it.

Monbiot also gives Porto Alegre in Brazil as an example of a more formal application of participatory budgeting. Here 20% of the infrastructure budget is allocated by 'the people'. About 50,000 people are involved in the development of a budget. Local public meetings review the previous year's budget and elect representatives to the coming year's budget council,

"Working with people in their districts, these representatives agree local priorities, which are then submitted to the budget council. The council weighs the distribution of money according to local levels of poverty and lack of infrastructure." (21)

Where participatory budgeting is done, there are sharper declines in infant mortality, better healthcare, better sanitation. The number of clinics, schools, and nursery places in poor areas improves. The supply of water improves. Monbiot quotes a woman in New York sharing her first experience of participatory budgeting there,

"...it was the first time.....probably ever in my adult life that I was like, 'this is democracy. This just feels like democracy, and this is the way decisions should be made in the city'" (22)

The state, in a civil society centred Britain, knows how to intervene when markets are failing. This *is* happening in orange Britain, but could become a stronger part of enabling a civil society Britain to develop. For example, Nottingham City Council took the view that the energy market is not working for consumers. They took action. They have set up Robin Hood Energy, the first local authority owned not-for-profit. It provides energy across Nottingham (and beyond) at the lowest possible price (23).

In Shetland, the state has done a deal with the oil industry who pay a sum per barrel of oil landed on Shetland. The money goes into a 'sovereign wealth fund'. In 2011 £11million a year was going back into civil society: first-class leisure centres in all the main population settlements, exceptionally good care for the elderly, property to let, a district heating scheme and more (24). Just imagine if these developments were teal led.

In Britain, we have some public services moving towards intelligent integration. For example, Yeovil's complex care team has this objective,

"The aim of the Complex Care team is to keep you in your home, for as long as possible through integrating your care with all the agencies involved, and designing a plan for your care, that has your wishes at the heart." (25)

We may have heard these laudable aims countless times before, but here there are structures, practices and processes supporting the objective. For example, they do same day assessment, treatment and returning home wherever possible. If it is not possible they have rented a floor in a care home for people not ready to go home. So, simple but very effective at building what needs to be done rather than sticking to outmoded boundaries.

The Weymouth and Portland integrated care hub is doing something similar,

"A pioneering partnership project is helping to deliver faster, more joined-up care for the frail, the elderly and people with long-term health problems in the Weymouth area. A host of different health and social care providers have come together to form the Weymouth and Portland Integrated Care Hub, which promotes closer working to deliver the right support to people at the right time – and as close to home as possible." (26)

Again, we are seeing structures, practices and processes supporting this aim. In the words of a local GP,

"I have seen huge changes in the ease of access to community services as a result of the hub. Now I make one phone call and a friendly health and social care co-ordinator listens to my needs and ensures an appropriate rapid response when needed, as well as arranging more routine aspects of care. This is 'joined-up care' working really well and tailored to our local population's needs. My frail patients have also benefited from the 'virtual ward' – whereas before, hospital admission would have been the only option, they can now be safely managed at home." (26)

Civil society activists can come right into the public service picture. Doctors come from 20% of schools (mostly fee paying). Given her background, Leanne Armitage has had to battle to become a doctor. Now she has created a foundation to help young people facing similar brick walls to break through (27). The NHS has found an ally!

A number of public services have partnered with the Scottish Violence Reduction Unit,

"Part of Police Scotland the VRU targets violence wherever it occurs whether it's on the streets, in schools or in our homes. Supported by the Scottish

Government the unit has adopted a public health approach, treating violence as
an infection which can be cured. ... ... The VRU believe violence is preventable –
not inevitable." (28)

The result?

"Since the VRU was launched in 2005, the murder rate in Glasgow has dropped
by 60%. The number of facial trauma patients passing through the city's
hospitals has halved, ... and is now around 500 a year." (29)

The passion and determination of people like John Carnochan, Will Linden and
others have made this happen. They have come right inside the public service
picture.

In Sussex the SERV riders and drivers volunteer their time, petrol and use
of their bike/vehicle to transport emergency blood and blood products to hospitals
throughout Sussex (30). Thornecombe's community responders have been
working with an ambulance service for 20 years, providing 24 hr care (31). The
NHS has found more allies!

All these examples involve leadership and community building.

Civil society at the centre

Figure 9

The civil society centred configuration

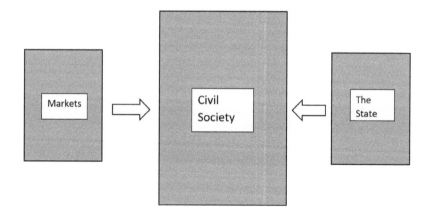

We come to the third part of a civil society Britain.

A key thing for civil society is for it to be recognised explicitly, across the society, for what it is: *the earth of everything else*. This is one of the things a teal political leadership nationally can achieve: civil society having a coherent public identity. This is where we live. This is life outside work. This is why we have a state, to provide what cannot be provided in civil society. Civil society has the most crucial parts of the ecology of support for realising potential: development of the self, family, friends, networks and communities.

It is through orange consciousness that organisations and politics have been taken *out* of this ecology, distorting the whole country in the process. Market thinking has inflicted inhuman rationales in organisations and supported this through the country's politics. A civil society centred Britain is about organisations and politics running *within* the framework of daily life in ways that harmonise with our natural ecology of support for realising potential. Civil society is about humanity, revitalisation and belonging. It's wellspring ultimately is the life of the universe, no less: selves connecting with that authentic inner wellspring which is itself part of a living universe.

In chapter 1 I said teal consciousness is the highest expression of consciousness, that we know today, that is workable within society, on a mass scale. Because society is dominated by amber, orange and green thinking, teal does this through great leadership. This is possible because the human being's integrity naturally drives in the direction of all four quadrants working together. We are here for self and others. We are surrounded by relationships and systems. We learn to view them as participating subjects *and* as social realities in a more objective way. As John Shotter shows us, our social realities also teach us to grasp the overall sense of meaning that is being shaped by 'us' or the 'we'. It is the four quadrants all connecting, right through the society. Individuals, families, friends, networks and communities all tend to work that way. Civil society Britain will bring organisations and politics within this. What is fundamental to this civil society OS is that it offers the most articulate expression of the teal consciousness.

Others have been far ahead of the arguments in this book for a civil society centred Britain. For example, in 2010 *Making Good Society* was published, on behalf of the Carnegie Trust, from a commission chaired by Geoff Mulgan into this central theme: putting civil society at the heart of Britain,

"Business without a strong civil society is more vulnerable, less adaptive and less efficient........Politics without a lively civil society lacks vigour and public confidence..Evidence shows us the limitations of public services that are not supported by a penumbra of commmunity organisations, mobilising ideas, help, campaigns and innovations. Government without civil society as a strong partner is poor at meeting or even spotting needs." (32)

And as if to summarise the historical movement I have charted out in chapter 7 they say,

"Too big a state crowds out enterprise and initiative. Too big a market crowds out compassion and co-operation.... (32)

It is in civil society that we see many of the qualities needed to address what has been thrown up by decades of market thinking,

"After a period when public debate has been dominated by the idea that people are at root selfish, acquisitive and materialistic, there is now a much more realistic appreciation that they are just as likely to be altruistic, compassionate and social, and that a good society finds outlets for these motives. It is in civil society that people's values of care, compassion, equality, solidarity and justice find their best expression. Civil society is where we express 'we' rather than just 'me', where we act with others rather than only doing things for them or to them." (33)

Just as initiatives and projects in the direction of teal are emerging in business and the state, in civil society such developments are emerging in greater numbers.

Place matters. Some communities have a very special genesis. Like the community on the island of Eigg. They bought their island in 1998! (34). Staying with the sea, Malcolm Baker is `the last fisherman` i.e. traditional fisher of the Rame peninsula, Cornwall. An unlikely friendship with an Australian youth worker led to young people spending time with Malcolm to mutual benefit. They communicate the whole experience in a film (35). On the Kennet and Avon canal the `liveaboard` community is now substantial and organised (36). When you live on a narrow boat you know the value of water and energy. In an urban context The Katherine Low settlement has an exemplary record of serving its local community for over 90 years (37). The Nottingham School of Boxing has been set up to help young people across the city build confidence, tolerance, discipline, respect, and self-esteem. It has saved peoples lives as they have become involved with a positive community of young people led by inspiring role models (38). There is more great leadership and community from the Manhood Academy with their tag line of `boys are born, men are made`, they are teaching black youth to become men and they are over-subscribed (39).

Civil society does not neglect children. Playing Out is a,

"parent and resident led movement restoring children's freedom to play out in the streets and spaces where they live, for their health, happiness and sense of belonging " (40).

Discover Children's Story Centre is a place where children and their families can enjoy playing, learning and making up stories together. They are creating a love of language, literature and stories with 0-11 year-olds and their families (41). Fun Palaces are by no means children only. It has evolved into *a campaign for cultural democracy, with an annual weekend of action every October"* (42).

It is in civil society that older people and very young children are being brought together for mutual benefit (43). A community within a community is the Glastonbury steward's team, who have learnt to improvise in order to keep a very large festival safe (44). The creativity and inventiveness of civil society is expressed too in Maslaha, tackling issues affecting Muslim communities (45). The murder of Jo Cox has led to extensive efforts to help repair the social fabric and combat loneliness (46). It was not government that supported victims of the Manchester arena attack, it was the international Peace Centre in Warrington (47).

Repair has also been taken literally by Farnham's Repair Café, one of 1,595 across the world (48). Fixing things for free has meant 2 tons diverted from landfill and saved people £40,000 in buying new products. Inventiveness knows no boundaries with the Hoe Street 'bank' in Walthamstow. This is a community run project aiming to be the forerunners of a larger movement of debt abolition. (49)

Civil society truly is the earth of creativity.

By outlining these three elements of a civil society centred Britain we can begin to see the value of local assemblies bringing together business, the state and civil society. Imagine Walthamstow's debt abolition, the community shop, and a freed-up benefits system putting their heads together? Discover Childrens Story Centre speaks to primary schools turning children on to reading and writing. I have given two examples of state services doing local integration, but these could go much further. This bringing together of people across the three parts of the OS is but one extremely beneficial implication a civil society Britain. There is another that I find truly inspirational.

The ripple effects

To have identified the state, business and civil society as central to a country's operating system is one thing. The implication is that *all the other areas of society get affected by that configuration.* My contention is that a civil society centred Britain will really bring new life to agriculture, energy, the environment, transport, exercise, food, science, technology, the media, towns and cities and the arts. We saw the power of thick networks in chapter 4. From small beginnings new things shot off in all directions. Imagine this principle applied to the country itself, changing its configuration and this rippling through, in 'thick network' fashion, to all these other areas. There are already developments going on in all these areas, doing just that. Let us start with agriculture.

A farmer's wife, feeling somewhat isolated, has used social media to bring fellow farmers wives together (50). Suffolk Community Farm has gone in a direction quite a few farms around the country have, opening their doors to their surrounding community,

"We do this by opening up the farm on Sundays 12-4pm to the public, holding workshops for people to take part in planting, letting them help with feeding the animals, or giving them the opportunity to build a bug hotel or bird box for their garden. To compliment this, we sell the excess produce that has been grown or produced on the farm, offer a place for refreshments and children to play in the open air whilst at the same time employing local people to make all this happen". (51)

They want to make a difference to the quality of life of the people in the community around the farm, *"Imagine if we had a community farm in every village or town – what a difference that would make!"*.

There are also eco villages, setting out to create alternative models for living on the land. Lammas as their website says, *"empowers people to explore what it is to live a one-planet lifestyle. It demonstrates that alternatives are possible here and now." (52)*

Riverford is making the transition from conventional ownership to employee ownership. As of June 2018, the 4 organic farms providing 50,000 vegetable boxes a week to households all over the country became 74% employee owned. The community of people doing this held their own launch festival. The person most in that teal-like CEO role, Guy Singh-Watson keeps pushing for Riverford to be a force for good. They run the farms on people power as they grow over 100 types of vegetable. There is no spraying to meet the supermarket requirements. They are completely independent. They have higher productivity, higher morale, and less debt. The farms are in a constant process of transformation. Guy's take on it all is,

"Most people are better, kinder, less greedy, and have more to give than our institutions allow them to demonstrate. We will help Riverford staff build the confidence to be the best possible versions of ourselves" (53)

Farms these days can go in any number of directions. Apsley, was a 400-hectare arable farm which would have been able to support 1-2 employees at most and break even. Instead it grows whole crop rye, maize, and sugar beet to feed a biogas plant. Apsley buys in crops from 43 other farms, making quite a community. It generates enough bio-methane to power 8000 home continuously. It generates electricity back into the grid. It sells on substantial amounts of C02. The bi-products become valuable fertiliser. Doing this employs 17 staff. Its probably not super teal, but they are responsibly generating and circulating wealth as a by-product of producing something well, that is needed. They recognise they are part of a larger whole (54).

Energy generating comes in all sorts of shapes and sizes. Temple Guiting took on the challenge as a village to try to become self-sufficient in electricity. It is very heart-warming to see an entire community working through the challenges with just the right kind of leadership (55). Energy4All serves 23 renewable energy co-ops around the UK with a combined membership of 23,000. This is some community, *"We have only just scratched the surface of the potential for community ownership of renewables in the UK. "* (56)

There is, in Britain, a people powered movement for trees and woods (57). It was launched on 6th November 2017, the 800th anniversary of the 1217 Charter of the Forest,

"More than 70 organisations and 300 local community groups worked together to help people across the UK to demonstrate the important role that trees play in their lives. These helped to define the 10 Principles of the Tree Charter, ... The Tree Charter has been supported by over 130,000 people and has been backed by ... ... community groups, schools, councils, celebrities and artists. Collectively, we've created something beautiful and inspiring which shows the love and respect felt for trees and makes a commitment to changing their future for the better."(57)

The Ellen McArthur Foundation is finding their ideas of how to create a `circular economy` are more and more being taken up (58). Isla bikes for one does so. And Apsley farm probably does.

How to combine keeping fit with repairing the social fabric? The GoodGym has found a way,

"We are a community of runners that combine getting fit with doing good. We stop off on our runs to do physical tasks for community organisations and to support isolated older people with social visits and one-off tasks they can't do on their own. It's a great way to get fit, meet new people and do some good. " (59)

In Todmorden it has been growing food that has brought amazing transformations: Incredible Edible. Watch Pam Warhurst`s video. This is her opening line, *"The will to live life differently can start in the most unusual places"* (60). Todmorden is a market town of 50,000 in the north of England. Now fruit, veg and herbs are sprouting up all over the place: in the railway station car park, in front of the police station and health centre, on canal towpaths and even in cemeteries,

"We are doing it because we want to start a revolution. Can you find a unifying language that cuts across age, income, and culture that will help people

themselves find a new way of living, see spaces around them differently, use resources differently, interact differently. ...the language is food" (60)

Incredible Edible was launched through a public meeting where they re-imagined life in their town as three spinning plates: community, learning and business plates. If all three could interact,

"We are starting to build resilience ourselves, we are starting to re-invent community ourselves, and we have done it all without a flipping strategy document...I have seen the power of small actions and it is awesome" (60)

If you think George Monbiot's example of Rotterdam's `thick network` was a one off, forget it. Incredible Edible does just that. One thing leads to another until all three of these plates are spinning. Thirty towns in Britain have got Incredible Edible at various stages.

BARN (Broadband for the Rural North) started with a hairdresser finding that their village needed a cabinet to get superfast broadband, which it didn't have (61). Satellite was ridiculously expensive. Eight villages grouped together raised funds and became shareholders in BARN. Access to farm land to dig trenches for cables was free. When BARN had reached its 600th customer it got its first employee, who was of course local. In the last 5 years they have got to 5,000 connected properties and employ 25 people. Neighbours, businesses, schools and many other organisations are connecting with pride. They all care for `their` network. Is there a capacity here to change rural economies? High tech jobs in a rural economy? In the substantial area covered by BARN young people feel they can stay where they are to run their own businesses.

Staying with technology, Simon Reeve's Big Life Fix has run two TV series where technically talented individuals create tailored aids for someone who, through disability, chronic untreatable ill health or a condition, is excluded from living anything resembling a normal life (62). This is a Britain fulfilling more of its potential.

The special place of the arts and culture

As we can see from the above many of us have indeed been fashioning something completely different from what our orange macro world would have us think, become and do. Within civil society, in Britain, at this time, I think the arts have a special role. Although politics and economics dominate the news, the centre of gravity, so far as individual lives are concerned, has shifted. Politics and economics do not equate with *giving free, unfettered play to one's unique talents or living with the full radiance of one's being!* In Britain, there is a shift going on away from politics and economics and towards culture and the arts and it is very much youth who are leading this. This is creating a civil society Britain.

It is not through market thinking that lives are touching one another. It is culture and the arts that are shaping the age precisely because they touch people's lives, enable new thoughts and awareness, and transform the human heart. The four quadrants connect and a whole way of living is born which satisfies the human heart, enables the individual to move forward in their lives with vitality and a constantly developing sense of meaning and purpose.

This is existential freedom. I can become who I can be. What is driving the age has moved on to this fuller human freedom: giving free play to my abilities and really living my life. This is being alive in a more complex and connected way. To that extent there is a really new kind of humanism afoot.

I am talking especially about music, writing, TV, the web, film, podcasts, performance, religion/spiritual teachings as well as all the arts. All these are experienced in civil society and the civil society on the web. People can connect like never before: on a scale, with an intensity and with a frequency not previously possible.

Art and culture have the power to unite people in spirit. Cultural events and activities assume a confidence in people's capacity for positive transformation. It is human beings who possess the wisdom to grasp the conditions they are experiencing. Culture and the arts feed and expand this capacity. They are offering a more advanced consciousness.

People can quickly find sources of internal growth and stimulation. We can all find books, courses, classes, concerts, performances, festivals, galleries, meetings and gatherings of all kinds. These are the sites of this new humanism. We can consolidate and further explore on our own through reading, surfing, listening/watching with headphones etc. We can share our discoveries, insights and understandings readily through social media.

It is youth who are at the forefront of this. At their most positive, we have a generation that values their own lives, their personal integrity, wants to be of benefit to others, wants what they do to benefit the environment *and* bring social benefit, *and* wants good organisation (with good tech built in).

Britain has novelists, playwrights, musicians, sculptors, painters and artists. This isn't just elite stuff. This is a country with the Royal Academy summer exhibition woven into the culture. Where would pop music be without Britain? Apparently, there are 1200 part-time bands in the UK. But if you want to go professional there is BIMM, the British and Irish Modern Music Institute,

"(BIMM) has colleges in eight cities where music matters most – London, Berlin, Dublin, Manchester, Bristol, Brighton, Birmingham and Hamburg – and is proud to be the largest and leading provider of contemporary music education in Europe."(63)

On the theatre front, repertory has come back to the Everyman in Liverpool (but `drama` is conspicuously absent from the vast majority of our schools). In the midst of public sector austerity, Tate Modern has spent £260 million (of which £58 million came from the public purse). The response: not 2 million visitors as expected, but 6 million! Tate Modern reaches out and nurtures artists (64). The arts are so vibrant in Britain, that new initiatives are springing up all the time, like the Chaiya Arts Awards (65), displaying really interesting, thought provoking works of art.

Symbolic of all this is the annual Edinburgh Festival Fringe, offering complete freedom. It nurtures the talent of the future and keeps things moving on (66). The Manchester International Festival is about building communities of support and entirely new works (67).

We have some very socially aware artists. For example, for a fusion of personal development, community developing and art, Grayson Perry, with his All Man performance pieces, wonderfully communicated with people in pain and confusion, not least men trying to surface their feelings without destroying themselves (68)

For those with the arts bug, if you can get into the BRIT school, with superb facilities, you can pursue your arts passion *and* get an education (69). The Northern School of contemporary dance, for over 30 years, has been a powerhouse of dance in this country. Their values are yelling the fostering of their version of a teal consciousness,

- *"The transformative power of dance and arts education; to uplift, inspire, stimulate our emotions and help us create a tolerant and cohesive society.*
- *Inclusive learning and collaboration in a spirit of mutual respect and generosity.*
- *Curiosity, self-reflection and open-mindedness*
- *Creative risk taking, innovation and investment in on-going artist and artform development*
- *Aspiration, self-motivation and dedication in striving for excellence*
- *Diversity – our differences as well as the things that we have in common, and that diversity inspires creativity and enriches our lives*
- *Our relationship to local, regional, national and international communities and the wider dance ecology*
- *The nurturing and investment that leads to independence and resilience*
- *Using resources in a way that is responsible and environmentally sustainable"* *(70)*

If you live in a town like Skipton you may find yourself out on the streets dancing. The market town did its very own dance spectacular led by Steve Elias. Have a look at the BBC film (71).

I am unable to get a reliable figure for the total number of choirs or choruses of all kinds in the UK. It is substantial. Gareth Malone has been bringing this to our attention on TV. If you are a student at a university, joining a choir will probably be an option. In fact, there are young farmers choirs too. The homeless literally have a voice through the Choir with No Name (72).

I think we can safely say that the culture/arts teal presence in Britain is being maintained and developed as a force in the country by significant institutions, structures, practices and processes.

To conclude

We have three ways to live in this world according to Tsunesaburo Makiguchi a pioneer of humanistic education in Japan in the early 20th century. The first is a dependent way of life where,

"...we are typically unable to sense our own potential, giving up any real possibility of transforming our situation, passively accommodating to others, immediate surroundings and the larger trends in society" (73)

There is also an independent way of life where,

"...people have the desire to find their own way forward but then have little interest in those with whom they are not directly involved. They are quick to assume that however trying the circumstances of another person, it is up to that person to find a solution through their own efforts" (74)

Britain certainly has a good number of people living these kinds of lives. Makiguchi illustrated this second, independent way of life with the example of someone placing a large stone on a railway track (75). This obviously is a highly destructive and negative act. If, knowing the stone is there, you fail to act and remove the stone, the train will be derailed. Not taking action (i.e. not doing good) amounts to perpetrating the destructive and negative. This very much is the mainstream ethical climate of Britain today, as well as the ambience and morals of the current spirit of the times. Seeming independence through individualism can actually mean isolation and indifference.

Makiguchi asserted that the way of life to strive for is a contributive one,

"..the world is a web of relationality in which nothing can be completely disassociated from anything else. Moment by moment the world is formed and shaped through mutual relatedness. When we understand this and can see in the depths of our being the fact that we live-that our existence is made possible-within this web of relatedness, we see clearly there is no happiness that only we enjoy, no suffering that afflicts only others....we ourselves- in the place where we are at this moment-become the starting point of a chain reaction of positive transformation. We are able to not only resolve our personal challenges but also

make a contribution to moving our immediate environment and even human society in a better direction" (76)

I had an experience of this when I got off a train in Bodmin, Cornwall to stay with a friend in Wadebridge for the weekend. He picked me up, and we turned the corner to find the usual road to the station blocked off for road works. All the traffic to and from the station was being redirected up one very narrow country lane with hardly any passing places. Cars were gingerly inching along until the whole thing just ground to a halt. My friend and I sat there, like everybody else, for a while, waiting for `someone` to get things moving. But nothing happened. We all just carried on sitting still in our cars. This for me is like orange Britain: concerned with the immediate, unaware that our self-centred micro reactions create collective realities.

Then my friend and I decided to get out and see what could be done, he went back towards the station and I went the other way, in the direction we were trying to go. As I walked along I spoke with every single driver. If there was a way to get out of the jam each driver said they would do it. I said I would come back to them. When I eventually got to the last car, I saw it could reverse and there was space to turn round. So, I asked that driver to do just that. And the next driver and the next driver until the jam started to free up and people could drive through. By then I was back at my friend's car, he had come back and was astonished. I felt *great!* It had been a real adventure and dramatically changed something involving lots of people, all of whom had been very grateful and wanted to help once they saw there was a way to resolve the situation. It made the weekend. This is teal Britain: people connecting well with one another, building trust, using leadership well, creating unity and feeling great.

This is such a story of our times. Ultimately this is the bedrock of transition: a kind of lived experience, where we free ourselves by engaging with others and they feel great because we have engaged with them and they with others, and as a result something of collective benefit is created. It can be in virtually any context that this becomes the central dynamic. This is not hard work. It is a joy. To arrive at a quite different state of affairs in our society is as a result of myriad such micro transitions. Let's hear from Incredible Edible's Pam Warhurst,

"In every single room in every single town that we have ever told our story it has been the same, people are ready and respond.....they want positive actions they can engage in. In their bones they know it is time to take personal responsibility and invest in more kindness to each other and to the environment" (as 60)

Previous changes in the configuration of power between the state, civil society and business have been engineered by elites. Civil society Britain is coming from the ground, from the people. But it does need leadership.

A civil society Britain depends on leadership with that all-important teal consciousness. Here the American educator, Parker Palmer, may have something to offer. He has worked on leadership through the Centre for Courage and Renewal. The Centre's mission is, *"To nurture personal and professional integrity and the courage to act on it"* (77). It has worked with over *40,000* leaders, and not just business leaders, but leaders of civil society organisations and state services too. The centre forms circles. A circle will be around 25 people who continue to meet together in facilitated programmes and retreats over the course of a year or more. These are safe places where people, who are otherwise strangers to each other, come together to explore their challenges of living in a heartfelt way. This is where they can connect, not just with each other, but with their own inner promptings and tensions. Perhaps we need our equivalent in the UK?

Moving to civil society Britain is a profoundly gradual renaissance. It goes at the pace with which teal consciousness spreads in the population. The impatient will want radical change by imposing a new ideology. And from the standpoint of those for whom Britain has become hell on earth we can see why some might be impatient. But we have been there.

With a radical politics there is always the danger of confusing ideals with substance. Britain today wants substance. I think the most sophisticated appreciation of gradualism comes from Daisaku Ikeda,

"There is a natural relation between rationalism and radicalism. If all events can be understood by rational processes, from which the blueprints for a rationalist utopia can be drawn, theoretically they can be speeded up, and the sooner the utopia is realised, the better. ... .Not only revolutionary radicalism but any worldview that bases itself on 'historical inevitability' fundamentally denies the human capacity to create our own destiny through our own efforts. We must always resist the temptation to treat individual lives or history as mere objective things or facts; their truth can only be known through active, living engagement and participation. To be of real and lasting value, change must be gradual and inspired from within. The application of external force will always destroy some aspect of our total humanity and compromise the balance and integrity of life" (78)

Ken Wilber's colour coded consciousnesses move in an upward, progressive direction (even if the politicians of nation-states drag their countries back in time!!!). For teal to become the leading edge of British politics means Britain being in sync with the general trend in humanity. Teal consciousness and what members of SGI-UK identify as the Buddha state inherent in all life, share much in common. The Buddhist humanism referred to in the book's opening dedication/quote is nothing but fundamental respect for all people. This is a natural accompaniment to cultures of thinking, being and doing.

The roots of the current shift into the next consciousness are deep and go back a long way in human history. In writing this book I have taken one of Nichiren's most famous writings, written in 1260, *"Establishing the Correct Teaching for the Peace of the Land",* as the model for a political writing from a Buddhist (79). The intention behind the word `correct` is humanistic and universal. What distinguishes this writing is its focus on `reforming the tenets we hold in our hearts` as the basis for peace in the world. Lacking this government is overwhelmed by what is coming from the lives of the people, even to the extent that it cannot really govern. This is part of what I see happening in Britain today, with the additional complication that the `tenets` government holds dearly are precisely the kind of thinking designed to aggravate the negative in what is `coming from the lives of the people`.

If we take any country in the world, each is subject to and has to respond to forces, developments and pressures coming from outside its borders. Britain is certainly no exception. The *greatest* freedom and power to shape what it is like to live in Britain comes from within our borders: from within the lives of the people. *The Britain Potential* is in our hands.

Notes

Websites were accessed between June 2017 and June 2018

Introduction

(1) See for example Ken Wilber and others. Integral Life Practice. Integral Books. 2008.

(2) Frederic Laloux. Reinventing Organizations. Nelson Parker. 2014.

(3) George Monbiot. Out of the Wreckage. Verso. 2017.

(4) See www.sgi.org. Also Clark Strand was for many years at the centre of Buddhism of many kinds in America. His account of the SGI movement called Waking the Buddha (Middleway Press. 2014) shows what a broad empowering movement this is and how it is changing the concept of religion.

(5) See www.sgi-uk.org

(6) See http://localtrust.org.uk/ . In July 2018 18 months worth of research by IVAR into the future of communities was published by Local Trust as a report: The Future for Communities. Available here http://localtrust.org.uk/library/research-and-evaluation/the-future-for-communities. There are also sites run by practitioners like Gemma Novis. See https://www.thefourcorners.org.uk/

(7) The roots of this go back 3,000 or so years to a teaching called The Lotus Sutra (pub Soka Gakkai. 2009). This explained that it was not just `the Buddha` who has the high state of life called Buddha. It is inherent in all people and all of life. It is the cosmic connecting life force of the universe. As Buddhism moved from India to China, during the 6th century Tien t`ai systematised the Lotus Sutra into the theory underpinning the SGI practice: three thousand worlds in a single moment of life. For a more detailed explanation of the mechanics of life please have a look at https://sgi-uk.org/Philosophy/History/T-ien-t-ai.

1 Potential and consciousness

(1) Frederic Laloux. Reinventing Organizations. Nelson Parker. 2014.pg 46

(2) Undoing the Demos. Wendy Brown. Zone Books. 2015: Pg 221

(3) See for example Ken Wilber and others. Integral Life Practice. Integral Books. 2008

(4) Sarah Wider in The Art of True Relations. Sarah Wider and Daisaku Ikeda. Dialogue Path Press. 2014. Pg 157

(5) http://www.thehorsecourse.org/

(6) Art of Living. Issue no 181. SGI-UK. July 2016: pg 31. To get back copies of the Art of Living go to www.sgi-uk.org and click on the shop

(7) Parker Palmer. Healing the Heart of Democracy. 2011. Jossey-Bass. Pg 18

(8) Richard Dagger. Civic Virtues. 1997. Oxford University Press. Pgs 38-39

(9) https://www.centreforsocialjustice.org.uk/policy/breakthrough-britain/family-breakdown

(10) New Scientist. 3rd January 2009: pg 25

(11) https://www.sheffield.ac.uk/psychology/staff/academic/peter-totterdell

(12) http://nottinghamtrent.academia.edu/JulietWakefield

(13) From project notes compiled in 1978/9 of fieldwork between 1974 and 1978.

(14) http://localtrust.org.uk/library/research-and-evaluation/the-future-for-communities

(15) The figures I have used here are:

Companies	State	Civil society	
1.3 million private sector **employing** businesses (a)	418 councils	160,000 voluntary organisations (b)	
70,000 social enterprises	9,061 NHS organisations		
6,500 co-ops	20,512 schools, colleges, universities		
	163 criminal justice organisations		
			totals
1,376,500	30,155	160,000	1.5+million

(a)There are 5.4 million private sector businesses, 4.1 million of which are just the owner.

(b)The 160,000 figure is a gross understatement being just the number of registered charities. A figure of 400,000 is suggested: see https://www.civilsociety.co.uk/voices/there-are-more-than-twice-as-many-charities-in-the-uk-as-you-ve-been-told.html

(16) Frederic Laloux. Reinventing Organizations. Nelson Parker. 2014: Pgs 3-4

(17) A talk at the Royal Society for the Arts entitled a new politics in an age of crisis. July 5th 2018. Video available here https://www.thersa.org/events/2018/07/a-new-politics-for-an-age-of-crisis

(18) New Economics Foundation, reported on the 28th March 2017, see http://neweconomics.org/2017/03/brexit-poll-control-crisis/?_sft_latest=press-releases

(19) Ken Wilber and others. Integral Life Practice. Integral Books. 2008

(20) Wilber and others. Pg 74

(21) Wilber and others. Pg 94

(22) Ilya Prigogine and Isabelle Stengers. Order out of Chaos. Bantam Books. 1984

2 Market based Britain

(1) The Spirit Level. Richard Wilkinson and Kate Pickett. 2009. Penguin.

(2) Paul Verhaeghe. What About Me? Scribe. 2014. David Marquand. Mammon`s Kingdom. Penguin. 2013. George Monbiot. Out of the Wreckage. Verso. 2017.

(3) Brian Robertson. Holacracy.2015. Penguin. Pg 11

(4) See the Guardian 3rd December 2012, https://www.theguardian.com/money/2012/dec/03/richest-10-uk-households-40-per-cent-wealth-ons and also the Daily Mail on 7th June 2017, http://www.dailymail.co.uk/news/article-3365981/Gap-Britain-s-rich-poor-soars-5trillion-wealthiest-assets-soar-21-cent.html

(5) Figures from the Money Advice Service. Reported by BBC News 29th September 2016, http://www.bbc.co.uk/news/business-37504449

(6) http://www.bbc.co.uk/news/business-38534238

(7) See Wikipedia https://en.wikipedia.org/wiki/Poverty_in_the_United_Kingdom. It is nurses, supermarket staff, and soldiers most turning to payday lenders. Figures from CashLady for the first half of 2017

(8) The report of the Malnutrition Task Force is reported at http://home.bt.com/news/uk-news/dismay-as-meals-on-wheels-axed-for-46000-older-people-in-last-three-years-11364016273544

(9) Reported 19th June 2016, http://www.express.co.uk/news/uk/681367/NHS-Scotland-cuts-spending-funding-lives-risk-Nicola-Sturgeon-Royal-College-Nursing

(10) Reported by BBC News 8th November 2016, http://www.bbc.co.uk/news/uk-england-37896836

(11) Reported on BBC News 20th November 2013 and see pressreader https://www.pressreader.com/uk/yorkshire-post/20160930/281505045710007 for details of the 40,000

(12) http://www.just-fair.co.uk/reports

(13) Reported in House of Commons Briefing Paper 02110 7th January 2016

(14) Reported in the Guardian on 25th January 2017,
https://www.theguardian.com/society/2017/jan/25/number-of-rough-sleepers-in-england-rises-for-sixth-successive-year

(15) There are many sources for this. The Mind website (/www.mind.org.uk) has a `mental health facts and statistics` page.

(16) NHS Digital released this data in June 2017. It was reported in the I 30-06-17

(17) Institute of Race Relations, http://www.irr.org.uk/research/statistics/racial-violence/

(18) 16th October 2014 Home Office Statistical Bulletin: Hate Crimes England and Wales, 2013/14

(19) An OECD survey reported by the world economic forum,
https://www.weforum.org/agenda/2016/12/if-you-live-in-a-nordic-country-then-you-probably-trust-others-a-mediterranean-country-forget -it. See also the World Happiness Report 2017.

(20) The survey is reported on the LSE website, http://blogs.lse.ac.uk/politicsandpolicy/the-great-british-class-survey/ . Guy Standing`s two most recent books on the Precariat are The Precariat. (2012) London: Bloomsbury Academic. And the Precariat Charter. (2014). Same publisher.

(21) Reported on the engaged employees page of the Gallup website,
http://www.gallup.com/services/190118/engaged-workplace.aspx

(22) Data from http://www.ukpublicspending.co.uk/

(23) In November 2015 £742 billion was going on public spending of which: £217 billion went on the benefit system; £117 billion on the NHS; £58 billion on education. Source: Budget statement to the House of Commons.

(24) https://www.theguardian.com/education/2015/aug/25/fine-schools-pupils-fail-gcse-maths-english-policy-exchange

(25) http://www.dailymail.co.uk/news/article-2571888/Thousands-families-face-inflation-busting-rises-parking-pest-control-year-one-council-planning-charge-parents-children-care.html

(26) https://www.theguardian.com/law/2015/dec/03/michael-gove-scraps-criminal-courts-charge

(27) http://www.pulsetoday.co.uk/your-practice/practice-topics/pay/uber-style-private-gp-appointment-service-primed-for-national-rollout/20032808.article

(28) George Ritzer: The McDonaldization of Society: 20th Anniversary Edition (2012); The Globalization of Nothing, Second Edition (2007); Enchanting a Disenchanted World, Third Edition (2009)

(29) https://en.wikipedia.org/wiki/Iron_cage

(30) Jean Boulton et al. Embracing Complexity. 2015. OUP. Pg 1

3 Family support

(1) Peter Berger. Facing up to Modernity:Excursions in Society, Politics, and Religion. Penguin. 1979. Pg 33.

(2) See the Guardian 26th November 2016, https://www.theguardian.com/society/2016/nov/26/ does-britain-take-too-many-children-into-care ALSO the CPAG website http://www.cpag.org.uk/child-poverty-facts-and-figures

(3) The `bank of mum and dad` was reported in the Financial Times 1st may 2017. https://www.ft.com/content/0bd5e826-2e49-11e7-9555-23ef563ecf9a. The budget speech is here https://www.gov.uk/government/speeches/autumn-budget-2017-philip-hammonds-speech

(4) http://www.adfam.org.uk/cms/docs/adfam_troubledfamilies.pdf

(5) https://www.theguardian.com/society/2014/jun/15/david-cameron-flagship-scheme-troubled-families

(6) http://www.adfam.org.uk/cms/docs/adfam_troubledfamilies.pdf

(7) All Participle related material including Relational Welfare available from their learning from their 10 years posted at http://www.participle.net/

(8) All material about family groups comes from the authors project papers and notes.

(9) Shirley Otto has remained focused on 3rd sector issues offering independent research and training.

(10) Homestart has a site at https://www.home-start.org.uk/

4 Networks and communities

(1) http://4freedoms.com/group/alinsky/forum/topics/alinsky-interview-with-playboy-magazine

(2) Madsen Pirie. Think Tank. Biteback.2012: pg 16

(3) Madsen Pirie. Pg 15

(4) The Future for Communities. IVAR. Local Trust. 2018. pg 7. See note 6 introduction.

(5) The Future for Communities. pg 56

(6) The Future for Communities. pg 57

(7) All material about the Estate comes from the authors project papers and notes.

(8) Sylvia Plath. The Bell Jar. Harper Perennial. 2006 . First published in 1963.

(9) All material about the Anti-racist network comes from the authors project papers and notes.

(10) https://www.waterstones.com/book/why-im-no-longer-talking-to-white-people-about-race/reni-eddo-lodge/9781408870587.

(11) Chantal Mouffe. Hegemony, Radical Democracy, and the Political. Ed James Martin. Routledge.2013.pg 204

(12) Cedric Robinson. Black Marxism. Zed books. 1983.

(13) Visit this Wikipedia entry for more information:
https://en.wikipedia.org/wiki/Hannah_Arendt

(14) Eds Ashok Ohri, Basil Manning, Paul Curno. Community Work and Racism. Routledge. 1982.

(15) Herman Ouseley. The System. Runnymede Trust and the South London Equal Rights Consultancy. No date.

(16) Peter Fryer. Staying Power. Pluto. 1984.

(17) Louis Fischer. The Life of Mahatma Gandhi. Harper Collins. 1997.

(18) Project notes

(19) Michel de Certeau. The Practice of Everyday Life. University of California Press. Trans Rendall, S. 1984. Pg xiv

(20) George Monbiot. Out of the Wreckage. Verso. 2017. Pgs 79-83

(21) Monbiot. Pg 20

5 Better organisations

(1) Frederic Laloux. Reinventing Organizations. Nelson Parker. 2014: Pg 3

(2) Frederic Laloux. pg 26

(3) Frederic Laloux: pg 27

(4) Frederic Laloux: pg 28

(5) https://www.youtube.com/watch?v=BeOrNjwHw58

(6) Frederic Laloux: pg 68

(7) Frederic Laloux: pg 151

(8) See, for example, Ken Wilber. The Integral Vision. Shambhala. 2007. Also Trump and the Post Truth World. Penguin. 2017

(9) View expressed by Laloux in the 6 dialogues published on the Integral Life site
https://integrallife.com/reinventing-organizations/

(10) Frederic Laloux: pg 156

(11) www.sgi-uk.org

(12) Theory of life developed in the 6th century in China by Tien T`ai. For more see
https://sgi-uk.org/Philosophy

(13) Richard Seager. Encountering the Dharma. University of California Press. 2006

(14) http://www.daisakuikeda.org/

(15) Arnold Toynbee and Daisaku Ikeda. Choose Life. Oxford University Press. 1976

(16) https://www.soka.ac.jp/en/ and http://www.soka.edu/

(17) http://www.daisakuikeda.org/sub/resources/records/degree/list-of-conferrals.html

(18) Details of the Human Revolution at http://www.daisakuikeda.org/sub/books/books-by-category/diaries-novels/human_revolution.html. Details of the New Human Revolution at
http://www.daisakuikeda.org/sub/books/books-by-category/diaries-novels/new-human-revolution.html

(19) There is a good introduction to Goffman`s Asylums at
https://en.wikipedia.org/wiki/Asylums_(book)

(20) Authors project notes

6 Politics

(1) Shotter, J. (2004a) Wittgenstein's philosophy and action research. IN Concepts and
Transformations, Vol 8 No 3, 295-301

(2) Shotter, J. (1997). The Social Construction of our Inner Selves. Journal of Constructivist
Psychology. Vol 10: Pg 15

(3) John Stewart. The New Management of Local Government. Allen and Unwin. 1986.

(4) Undoing the Demos. Wendy Brown. Zone Books. 2015: Pg 88

(5) David Marquand. Mammon`s Kingdom. Penguin. 2015. Pg 217

(6) http://localtrust.org.uk/

(7) https://www.transitionnetwork.org/

(8) The East London Communities Organisation (TELCO for short), reflects the kind of
community organising Saul Alinsky advocated. See this entry in Wikipedia:
https://en.wikipedia.org/wiki/Saul_Alinsky. A key text is Reveille for Radicals.

(9) http://iffrome.org.uk/

(10) http://www.totnespulse.co.uk/devon-united-doing-democracy-differently-by-pam-barrett/

(11) https://p2pfoundation.net/

(12) www.labgov.it/2017/01/25/bologna-as-a-laboratory-for-urban-commons-urban-change-talk-berlin/

(13) Laloux. Pgs 279-282.

(14) Su Maddock. Making Modernisation Work: New Narratives, Change Strategies and People Management in the Public Sector. The International Journal of Public Sector Management. 2002. Vol 15 No 1: 13-43

(15) Maddock: pg 26

(16) Daisaku Ikeda. Annual Peace Proposal. 2017: pg 3. Available here http://www.sgi.org/content/files/about-us/president-ikedas-proposals/2017-peace-proposal.pdf

(17) John Shotter. Conversational Realities: Constructing Life through Language. Sage: London. 1993, pg 7

(18) See note 13 chapter 1

(19) Carol Gould. Rethinking Democracy. Cambridge University Press. 1995.

(20) Carol Gould: pg 147

(21) Carol Gould: pg 26

(22) Carol Gould: pg 222

(23) https://www.bbc.co.uk/programmes/b0b2mgjb

(24) https://renewbritain.org/our-vision/

(25) https://www.japansociety.org.uk/event/anne-mette-fisker-nielsen/

(26) Inigo Errejon and Chantal Mouffe. Podemos:in the name of the people. Soundings. 2016.

(27) https://services.parliament.uk/bills/

(28) George Monbiot refers to this in Out of the Wreckage Pg 141 and references Patrick Fournier and Henk Van Der Halk. When Citizens Decide:Lessons from Citizens Assemblies on Electoral Reform. OUP. 2011.. See also Monbiot pg 155 and 152-3.

7 The historical dimension

(1) Daisaku Ikeda in Sarah Wider and Daisaku Ikeda. The Art of True Relations. Dialogue Path Press. 2014. Pg 15

(2) Professor Jeremy Black Why The Industrial Revolution Happened Here. BBC 4. 7th Jan 2017. http://www.bbc.co.uk/programmes/b01pz9d6

(3) This and following sections draw from Derek Fraser: The Evolution of the British Welfare State. Palgrave. 2003. Especially chapter 5.

(4) Jeremy Rifkin. The Empathic Civilization. Polity Press. 2013. Pg 336

(5) From Derek Fraser note (3) above

(6) Derek Fraser. Pg 120

(7) David Vincent. Poor Citizens. Longmans. 1991. Pg 101

(8) Derek Fraser. Pg 189

(9) Derek Fraser. Pg 190

(10) Keynes was the pre-eminent economist of the welfare state. Keynes theories centred on the state pumping money into the economy during times of depression. His thinking had been adopted by Roosevelt in America. Roosevelt had created a substantial range of government organisations to employ Americans thrown out of work by the great depression. This had enabled the American economy to `survive`. Americans generally wanted a free market economy and so pressure against Roosevelts state centred measures built and built. It was really world war two that took the American economy out of depression. The significance of Keynes returning to Britain was that a) he could `prove` the success of his approach through the American experience b) he was placed right at the heart of government ready to enact similar policies here. But as the American experience suggested, there would always be pressure to make markets central rather than the state.

(11) William Beveridge. Social Insurance and Allied Services.

(12) See this entry in Wikipedia: https://en.wikipedia.org/wiki/Scientific_management

(13) See this entry in Wikipedia: https://en.wikipedia.org/wiki/Rational-legal_authority

(14) See this entry in Wikipedia: https://en.wikipedia.org/wiki/Henri_Fayol

(15) See this entry in Wikipedia:
https://en.wikipedia.org/wiki/Luther_Gulick_(social_scientist)

(16) Daniel Stedman Jones. Masters of the Universe. Princeton University Press. 2012. Pg 2

(17) Friedrich Hayek. The Road to Serfdom. Routledge. 1944.

(18) This is in Hayek`s The Constitution of Liberty.

(19) Stedman Jones pg 4

(20) Stedman Jones pg 80

(21) Stedman Jones. pg 216

(22) Lord Scarman. The Brixton Disorders: 10-12 April 1981. 1981. HMSO.

(23) From a booklet by Nicholas Ridley called The Local Right: Enabling Not Providing. (Centre for Policy Studies Study no 92. 1988) . In it central government signalled a major change for local authorities who were to now regulate and monitor a multitude of services by contracted providers, rather than providing services themselves.

(24) Authors` project papers.

8 The decisive role of the public services

(1) Thomas Sedlacek. Economics of Good and Evil. OUP.2013.pg 320.

(2) The Citizen`s Charter. HMSO. 1991

(3) Council on Social Action 2008. See the archive at http://webarchive.nationalarchives.gov.uk/+/http://www.cabinetoffice.gov.uk/social_action.a spx

(4) Michael Power. The Audit Society. Oxford University Press. 1997. pg123.

(5) Power. pg 13.

(6) See the Office for National Statistics total claimant statistics at https://www.ons.gov.uk/employmentandlabourmarket/peoplenotinwork/outofworkbenefits/ti meseries/bcjd/unem

(7) See https://inews.co.uk/essentials/news/uk/benefit-sanctions-pushing-people-towards-survival-crime/. This study was funded by the Economic and Social Research Council (ESRC) and is reported here http://www.esrc.ac.uk/research/our-research/welfare-conditionality-sanctions-support-and-behaviour-change/

(8) See https://www.theguardian.com/society/2015/jan/20/jobs-revival-benefits-work-jobseekers-allowance

(9) Find the form here https://www.gov.uk/government/publications/capability-for-work-questionnaire

(10) See https://www.christiantoday.com/article/ tens.of.thousands.struggling.over.benefit.delays.christian.mp.reveals/83934.htm

(11) Reported at http://www.bbc.co.uk/news/business-37356646

(12) Paul Verhaeghe. What About Me? Scribe. 2012.Pg227

(13) https://www.ifs.org.uk/uploads/publications/budgets/gb2017/gb2017ch5.pdf

(14) https://www.ifs.org.uk/uploads/publications/bns/BN200.pdf

(15) Henry Marsh. Admission. 2017. Orion Books. Pg 39.

(16) Jean Mathews. Discursive Warfare in the NHS. 2009. 6th Critical Management Studies Conference. University of Warwick

(17) Marsh. pg 42

(18) http://www.rcgp.org.uk/news/2016/september/
patient-safety-in-general-practice-could-be-at-risk-unless-chronic-shortage-of-gps-is-turned-around.aspx
Also https://inews.co.uk/nhs/revealed-nhs-gp-recruitment-crisis-40-approach-retirement/
Also Reported in the Independent, http://www.independent.co.uk/news/uk/politics/
theresa-may-seven-day-week-gp-surgeries-jeremy-hunt-nhs-hospitals-accident-and-emergency-a7526951.html
Also Reported in the Guardian, https://www.theguardian.com/society/2017/may/13/royal-college-nursing-nhs-recruitment-crisis

(19) See pg 16 of
http://www.cqc.org.uk/sites/default/files/20170302b_stateofhospitals_web.pdf. Also
http://www.express.co.uk/news/uk/759804/nhs-crisis-cancelled-operations-highest-on-record

Also This report in the Guardian puts the figure at 380 since 2010,
https://www.theguardian.com/society/2017/jan/11/care-home-closures-funding-crisis. See
also a report in the `I` on 6/7/17 on the Care Quality Commission report on care homes
inspected in the previous 3 years of which 67% were rated as good, 29% requires
improvement and 3% as inadequate.

(20) Paula Hyde and Daniel Madge. The Rational Abuse of Organizations. .2007.5[th] Critical
Management Studies Conference. University of Manchester.

(21) See http://www.publicworld.org/projects/Bringing_Buurtzorg_to_Britain_and_Ireland
...i.e Buurtzorg has trained nurses working in London and West Suffolk. The RSA has been
active in Buurtzorg`s approach being taken up in Britain.

(22) See https://www.theguardian.com/healthcare-network/2015/jul/16/we-wouldnt-go-back-into-the-nhs-plymouths-pioneering-social-enterprise

(23) Kathleen Galvin and Les Todres. Caring and Well-being. Routledge.2013. Pgs 11-12 for
the framework.

(24) Dr Elizabeth Taylor. Getting the Measure of Therapy on Stroke Units. Humanising
Care, Health and Wellbeing conference. Bournemouth University 2017.

(25) To contact the co-ordinator of the network see
https://www1.bournemouth.ac.uk/events/humanising-care-health-wellbeing-conference

(26) http://myhomelife.uws.ac.uk/scotland/

(27) See http://www.imuk.org.uk/families/what-we-do/

(28) See http://www.babicm.org/about-us.html

(29) Paul Verhaeghe. What About Me? Scribe. 2012.Pg226

(30) Verhaeghe.pg 227

(31) August 22nd at 8pm Radio 4 broadcast `The Edge of Life`. See also the website of the Zero Suicide Alliance, a collaboration between NHS Trusts, business and charities https://www.zerosuicidealliance.com/ ....commited to preventing suicide in the UK.

(32) http://www.independent.co.uk/news/uk/home-news/average-house-price-passes-300000-mark-for-the-first-time-a6942946.html

Also http://www.itv.com/news/2017-03-02/new-build-homes-unaffordable-to-80-of-working-families/

Also Help to Buy reported in the `I` 29/5/18. Bank of mum and dad reported in the `I` 29/5/18.

(33) See note 20 chapter 2. The combined figures for the precariat and service sector are 34%

(34) https://www.theguardian.com/society/2016/aug/20/private-landlords-9bn-housing-benefit-taxpayers-national-housing-federation-report

(35) The bus has a website http://thebusshelteriow.co.uk/about-us/. It was reported by the BBC: http://www.bbc.co.uk/news/uk-england-hampshire-38055088

(36) http://www.citizensuk.org/apply_clt_stclements

(37) https://en.wikipedia.org/wiki/Walter_Segal

(38) https://www.theselfbuilder.com/self-build/buildingextending/772-from-kevin-mccloud-july

(39) http://www.owch.org.uk/. it was Tudor Trust together with Hanover Housing that helped them achieve this

(40) https://www.adactushousing.co.uk

(41) A Place of Refuge. Tobias Jones. Quercus. 2015.

(42) https://www.theguardian.com/business/2016/jan/27/legal-general-to-build-and-rent-out-3000-new-uk-homes. And https://www.theguardian.com/business/2010/dec/17/renting-build-to-let-boom

(43) http://www.housing.org.uk/

(44) In 2013 the numbers of state schools funded directly from central government, as academies and free schools, really started to rise. The previous three years the totals were:
        465 in the academic year 2010/11;
        1657 in the academic year 2011/12;
        2804 in the academic year 2012/13.
But by the end of the academic year 2013/14 the total stood at 4,548.

For more data see https://www.local.gov.uk/sites/default/files/documents/academies-and-la-maintain-3ca.pdf

(45) Ken Robinson. Creative Schools. Penguin. 2016. Pgs 9-10.

(46) Robinson. pg 7 PISA Key Findings. From the OECD website

(47) http://www.bbc.co.uk/news/av/uk-wales-38122714/welsh-students-try-south-korea-s-hagwon-night-schools

(48) See https://www.theguardian.com/education/2016/may/06/
government-backs-down-over-plan-to-make-all-schools-academies

(49) http://www.independent.co.uk/news/education/education-news/ nearly-four-in-ten-qualifying-
teachers-quitting-the-classroom-after-one-year-10147043.html

(50) https://www.theguardian.com/education/2014/jan/15/ofsted-chief-teachers-quitting-scandal

(51) http://www.sands-school.co.uk/. There is a video at https://vimeo.com/69974810.

(52) http://www.sands-school.co.uk/

(53) http://www.valuesbasededucation.com/ . Here are some examples and a write up in the
Guardian:www.fieldingprimary.com/values-based-education/ Also
www.ledbury.hereford.sch.uk/values-based-education Also
http://www.downley.bucks.sch.uk/_files/78503BD8369EB3CC42F0717EA90AF2C0.pdf
Also https://www.theguardian.com/education/2012/aug/06/rise-values-based-learning-schools

(54) The school's website is at http://www.fevershamprimaryacademy.org/. Details of the
Kodaly method of children learning to play music is at
https://en.wikipedia.org/wiki/Kodály_method. The school featured on the BBC One Show
on 28/11/17 https://www.bbc.co.uk/iplayer/episode/b09gsfbb/the-one-show-28112017

(55) David Weir and others. The Shudda Brigade. 2007.5[th] Critical Management Studies
Conference. University of Manchester.

(56) http://www.apccs.police.uk/latest_news/budget-cuts-will-radically-change-policing/

(57) This site gives an idea of front line views of currently serving officers in the Met.
https://www.glassdoor.co.uk/Reviews/Metropolitan-Police-Service-work-life-balance-
Reviews-EI_IE241763.0,27_KH28,45.htm

(58) http://www.independent.co.uk/news/uk/crime/prisoners-being-left-in-squalid-
courtroom-cells-by-private-escort-companies-and-told-they-have-only-a6723336.html

(59) https://www.nao.org.uk/wp-content/uploads/2016/03/Efficiency-in-the-criminal-justice-
system.pdf Also https://www.theguardian.com/uk-news/2016/may/27/justice-system-
failing-witnesses-victims-crime

(60) http://news.sky.com/story/uk-has-highest-prison-population-in-the-eu-report-says-
10801556 Also Patrick Coburn in The `I` 17th June 2017 pg 20

(61) http://howardleague.org/news/prisonofficernumberscut/

(62) https://www.bbc.co.uk/programmes/p03y1s83

(63) https://www.theguardian.com/society/2001/feb/02/crime.penal5. See also Noel Smith. A Rusty Gun

(64) https://www.bbc.co.uk/programmes/b06jmbv7

(65) John Braithwaite. Crime, Shame and Reintegration Cambridge University Press. 1989. https://www.researchgate.net/profile/Gerry_Johnstone

(66) See note 5 chapter 5

(67) Project notes

(68) Ralph Stacey. Managing Chaos. Kogan Page. 1992.

9 Civil society Britain

(1) Frederic Laloux: pg 285

(2) Darren McGarvey. Poverty Safari. Luath Press. 2017. Pg 200

(3) Daisaku Ikeda. Selected Lectures on the Gosho. NSIC. 1979. Pg 106

(4) http://www.chobani.com/story

(5) https://www.theguardian.com/sustainable-business/2017/sep/01/meet-the-uk-energy-company-that-will-give-profits-back-to-customers

(6) https://www.riversimple.com/

(7) http://www.islabikes.co.uk/why-islabikes. Have a look at their imagine project. http://www.islabikes.co.uk/imagineproject

(8) Brian Robertson. Holacracy.2015. Penguin. In June of 2015, Robertson released a book, Holacracy: The New Management System for a Rapidly Changing World, that details and explains the practices of Holacracy

(9) http://www.holacracy.org/constitution

(10) https://www.ft.com/content/bf358e0e-1f36-11e5-ab0f-6bb9974f25d0

(11) https://www.legislation.gov.uk/ukpga/2004/27/contents

(12) Community Interest Company Association, 2016. What is a CIC? (online) Available at http://www.cicassociation.org.uk/about/whatis-a-cic

(13) http://www.thirdsector.co.uk/analysis-rise-rise-community-interest-companies/governance/article/1348096

(14) https://www.companyshop.co.uk/community-shop/

(15) https://www.uk.coop/

(16) Here are some examples: Wilkin & Sons, employee owned since 1989; Gripple, employee owned since 2011; Union Industries, employee owned since 2014; Childbase Partnership, employee owned since 2000; Cambridge Weight Plan, employee owned since 2014.

(17) Details at https://www.riverford.co.uk/aboutus/employee-ownership

(18) http://www.enliveningedge.org/about/ This is a community whose aim is to nourish the growing ecosystem of teal organisations

(19) See https://www.theguardian.com/tv-and-radio/2017/jun/15/the-passengers-that-took-on-the-train-line-review-fascinating-journey-to-inevitable-disappointment

(20) George Monbiot. Out of the Wreckage. Verso. 2017. Pg 156

(21) Monbiot. Pg 128

(22) Monbiot. Pg 129

(23) https://robinhoodenergy.co.uk/. Provides energy across Nottingham (and beyond) at the lowest possible price

(24) https://www.scotsman.com/news/gavin-mccrone-shetland-shows-the-way-to-oil-wealth-1-1803090.

(25) https://www.yeovilhospital.co.uk/patients-visitors/symphony-care-hub/ . Same day assessment, treatment and returning home. If not possible the NHS rents a floor in a care home for people not ready to go home.

(26) https://www.dorsethealthcare.nhs.uk/about-us/news-events/press/new-care-hub-transforms-services-people-weymouth-and-portland

(27) https://www.linkedin.com/company/armitage-foundation/

(28) http://www.actiononviolence.org.uk/

(29) https://www.theguardian.com/news/2018/jul/24/violent-crime-cured-rather-than-punished-scottish-violence-reduction-unit

(30) http://servsussex.org.uk/ SERV Riders and drivers volunteer their time, petrol and use of their vehicle to transport emergency blood and blood products to hospitals throughout Sussex.

(31) https://www.swast.nhs.uk/news/THORNCOMBE-FIRST-RESPONDERS-CELEBRATE-20-YEARS.htm)

(32) https://www.carnegieuktrust.org.uk/publications/making-good-society/ Pg 147 of the report

(33) https://www.carnegieuktrust.org.uk/publications/making-good-society/ Pg 148

(34) http://www.isleofeigg.org/

(35) https://lastfisherman.co.uk/

(36) http://kanda.boatingcommunity.org.uk/tag/liveaboards/ This is a community living sustainability

(37) http://www.klsettlement.org.uk/ Building stronger communities by tackling poverty

(38) http://www.nottinghamschoolofboxing.co.uk/

(39) http://www.manhoodacademy.co.uk/

(40) http://playingout.net/.

(41) http://www.discover.org.uk/

(42) http://funpalaces.co.uk/

(43) http://www.ageconcernhampshire.org.uk/age-fusion/

(44) http://glastonburystewards.co.uk/wp/wp-content/uploads/2015/05/Welcome-to-On-Site-Stewarding-2015-v3.pdf. As they say "It's a real strength that we have experienced stewards coming back again and again, learning more about the Festival, and helping everyone have a safe and brilliant time". Wonderfully organised humanistic protection.

(45) http://www.maslaha.org/ New ways of tackling long-standing issues affecting Muslim communities

(46) https://www.greatgettogether.org/ On the weekend of the 17/18 June 2017 120,000+ events were held celebrating the life of Jo Cox, as a deliberate effort to counterbalance division. Their motto, "we have far more in common than divides us".

(47) https://www.peace-foundation.org.uk/peace-centre/

(48) https://repaircafe.org/en/visit/ ALSO http://cfsd.org.uk/events/farnham_repair_cafe/

(49) https://www.theguardian.com/world/2018/mar/23/hoe-street-central-bank-walthamstow-london-debt

(50) http://farmerswifeandmummy.com/category/farming-2/

(51) http://www.debencommunityfarm.co.uk/the-farm/. As their website says, "We are not out to conquer the world – just make a difference in the quality of life of the people who live, work and play in the community around us. Our aim is that others will be inspired by what we do, take away ideas, and use them or adapt them for their own needs.

(52) http://lammas.org.uk/en/welcome-to-lammas/

(53) https://www.riverford.co.uk/aboutus/employee-ownership

(54) http://www.apsleyfarms.co.uk/

(55) http://www.templeguiting.gloucs.sch.uk/temple-guiting-green-energy-project/

(56) http://energy4all.co.uk/about-us/

(57) https://www.woodlandtrust.org.uk/get-involved/tree-charter/

(58) https://www.ellenmacarthurfoundation.org/about

(59) https://www.goodgym.org/

(60) Play the video http://incredibleediblenetwork.org.uk/incredible-beginnings

(61) https://b4rn.org.uk/

(62) https://www.bbc.co.uk/programmes/b09g5hwf

(63) https://dreamfoundation.eu/institutions/institution/120-british-and-irish-modern-music-institute

(64) http://www.tate.org.uk/whats-on/tate-modern/tate-exchange/workshop/pop-pardip This is London based. They are also nurturing artists in Manchester, Leeds and other parts of the UK

(65) http://www.chaiyaartawards.co.uk/

(66) https://www.edfringe.com/

(67) http://mif.co.uk/about-us/

(68) http://www.channel4.com/info/press/news/grayson-perry-all-man

(69) http://www.brit.croydon.sch.uk/

(70) http://www.nscd.ac.uk/about/vision-mission/70

(71) http://www.bbc.co.uk/programmes/p04p0yft

(72) http://choirwithnoname.org/ .Re-integrating people with society through performing arts. Reported in the `I` 21/2/2017

(73) Daisaku Ikeda. 2016 Peace Proposal 2016 pg 5 and available here http://www.sgi.org/about-us/president-ikedas-proposals/peace-proposal-2016/index.html

(74) Daisaku Ikeda. 2016 Peace Proposal 2016 pg 5

(75) This was used in the opening quote of chapter 8.

(76) Daisaku Ikeda. 2016 Peace Proposal 2016 pg 6

(77) Parker Palmer. Healing the Heart of Democracy. 2011. Jossey-Bass. Pg 158

(78) Daisaku Ikeda. A New Humanism. I B Tauris. 2013. Pg 202

(79) Nichiren. On Establishing the Correct Teaching for the Peace of the Land. The Writings of Nichiren Daishonin. Soka Gakkai. Pg 6.

<u>This work to create a new politics, which embraces life more fully, is just getting started. If you want to be informed about developments across the country inspired by a new stage of human consciousness, I would like to offer you an open invitation to get in touch.</u>

One jumping off point for that is a website:-

www.thebritainpotential.co.uk

You can also follow the book on Facebook

www.facebook.com/thebritainpotential

You can email me at:-　**jim.cowan@thebritainpotential.co.uk**

I really want to hear about developments that take us forward in the way the book describes - I know the book just scratches the surface.

Also, ideas you may have for enabling the book to reach people who are interested in this way of thinking.

Last but by no means least I would love to hear what reading the book has meant for you.